BOOK YOUR OWN TOUR

BOOK YOUR OWN TOUR

FIRST EDITION

LIZ GARO

ROCKPRESS PUBLISHING
P.O. BOX 99090 SAN DIEGO CA 92169 USA

ISBN 1-884615-12-0
Library of Congress Catalog Card No. 94-067300
First printing.

Edited (sort of) by Gary Hustwit
Cover and book design by Gary Hustwit and Liz Garo.
Front cover photo by April Hazen, back cover photos by Mark Waters (top) and Janine Cooper (middle).

Vans of the Stars segments reprinted with permission from *Cake* Magazine, the Non-Music Music 'Zine. Call 612-781-9178 to subscribe to this very cool monthly from Minneapolis. Artwork by the bands.

This book is dedicated to:
Downy Mildew: Charlie Baldonado, Jenny Homer, Nancy McCoy, Iain O'Higgins, John Hofer, Cole Coonce, Rob Jacobs, Sal Garza, Janine Cooper, and to Happy Goes Mad Booking.

Applause and thanks to:
Ellen Stewart (Go Ahead Booking), Mark Linn (Do Easy Booking), Eric Seltz (Red Ryder Booking), Joel Mark (Lovely Booking), Suzanne McCarthy (Flower Booking), Todd Cote & Kevin Wortis (Rave Booking) and Andrew Bennett.

Thanks to: Restless Records, Charlie from Popdefect (Al and Nick too, for being part of the ultimate touring band! See their true-to-life road movie *Live With This* for the real tour story), April Hazen, Campbell, Friends of Dean Martin & Giant Sand, Van Christian & Naked Prey, John Andrew Fredrick and The Black Watch, Aaron Deri for straightening my thots and sentences, aMINIATURE, Mercy Rule, Carol Schutzbank, Keith Lyle, Randy Kaye, Marcy Blanstein, Jabberjaw (for bringing the best bands to L.A.), Ben Wood, Bob Gulla, Eric Gladstone, Foreskin 500, Melanie & John of Basura Records, Fig Dish, Zuzu's Petals, *Cake* Magazine, and to Greg Adamson of Deadhorse Fascination.

Never-ending appreciation for:
The people who compiled the directories: Christian Hoffman, Jennifer Roy, Sandra Zane and Ana Martinez, and to Gary Hustwit, who asked me to put this thing on paper in the first place.

Rockpress thanks:
Denise Hustwit, William Hustwit, Jennifer Roy, Sandra Zane, Ana Martinez, Mix Bookshelf, The Charms, aMINIATURE, Joe Austin, Chank, Restless Records, Cargo Records.

TABLE OF CONTENTS

INTRODUCTION

"So you want to take your band on the road..." Without a doubt, touring is the best way for an unknown independent band to get noticed and make some noise. Touring provides you the chance to meet other bands, musicians and people who are doing just what you're doing. It's the basis of networking and building a foundation of support across the country. This book will give you contacts information for venues, radio stations, press, record stores and other people you will need to talk to in order to book a tour, combined with the how-to knowledge you need to succeed.

This touring guide assumes that you are an independent band with maybe only a single released or a decent demo. Maybe the one person in the band who holds a steady job was able to pay for a full-length CD and put some extra coin in for promotion. Perhaps you've had some success at your local club and college radio station and maybe you have a friend in a band a few hours away who says your band can open for them. These could all be good enough reasons to get on the road. You'll probably be doing this tour on limited funds, which means that you and your band are going to be doing all the work.

Depending on your level of experience, some of this information in this book may seem obvious, while other bits should help you in your plans to conquer the rock 'n' roll highway from Route 66 and beyond...

Why tour?

Touring is usually not as glamourous as it may sound — it's not all wild stories or one big happy roadtrip. On your first tour, plan on playing to empty clubs most of the time. Touring is performing in a tiny bar on an unfamiliar stage with maybe only the bartender and doorman in the audience. It's driving with the same four people for over eight hours a day and seeing the country through a van window.

But, touring *is* ultimately an important element in any artist's "career" and has the potential to strengthen the you both personally and musically. It is one more way for people to find out about your music, read your name somewhere and get a chance to hear you. When a band tours, it helps generate what is known in the music industry as a "buzz" — which basically means if your music is strong, credible, entertaining and you put on a good live show, people will start talking about you. And, don't ever underestimate word-of-mouth advertising.

In a nutshell, this is what you can get out of a tour:

★ You'll improve your playing, performance and band interaction on stage.

★ Band bonding (although keep in mind that more than a few bands have called it quits after a disastrous tour!).

★ You'll build a fan base that creates an audience for your music which eventually makes a band more valuable and can lead to other opportunities.

★ Garnering press clips and college radio airplay.

★ Networking: Meeting bands, club owners, record store clerks, etc., and exchanging information about what's going on in any given music scene.

★ You'll play your music to a new audience who aren't already your friends or family.

Keep your expectations realistic. Touring is a pain in the ass. Look at it as a short-term experience with the potential to help you towards your long-term goal.

A band that gets this tour thing wired, and does it enough times so that they can stay on the road successfully, can actually make some kind of living out of it!
(be inspired by these bands who've done it on their own: Southern Culture On The Skids, Unwound, Doo-Rag!)

GETTING STARTED

To start booking your tour, follow this brief outline of steps to organize your plan of attack. Be prepared for a phone bill increase, trips to the post office and an obsession with road maps:

1) **Map out the itinerary**
2) **Send promotional materials to clubs**
3) **Confirm the Gigs**
4) **Promote the Gigs**
5) **Budget Your Tour**
6) **Choose band responsibilities**
7) **Drive**

The success of almost any venture depends on set-up and preparation, and touring is no exception. It's important to give yourself enough lead time to make plans, send out materials and to make sure that the van is running and ready. If this is your first tour you will be at the mercy of the people who book the club which means you will basically have to take whatever shows you can get. The goal of touring is getting exposure and playing as much as possible; the money may be crap and there will be long drives in between but playing a lot and meeting new people will be to your benefit in the end. Remember, the goal is *exposure*.

★ The preparation process should start about four months in advance of when you want to tour.

Info you'll need to get started

Getting accurate information on where to play and who to talk to is an ongoing process. There can be a quick changes regarding who is booking a club and new venues come and go. The information in this book is one place to start. Most of the venues that are listed in these pages have launched careers and the itineraries cover key towns and cities that have supported young bands. Every band is going to want something different, so use the information here as a basis to create the tour that works best for you.

Talk to other bands who have toured and ask questions about their experiences on the road: Where do you play in Louisville? Is there anything between Washington and Wyoming? Investigate the particulars about a club: Who do you talk to? Where do you load-in? What's the sound system like? How big is the stage? When you're in a band and on the road there is a community of people out there who have information that can help you. Don't be afraid to ask.

Other places to find info:

★ Go to the library or a well-stocked newsstand and look up the daily and weekly newspapers of the cities you plan to go to. Look at their entertainment sections, and see what type of bands play at the local clubs. You can call the publication and ask to get a sample copy to really peruse. Also, at the library, look through the *Bacon's Guide to Periodicals.* This book lists all the weekly and daily publications in the country.

★ Get a copy of *Pollstar,* a weekly publication geared to booking agents and clubs. It lists bands' touring itineraries and gives information about what's going on at different clubs. You can also find phone numbers for concert promoters, and *Pollstar* puts out an annual music industry directory. The phone number for *Pollstar* is 209-224-2631.

★ If you are part of the computer age, take advantage of the music sections on on-line services like America Online and Compuserve. Also, alt.music.alternative on the Internet is a cyberspace hangout for touring bands, and there are usually folders on touring and booking your own tour.

★ *Musician* magazine puts out a special issue called *The Musician's Guide To Touring and Promotion.* Call them at 212-536-5208 or write to 1515 Broadway, 11th Fl., New York NY 10036.

★ *Maximumrocknroll* magazine in San Francisco also has a booking issue titled *Book Your Own Fucking Life.* This has got a lot of information for punk and alternative bands. Write for information: P.O. Box 460760 San Francisco CA 94146.

The bottom line here is to get as much information as you can before you start booking your tour. The more informed you are, the easier and more successful your tour will be.

Tour-speak

The following are a few examples of some common vernacular used when dealing with an agent or club. Again, none of this is earth-shattering but there could be a few helpful words in here. And of course, it never hurts to increase your vocabulary.

Advancing the show: Calling the club a few days before the scheduled show to confirm directions, load-in time and soundcheck time. This is to just double-check everything that's been previously confirmed.

Booking Agent: A person who represents several bands and books tours for them for a fee, usually between 10% and 15% of the total $ amount from the shows booked. Booking agents can work independently or be part of larger agencies such as C.A.A. or William Morris.

Avails: What days or shows a club has available for a support band or opening spot.

Buy-Out: When the club or promoter gives you a certain dollar amount per band member instead of feeding you. Not all clubs do this and it is something you will have to ask for.

Contract: The written agreement between the band and promoter or club. You should bring a copy of the signed contract with you to the performance.

Holds: When the club pencils you in or holds a date for you. A hold does not mean you have the show, it indicates that you may be able to play on that date.

Itinerary: The route of where you are touring that includes the city, state, date of show, club address and phone number.

Per Diem: A daily allowance (spending money) paid to each band member out of the band fund. This is also known as the "PD."

Promoter: Individual who secures show date and handles all the details.

Press Release: A one-page announcement with information about a band and what they are doing, where they are playing, etc.

Rider: The rider is the band's request for any sound system specifications and/or food and drink requests. We've all heard the stories of David Lee Roth from Van Halen demanding only green M&M's backstage. Don't expect too many clubs asking for riders, but it's good to know what they are when you make the big time.

Set-Up: This is the time used for promotion prior to the date. Set-up time is used to contact the press, radio and record stores to promote the gig.

MAP OUT YOUR ITINERARY

The Working Itinerary

The working itinerary is what you use to map out your destinations. It should outline the route a band wants to take. The working itinerary will have a starting point, a middle (turnaround point) and an ending point (there's no place like home). It should allow for flexibility and for more than one venue or city in any given time-frame.

The working itinerary will be revised and updated as shows get confirmed and cancelled. Plan the tour in two different directions; such as possible shows north of your starting point and possible shows south of your starting point.

A band on the road needs to be resourceful, so if a show falls through while you're on the tour, see if you can play at the local coffeehouse or at a party. Last minute shows may not always be an ideal situation, but they can sometimes help put much needed money in a band's pocket. A rule to remember is that if you're on the road, you will always need more gas money.

Let's say you are taking the route from Los Angeles to Seattle. This west coast route offers a band the chance to play some key college towns (San Diego, Chico, Eugene) as well as some major music scene markets (Seattle, Los Angeles, San Francisco). Balance the tour so there are shows on the way to your turnaround point as well as shows on the way back. If you have sent singles out to college radio stations, book shows in those cities in which you're getting airplay.

A working itinerary may look like this:

April 2,3,4 — Santa Barbara; Fresno; San Luis Obispo, CA.
April 4,5,6 — Fresno; San Luis Obispo; San Jose; San Francisco, CA.
April 7 — San Francisco, CA.
April 8 — (day off)
April 9 — Sacramento, CA.; Stanton, CA
April 10 — Driving day or Arcata, CA

April 11 — Eugene, OR; Pullman, WA.
April 12 — Portland, OR, Eugene, OR.
April 13 — Portland, OR, Tacoma, WA
April 14 — Tacoma, WA, Spokane, WA
April 15 — Seattle, WA; Olympia, WA.
April 16 — day off
April 17 — Portland, OR; Bellingham, WA.
April 18 — Eugene, OR; Chico, CA; Arcata, CA.
April 19 — driving day
April 20 — Santa Clara; San Jose, CA.
April 21 — Berkeley; San Jose; Monterey, CA.
April 22 — San Luis Obispo; Santa Barbara; Fresno, CA.
April 23 — San Diego, CA. Home.

Once you get a show confirmed, you'll have a clearer picture of where you'll go. In this sample itinerary, if Santa Barbara gets confirmed for April 3 and Fresno for April 4, you can now try for San Luis Obispo on the way down. Try to get your starting point and what I refer to as your turnaround point first, then fill in from there. For example:

April 3 - Santa Barbara (starting point)
April 4 - Fresno
April 17 - Seattle (turnaround)

This gives you two weeks to make it up north — what you don't get on the way up try to schedule on the way down. Make sure your itinerary leads somewhere. Avoid zigzagging or backtracking tour routes. Pick a direct line and follow it.

The final itinerary should include the date of the show, city, state, name of promoter, phone number and club address. When the tour is all booked make sure each person in the band has an itinerary as well as the loved ones who are being left at home.

Touring Regionally

The mechanics of touring are pretty much the same no matter how far you go. To get yourself started, try booking and promoting regionally then tackle touring on a national level. Touring regionally gives you a concentrated area to work, and chances are, if you've made some decent noise from your home-base, the next town two-hours away has heard you as well.

Map out a route close to home and work it nonstop. For example, if you are based in Los Angeles and you have a single out and you want to tour, concentrate on the Southwest (Arizona, New Mexico, Colorado) or the Pacific Northwest (Oregon, Washington) or even just the west coast (everything between Los Angeles and San Francisco).

You can build your audience and rapport with a club by repeat performances over a period of time. Repetition is recognition. You get the most from touring when you play the same markets over and over. Play a club once and go back in another 6 to 8 weeks. Aim to create and develop a following in every city that you go to. (More of this under Promotion)

Another way of keeping track of your itinerary is by xeroxing the month(s) from a calendar. Make all your notes in the boxes. This can help you keep track of what cities you're playing on what days, for example try to play Seattle on a weekend instead of a Monday night. See the examples of itineraries on the following pages.

Sample Tours

The following are a few sample tour itineraries for different parts of the country. Don't feel bound by these, they are just meant to be guidelines.

Tour One
Starting from the Seattle, WA area, going on an approximately four-week tour of the Midwest, South and West Coast.

Yakima, WA
Missoula, MT
(2 days for driving)
Denver, CO
(1 day for driving)
St. Louis, MO
Des Moines, IA
Iowa City, IA
Minneapolis, MN
Chicago, IL
La Crosse, WI
(1 day for driving)
Cincinnati, OH
Louisville, KY
Knoxville, TN
Memphis, TN
Lawrence, KS
Norman, OK
(2 days for driving)
Phoenix, AZ
Tuscon, AZ
San Diego, CA
Los Angeles, CA
San Francisco, CA
Portland, OR
Seattle, WA

Band of Susans - Lovely Booking
Here Comes Success US 95

Show Date	Venue	Promoter
C - Thursday - 03/23/95	Middle East 472 Massachusetts Ave Cambridge, MA 02139 617 3545434/617497 0576 Fax:617 547 3930 Cap:150/Tkts:/Adv:/Age:21+	Middle East
C - Saturday - 03/25/95	9:30 Club 930 "F" St. N.W. Washington, DC 20004 (202) 638-1680 AgentLine/(202) 638-2008 Fax:202 667 4527 Cap:/Tkts:/Adv:/Age:All Ages	9:30 Club
C - Sunday - 03/26/95	Flood Zone Brett Cassis 11 South 18th Street Richmond, VA 23223 804 643 6006/ Fax:804 782 0043 Cap:800/Tkts:/Adv:/Age:All Ages Load:5 pm, Check:5:30 Set:11/	Larry Glover 232 South Cherry St Richmond, VA 23220 804 643 5216/ fax:
C - Monday - 03/27/95	The Point James St James & Miki 420 Moreland NE Atlanta, GA 30307 (404) 659-3115/(404) 659-3522 club Fax:(404) 659-4530 Cap:/Tkts:$5/Adv:/Age:21+	In House
C - Tuesday - 03/28/95	Butchertown Pub Elaine Ford 1335 Story Ave Louisville, KY (502) 583-2242/ Fax: Cap:/Tkts:$2/Adv:/Age:21+ Load:7, Check:8 Set:11:30/60 mins	Elaine Ford 1603 Norris Pl Louisville, KY 40205 502 459 7279/ fax:
T - Thursday - 03/30/95	Washington University Dawn Barger 1 Brookings Drive St Louis, MO 63130 Cap:500/Tkts:/Adv:/Age:	The Gargoyle Committe 1 Brookings Drive Box 1068 St Louis, MO 63130 314 935 5917/ fax:

Above: Put all the details for each show in a "master itinerary" such as this. Be sure to bring several copies with you on tour. The "C" shows are confirmed, "T" is tentative.

FOR IMMEDIATE RELEASE

CONTACT: Liz Garo/Restless Records
213.957.4357, x237

RESTLESS PRESS RELEASE

CRAIN TOURS IN SUPPORT OF RESTLESS DEBUT, *HEATER*

MARCH 14, 1994 -- Crain snaps, crackles, crunches and distorts noisey pop. From Louisville, Kentucky, this trio of sonic noisemakers embark on a national tour in support of their Restless debut *Heater* (produced by Chicago's magician knob-turner Whodini).

The energetic three-piece will be playing with enough assorted (or is it sordid?) indie-rock luminaries that would make any mother proud.
Go get yourself a healthy dose of punk rock and go see Crain.

DATE	VENUE	CITY/ST.	SUPPORT
3/24	Casbah	San Diego, CA	Unwound
3/25	UC Irvine	Irvine, CA	afternoon
3/25	Eagles Coffeehouse	Los Angeles, CA	night
3/26	Jabberjaw	Los Angeles, CA	Unwound
3/27	UFCW	Santa Barbara, CA	Unwound
3/29	Bottom Of The Hill	San Francisco, CA	Unwound
3/30	Berkley Square	Berkley, CA	Unwound
3/31	John Henry's	Eugene, OR.	Unwound
4/1	Reed College	Portland, OR	Unwound
4/2	Velvet Elvis (day)	Seattle, WA	Unwound
4/2	Moe (evening)	Seattle, WA.	
4/3	TBA	Olympa. WA.	Unwound
4/4	Starfish	Vancouver, BC	Sparkmarker
4/8	Cave/Carlton College	Northfield, MN	TBA
4/9	Hairy Mary's	Des Moines, IA	TBA
4/10	Uptown	Minneapolis, MN	TBA
4/13	Dead Pigeon	Muncie, IN.	
4/15	Lounge Axe	Chicago, ILL.	TBA
4/16	TBA	Indianapolis, IN.	Unwound
4/17	Uncle Pleasants	Louisville, KY.	Unwound
4/22	Middle East	Cambridge, MA.	Unwound, Kudgle
4/24	Last Call	Providence, RI.	Unwound
4/27	Forham University	Bronx, NY.	

1616 Vista Del Mar Avenue, Hollywood, CA 90028-6420 tel 213-957-4357 fax 213-957-4355

Above: A sample tour itinerary that can be sent to the press.

Tour Two

Here's an itinerary that starts from the West Coast and covers the Southwest and Midwest. Estimated time is three weeks.

Los Angeles, CA
San Diego, CA
Tuscon, AZ
Albuquerque, NM
(2 days for driving)
Tulsa, OK
Lawrence, KS
Kansas City, MO
St. Louis, MO
Chicago, IL
Iowa City, IA
Lincoln, NE
Denver, CO
(2 days for driving)
Las Vegas, NV
Indio, CA
Los Angeles, CA
Fresno, CA
San Francisco, CA

Tour Three

Here's a solid one-week Midwest tour starting in Chicago.

Chicago, IL
Champaign, IL
Kansas City, MO
Lawrence, KS
Lincoln, NE
Des Moines, IA
Minneapolis, MN
Iowa City, IA

Tour Four

Here's a tour that starts in the South, covers the East, Northeast and ventures slightly to the outskirts of the Midwest. Estimated time is 2 to 3 weeks.

Athens, GA
Knoxville, TN
Chapel Hill, NC
(2 days for driving)

Washington, DC
New York, NY
Boston, MA
Hoboken, NJ
Philadelphia, PA
Cleveland, OH
Cincinatti, OH
Louisville, KY
Nashville, TN
Atlanta, GA

Tour Five

Here's a two-week East Coast and Midwest tour.
Boston, MA
New York, NY
Washington, DC
Richmond, VA
Louisville, KY
Cincinnati, OH
Cleveland, OH
Buffalo, NY
New York, NY

Tour Six

This tour starts in Texas, goes through the Southwest, part of California and scattered bits of the Midwest in approximately 2 to 3 weeks.

Houston, TX
Austin, TX
Dallas, TX
(2 days of driving)
Albuquerque, NM
Phoenix, AZ
Los Angeles, CA
Las Vegas, NV
Salt Lake City, UT
Denver, CO
Lawrence, KS
Kansas City, KS
Tulsa, OK

Timing

To quote tour sage Mike Watt: "Never start a tour after Halloween." In general, Winter is not the time to be on the road. The most popular times to tour are probably Spring (March through June) and early Fall (September, October). Summer can be a good touring time, but be aware that school's out, turning some college towns into grave-yards. Also, many college radio stations will be run by skeleton crews and some will completely shut down during the summer.

Driving Miles & Directions

★ Be as accurate and as aware as possible of the miles in between shows. Always add on at least an extra hour or so when figuring out your driving time — for food stops, stretching your legs, getting lost to sound check. Try to avoid a lot of long drives — especially overnighters!!! — there have been too many accidents and casualties caused by bands having to drive 20 hours in a day. No gig is worth someone falling asleep at the wheel and rolling the van with sometimes fatal results. Pace yourself. Try not to book shows over eight hours driving time apart — if you drive more than that you are usually too burnt by the time you get to the club to give a good performance.

★ To calculate your miles you can use a disk-o-meter, found at most travel stores. The disk-o-meter is basically a tool that calculates the mileage between cities.

★ There are several software programs for Macs and PCs that will give you miles between your destinations, estimated driving time, gas consumption, and even print you out custom maps for your whole tour. The Mac version is called Route 66. Call your local software store.

★ Know how to read a map and refer to them constantly. Be sure you have a road atlas which supplies more detailed travel information.

★ Make sure someone in the band belongs to the Automobile Club — this will come in handy more than one occasion! With a Triple A card, in addition to getting maps and information about different states, you can get a TRIPTEK which supplies directions to all your stopping points.

MUSIC CONFERENCES AND COLLEGE GIGS

Music conferences and college gigs can be cornerstones to book a tour around. College gigs usually offer decent money and music conferences can be a place for exposure and a source of information as to what's going on with record labels and other bands.

Colleges

The college gig is a coveted one. Because there is usually a set "entertainment budget" at a school, a band can usually earn more money playing one show at a college than the total of five crappy club gigs. When you're trying to get a show at a school, there are a few things to keep in mind:

★ The shows are often booked far in advance by a student body group usually tagged "entertainment council" or "program board." The Spring Semester Program Board may already have everything booked through Fall.

★ Each campus is different and there may be more than just one venue to play. Be open to afternoon shows as well as the night gigs.

★ Since college gigs have the potential to be high paying, let them make you an offer.

If you're receiving any college radio airplay, contact those stations and ask about on-campus shows. You can also simply call any college and ask for the Program Board or whoever handles campus activities.

The National Association of Campus Activities (NACA) is a wealth of information on College Program Boards, and they also organize meetings where college bookers come and watch performances by dozens of bands, then arrange shows with those bands on their respective campuses. Call them at 800-845-2338 or write to: 13 Harbison Way, Columbia SC 29212.

Music Conferences

There are many music conferences throughout the year and they are often in markets where a band would want to play. In addition to showcasing lots of bands, the music conferences are attended by record labels, managers, booking agents, club promoters, radio promotion people and others who have some involvement in the music business. There are panels and seminars during the day that discuss everything from the marketing of an act to how to get college radio airplay to the politics between a publicist and magazine editor.

To play one of the conferences, a band has to submit a tape to the particular convention about four months ahead of time (this varies, call), and wait to hear if they've been accepted and then take whatever slot is given. If you do get accepted, it may sound great to get a Thursday night at Brownie's in New York at 11pm during the College Music Journal Convention (AKA the CMJ), but that could also be the same day and time that Pavement or some other huge draw is doing a surprise gig at CBGBs. The thing to remember is that these music conference shows may seem really appealing and exciting but there is no guarantee that they're going to be life-changing experiences.

The competition is tough at conferences but it does give some insight (if you care to look) at the industry game. For developing bands, South By Southwest (SXSW) and CMJ offer the best exposure and you're usually dealing with a compassionate staff who are willing to at least try and help you out. The New York University Indie Fest, Independent Music Seminar and the Independent Label Festival are all geared to showcase unsigned bands and talent. There are enough music conventions every year throughout the country that a band could play at least one if they are persistent and thorough in tracking down the information.

Music Conferences Directory

February

Gavin Convention
140 Second St.
San Francisco, CA 94105
415-495-1990
All musical styles, signed bands only. Panels, trade show.

March

Loud Music Festival
86 Buckingham St.
Cambridge, MA 02140
617-491-1058
Alternative. Concerts and panels.

SXSW
PO BOX 4999
Austin, TX. 78765
512-467-7979
The best place to find agents and club owners; also one of the most enjoyable of the conferences. There is a fee to submit music for showcase slots, call for info. SXSW also organizes the NXNW, NXNE, and the Mississippi River Music Festival.

April

Crossroads Jam
P.O. Box 41858
Memphis, TN 38174-1858
901-526-4280
Panels, trade show, workshops, all styles of music.

Independent Music Fest
566 La Guardia Pl. Room 103
New York, NY 10012
212-998-4999
Sponsored by NYU.

May

Music West
21 Water St. #306
Vancouver BC V6B 1A1 CANADA
604-684-9338
Trade show, panels, mostly alternative/rock.

SFO
140 Second St.
San Francisco, CA 94105
415-495-1990
All musical styles, unsigned bands only. Panels, trade show.

Undercurrents
P.O. Box 94040
Cleveland, OH 44101
216-463-3595
Panels, trade show, concerts, mostly alternative.

Winter Music Conference
3450 NE 12th Terrace
Ft. Lauderdale, FL 33334
305-563-4444

June

North By Northeast (NXNE) Toronto, Canada
PO BOX 4999
Austin, TX. 78765
512-467-7979
This seminar is in Toronto, but organized by SXSW in Austin.

Northwest Music Conference
300 Lenora Street
Suite #B-261
Seattle, WA. 98121
206-528-6210

St. Louis Regional Music Seminar (RMS)
2327 Tennessee 1N
St. Louis MO 63104
314-773-5454
Primarily features regional acts, but will also book out-of-towners. Panels, trade show.

July

Indie Label Festival
600 S. Michigan Ave.
Chicago IL 60605
312-341-9112
Unsigned or independent labels bands only, mostly alternative.

September

CMJ Convention
245 Great Neck Road / 3rd Floor
Great Neck, New York 11021
Sponsored by the radio trade publication *College Music Journal*. The CMJ is becoming the 'conference of choice' for new, developing bands. This conference primarily offers exposure and insight into college radio.

Cutting Edge Music Conference
710 S. Broad St.
New Orleans, LA 70119
504-827-5700

Mississippi River Music Festival, St. Louis, Missouri
PO BOX 4999
Austin, TX. 78765
512-467-7979
Organized by the SXSW although it takes place in St. Louis.

North By Northwest (NXNW) Portland, Oregon
PO BOX 4999
Austin, TX. 78765
512-467-7979
This seminar is in Portland, but organized by SXSW in Austin.

October

Independent Music Seminar (IMS)
P.O. Box 99090
San Diego CA 92169
619-234-9400
Alternative. Independent label or unsigned bands only. Concerts and panels.

Philadelphia Music Conference
P.O. Box 29363
Philadelphia PA 19125-0363
215-426-4109
Panels, concerts, trade show.

SENDING YOUR MATERIALS TO THE CLUBS

Promo Packages

After the itinerary is mapped out you need to get packages to the clubs and/or promoters for solicitation. Send out "promo packages" around 3 - 4 months from when you want to go out and tour (i.e. if you want to tour the month of April you should get your plans and promo packages mailed out by mid-January/early February at the very latest — you always have to allow time for a package to get lost, remain unopened, thrown away, etc.).

★ The promo package doesn't need to be overdone, slick or fancy — just to the point. Nine out of ten times the people who book clubs are so inundated with tapes that they aren't going to have a chance to go through the five different 8x10 glossies you've sent, the 20-page press kit and the personal history of each member of the band. Keep things informative and to the point.

★ What you need to send is: a bio that is simple and highlights/captures anything that may be a selling point about the band: the guitar player used to be in such-and-such band, the band has a strong local following or the band is getting college airplay in that particular market. Send any press clips you have already received: a live review in your local paper, record reviews from fanzines. You *don't* need to send every mention of your band, but you *can* be clever, irreverent, funny and creative. Just make sure that the information is simple and clear.

★ Include a simple letter stating who you are and what date your band is looking to play at that club. Give the promoter a couple of choices of when you want to play. Be flexible and receptive to what is thrown at you — that may mean playing at 1AM on a Tuesday night.

★ Make sure there is a contact name and phone number on your letter, and on your cassette or CD that you send. Never make contacting you an effort!

heavy vegetable

Hi, I'm Rob from heavy vegetable. I guess this is our bio thingy. We are from Encinitas, California, a town which is mostly record and health food stores. This suits us just fine. We live right above a liquor store and everything! Anyway, as I said, I'm Rob and I play guitar and sing, Manolo plays drums, Travis plays bass and sings sometimes, and Elea sings too. We don't seem to have any definable "sound". You can't read what a band sounds like anyway. We just play what we feel, and people whose opinion I respect enjoy it. I will admit, though, that we live in fear of being thought of as another "San Diego ROCK Band". You won't find any songs about fast cars and fast women, but you'll probably find a couple about wasting pigs. Sorry, we don't have a gimmick either, unless being yourself and writing what you know is a gimmick. Actually, that might be one nowadays, it's a sick fucking world. As far as our individual personalities are concerned, we're the kind of people you would have beat up if you were a "cool" kid in high school. We are just four bored dorks who like to play music as a substitute for getting all self absorbed and depressed. Hope you enjoy our music and thank you for your time. HV

...here are some recordings with us on them;

a bunch of stuff - 7" (way out 006)
heavy vegetable/powerdresser split - 7" (goldenrod)
ask for disorder (compilation) - CD (lsr/dutch east 2035-2)
heavy vegetable (acoustic)/fugbear split - 7" (rugcore)
mud on the wheel (acoustic compilation) - CD (earth music/cargo)
saint doug, 91X compilation - CD (91X)
musica del diablo (live compilation) - CD (casbah/cargo)
the amazing undersea adventures of aqua kitty and friends
CD (hed-027/cargo) LP (goldenrod)

for more information contact:
bryan spevak/publicity
robbie lloyd/radio promotion
cargo records
4901-906 morena blvd.
san diego, ca 92117-3432
619-483-9292 phone
619-483-7414 fax

Montreal • San Diego
Chicago • London

Above: A sample band bio (one-sheet).

CLOWNHEAD HAMMER

What the hell IS this? It's loud and melodic, dischordal and groovy, funky and ugly, distinctly indistinct. But, strangely enough, people seem to like this stuff. It's got teeth, fur, wire and wood and it's called CLOWNHEAD HAMMER.

The drums come from the far east, the bass and guitar come from the mid-west, the voice from the west coast and the percussion from where ever they can get it. The band has been together for two years, rehearse five nights a week, are still on speaking terms and frequently find themselves loving what they're doing.

Touring seems to be the immediate goal of the band. After a small jaunt through the mid-west playing for crowds, (yes, crowds), the response was so positive that coming back to "critics corner", (a.k.a. L.A.), was not the most popular subject within the band. But, home is where the house is, so...

CLOWNHEAD HAMMER has graced, or grazed, the stages of several of L.A.'s most popular clubs, making occasional acoustic stops at some of the better known coffee houses around the city.

CLOWNHEAD HAMMER's debut CD is currently available at The Wherehouse(CA), Moby Disc(CA), Aron's Records(CA), Disc and Tape Masters(ND, MN), and Marguerite's Music(MN). The band and their music are also getting national and international exposure through P.A.I.N.(Perfect Alternative Independent Network), I.U.M.A.(Internet Underground Music Archive), and college & independent radio stations.

It's disturbing, it's memorable, it's uniquely familiar-
it's CLOWNHEAD HAMMER.

P.O. Box 5066 Sherman Oaks, CA 91413

Above: Another sample bio.

★ Don't waste a lot of time trying to "touch base" before they've received your package. It's more important to get your material in the mail and then start calling and bugging them to listen to it, rather than trying to speak to the club first.

★ Send out packages to all the clubs in a market that may be a possibility for you to play. Call and follow-up on as many clubs as possible. Don't wait for a confirmation from one club before you talk to another one.

CONFIRMING THE GIG

The person you'll be talking to for a gig is either the club booker or a promoter. In general, the club booker is the person who books all the talent at a particular venue. The promoter is someone puts on shows on a particular night at a venue, or may have several venues that they book.

About a week to ten days after sending a package, follow-up with a phone call to the club. Some club bookers have set days and times that they take calls, others are at the venue all the time and then there are those who are impossible to get in touch with. If you do have trouble reaching someone, and you will, find out if there is a fax number at the club and contact them that way or check to see if there is another number where the person can be reached. A rule that must be repeated: be patient and persistent.

How you interact with other people is one of the keys to getting your band from point A to point B smoothly, easily and successfully. Granted, booking a tour for your band is probably the most important thing to you right now, but the promoter also has to deal with the blown sound system from last night's band and the big agent that just called threatening to pull a sold-out show if the artist rider isn't met and the delivery truck is late with the weekend's beer order. Keep in mind that people who spend lots of time on the phone usually have just as much going on in their head, in their ear and on their desk. They can sometimes be quick in their response (i.e. rude) or forgetful (i.e. they'll tell you one thing one week and won't remember anything they said to you the next week).

Not all promoters are the same; you'll find ones that are helpful and believe in the band, ones that don't care, ones that want to just make money, ones that will do you a favor, and ones that will finally give you a show just to stop you from calling. When booking a tour, your "people skills" will be put to the test over and over.

★ When you call the club let the booker know your name, band name and a brief description of what your music is about. Let the booker know the time frame in which you are looking to book a gig.

★ Organize your information, and keep a record of all your phone calls, whether it's on 5x7 cards, in a spiral notebook or on a computer. Keep a record of the venue name, address, phone number and contact person. Take notes on every conversation you have, even if you just left a message. This will remind you of the status of each potential show.

★ You probably won't get a confirmed date on your first call. Try to at least get them to hold a date or "pencil something in" for you. This means that they will have you down as a consideration for a certain night. Consider every club (that's musically right for your band) in a city as a possible place to play. Try not to limit yourself to wanting to play only one venue.

★ Don't be an asshole, don't over-pitch your band, be patient and persistent when calling clubs and trying to get a date.

★ When you finally get a date confirmed you need to get the details: address of club, load-in, soundcheck, stage times. Will you get beer? What's the guest list? How much will you get paid? Some promoters will have you get back to them to get all the details but be sure to get all information as soon as possible.

★ As a developing band, playing a club for the first time and booking the shows without an agent, you aren't going to have a lot of leverage to get money. Depending on the club and what potential buzz your band is generating, a band can usually get anywhere from $50 guaranteed to a couple hundred dollars. More than likely you will get a percentage of the money taken at the door, but always try for a guarantee, or at least a partial guarantee (i.e. $50, plus 50% of the door over $400). See the Money Matters section for more on this.

The Pitch

When you finally get the club booker or promoter on the phone, the conversation may go something like this:

BAND: Hi this is (your name here) from (band name here). We're looking for a show at the end of April and . . .

CLUB: Did you send a tape? Does anyone know who you are?

BAND: We've sent a tape and we have a single out on (your cool indie label name here) that we've sent to the college radio station and . . .

CLUB: What do you sound like?

BAND: Loud, lots of guitars, 4 piece, some people say we're like Sebadoh . . .

CLUB: Yeah, well who isn't? What dates are you looking for?

BAND: Either April 8, 9, 10 or April 19, 20, 21 *(this designates a band playing the venue either on the way out or back in their route)*

CLUB: Let me see if I can find the tape. You sent something, right? Call me if you have any radio info. I'll see if I can pencil you in somewhere for that Tuesday, April 8th. I'm either doing two local bands that night or a show with Jawbreaker. I don't know, maybe you can open for them. I'll have to find the tape. Does anyone know who you are?

BAND: We're getting played on the college station and we love Jawbreaker, if we could open for them that would be great. We have posters and stuff that we would send out.

CLUB: Okay, let me see what I can do.

BAND: So that would be Tuesday, April 8?

CLUB: Yeah, maybe. Maybe the 9th. Just call me in a week or so . . . .

These kind of noncommittal conversations could go on for a few weeks. Be persistent. Check out the other clubs in the area. Be persistent. Send the club more information if you have it. Be persistent. If the college radio station is playing your single, have someone from there call the club for you and maybe help you get an opening spot for that Jawbreaker show. Be persistent.

Once you get a date confirmed, get those details from the promoter: day and date of show, payment, club address, load-in time and soundcheck time, what bands you'll be playing with and what time you'll play. Put all the information into a contract and make a copy for yourself and mail a copy to the promoter. Ideally, the promoter should sign it and return it to you before the gig. Whether it's signed or not, bring a copy of this agreement with you when you are collecting the money at the end of the night. Always count the money when they hand it over to you in case there is any discrepancy in the amount.

Also find out where you should send your posters and fliers, and get the addresses of any local magazines or newspapers that do concert listings.

I've included two sample booking contracts on the following pages. Copy and use them as is, or write your own contract based on them.

PERFORMANCE AGREEMENT

This agreement is for the services of_____(herein called "artist") and _____(herein called "purchaser") for the engagement descibed below is made this day_____, 19__, between the undersigned artist and purchaser.

1. Place of Show_____
2. Date(s) of Show_____
3. Times: Load In_____Sound Check_____ Start_____
4. Number and Length of Sets_____
5. Sound System_____
6. Compensation: Performance_____
                    Lodging_____
                    Meals_____
                    Transportation _____
                    Other _____
                    TOTAL _____
7. Payment is to be made in cash__or check__ no later than_____
8. Sales of merchandise by artist will be on the following terms_____
_____
9. Other_____
_____

10. The recording, reproduction or transmission of Artist's performance is prohibited absent written consent of Artist. Artist's obligations under this contract are subject to detention or prevention by sickness, accident, riots, strikes, epidemics or any other Act of God which could endanger the health or safety of the Artist. If any of the Artist's compensation is based on door receipts, Purchaser agrees to provide the artist a statement of gross receipts within two hours of the conclusion of the performance if asked, and Artist shall have the right to have representation at the door or the box office at all times. Said representation shall have the right to examine box office records relating to the above performance only. In the event Purchaser fails to fulfill its obligation provided herein, Purchaser will be liable to Artist in addition to the compensation provided herein. Either party may cancel this agreement without obligation to other if notice is received 21 days in advance of show. In witness whereof, the parties sign this contract this_____day of_____ 19___.

_____ Purchaser   _____ Artist

Above: A sample booking contract.

HAPPY
GOES • MAD
BOOKING

Contract #___

This contract for the personal services of the musicians for the engagement described below, is made this _____ day of _____, 19___ between the undersigned purchaser of music (herein called "Purchaser") and the undersigned musicians (herein called "Artist").

1.   Place of Engagement: _____

2.   Artist: _____

3.   Number of Musicians/Crew   _____

4.   Day and Date of Engagement   _____

5.   Club Capcity _____   Ticket Price _____

6.   Gross Potential   _____

7.   Guest List   _____

8.   Compensation Agreed Upon   _____

9.   Purchaser Shall Make Payments as Follows _____

     _____

     _____

10. All contract riders attached hereto are hereby made a part of this contract.

11. A cancellation fee equal to 50% of the guarantee compensation shall be paid to Artist if show is cancelled by purchaser for reasons other than riot, strike, epidemic, an act of God or other legitimate condition beyond Purchaser's control.

12. No portion of the performance shall be recorded, reproduced or transmitted from the place of performenace, in any manner or by any means whatsoever, without specific written approval or Artist or Artist's representative.

13. All claims and disputes which may arise between the Purchaser and the Artist regarding application or interpretation or any terms or conditions of this contract shall be referred exclusively to binding arbitration.

14. Signed contracts and rider must be received no later than _____

_____   _____
       PURCHASER   ARTIST

_____   _____

_____   c/o   HAPPY*GOES*MAD booking
                                            749 Tularosa Drive
                                            LA,CA. 90026

Above: A sample booking contract.

MONEY MATTERS

There are no set rules on how a band gets paid — just be sure to walk out that club door with at least a few dollars in you pocket to help get you to your next destination, or buy a decent pizza or burrito. The ideal situation is to play for a guarantee, but that isn't always possible. A band that is touring to support a single or a record always stands a better chance of getting exposure and money. Here's a few thoughts on the money thing:

★ You are doing this on your own so you don't have the leverage of a booking agent, or the marketing budget of a record label. That doesn't mean you can't try for a guarantee. The guarantee is money that you will receive regardless of how many people come to the show. If your band already has a buzz going or has a single charting on college radio, there's a good chance that you can get a set amount of money. Keep in constant communication with the club in regards to what promotion your band is doing and what attention you are generating, in the club's city and nationally. If the club thinks your band will draw a decent amount of people, they may offer you a couple hundred bucks outright. Gigs with guarantees are always what you aim for.

★ If your band is unproven in a particular market or venue you will most likely get offered a door percentage. This is where those math classes you took may actually come in handy. Figure this: there are four bands on the bill, with a six dollar cover charge. Let's say each band gets 25% of the door that night, after the club's expenses which total $150. Expenses that a club factors in can include PA rental, soundman, doorman, flyers or advertising. If the club is taking a piece of the door for expenses, always find out what the total will be for those expenses (or at least an approximation) when you're booking the show. After the gig, get the door count of how many people paid to get in and how many were let in free on the guest list (when playing for a percentage, always try to keep the guest list small).

Let's say the total the number of people who paid to get in was 63.

Multiply the door count by the ticket price:
63 paid @ $6 a head = $378

Subtract the expenses:
$378 – $150 (expenses) = $228

Multiply your percentage by the dollar amount:
25% of $228 = $57

Here's another example:
Your band is getting 40% of the door with a five dollar cover charge and no expenses taken out. 48 people pay to get in.

48 x $5 = $240
40% of $240 = $96

★ Another payment plan that some clubs offer (although it should be avoided if at all possible) is giving you a few dollars for every person that specifically says they are here to see your band. The problem with this is that you are dealing with a doorman you don't know or trust and if you're playing a city for the first time as an opener for the big local band, people probably won't even know who you are. You won't run into this policy very often, but if you do, at least try to get a straight door percentage.

There are also certain payment compromises that you will undoubtedly run across. If a club can't pay you very much, they may offer you a free hot meal and a place to stay, or some other kind of added incentive to enhance the experience.

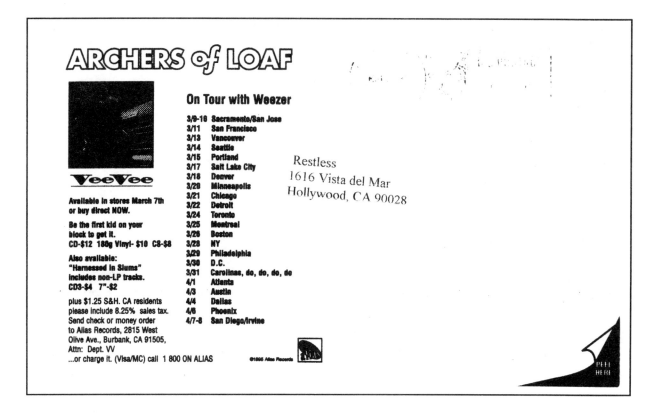

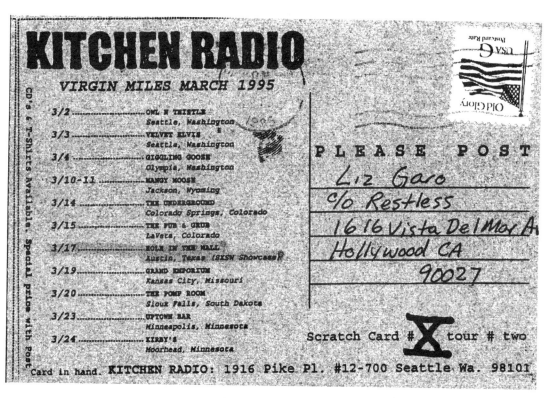

Above: Sample tour promo postcards from an indie label (top) and an indie band. Notice that the Archers postcard includes complete record ordering info. On the Kitchen Radio card, they've highlighted the 3/17 date that they want the recipient to attend, and note the "Special price with postcard" offer.

PROMOTING YOUR SHOWS

Materials you'll need to promote your shows:
1. **Press Release**
2. **Postcards**
3. **Posters, photos, other promo items**

Promoting the show

★ After the show is confirmed, make sure the club has all the materials they need. Chances are they will want photos, another tape, some press and whatever posters, t-shirts, stickers and other propaganda you may have.

★ Write up a one-page press release briefly talking about the band. Include any good quotes from any press clippings, list all the tour dates and fax it to the calendar section of the daily and weekly papers in each market you're playing.

★ Do something similar on a postcard and mail it to press, radio, record stores and send a stack to the club.

★ Make posters to send to the club: you can do relatively cheap color xeroxes or even black and white copies on 11 x 17 paper. With the advent of computers and 24-hour Copymats and Kinkos on every street corner throughout the country, you can easily make something that can be hung on a wall. Use magazine pictures, cartoon images or big bold words that present the band's name. Make it eye-catching!

Set-up

The goal of tour set-up is to effectively "work" three areas: press, radio and record stores. This gets your band name out there, starts to generate interest and is the first step in building/finding your audience. These areas will prove to be valuable sources of information and are usually operated by people who know the "scene" and know what is happening in the music world.

FOR IMMEADIATE RELEASE

THE USELESS PLAYBOYS - Richmond, Virginias' "post-mortem swing-noir" combo - are on the road again, this time in support of a self-produced single (Jungle Fever/ Caravan) on their own SAFARI RECORDS, a picture disc single (Bim Bam Baby/ Cool) on artist Frank Koziks' San Francisco independent label, MANS' RUIN, and an upcoming full length CD entitled I Am Curious Santo for Austins' CONTINENTAL RECORDS. Following up their very successful tour with The Reverend Horton Heat, The Playboys will be traveling coast to coast throughout February and March, highlighted by a featured appearance at this years' South By Southwest conference in Austin. The dates of the tour are as follows:

FEB.14-Memphis bar & grill- Richmond,VA,	MAR.8-Freemont St.-Las Vegas,NV.
16-Proud Larry's-Oxford, MS.	10 & 11-Stubbs BBQ-Lubbock,TX.
18-Metropolis-Lafayette,LA.	13-Emo's-Austin,TX.
19-Emo's-Houston,TX.(tent.)	14-The Continental-Austin,TX.
21-Orbit Room-Dallas,TX(tent.)	16-The Continental-Austin-(SXSW)
23-Golden West Saloon-Albuquerque,NM.	17-Hot Wheels-Houston,TX.
24-Club Congress-Tuscon,AZ.	18-Velvet Elvis-Houston,TX.
25-The Foothill-Long Beach,CA.	19-House of Blues-N.O.,LA.(tent.)
26-Linda's Doll Hut-Anaheiem,CA.	20-Saturn Bar-N.O.,LA.
28 thru March 1st-L.A.-TBA	24-Sluggo's-Pensacola,FL.
MAR.2-The Viper Room-L.A.,CA.	25-Star Bar-Atlanta,GA.
3 & 4-San Francisco-TBA	31-Berkeley Cafe-Raliegh,NC.
6-The Rhythm Room-Phoenix,AZ.	APRIL 1st.-Memphis bar & grill-HOME.

For the uniniated, here are just some of the things that have been written about the Useless Plaboys in the past:

"The Useless Playboys take the stage like hipsters from a lost era, or even another planet...Geier's crooning, which has impressive range and savoir-faire for a man wearing size 13EEE saddle shoes, blends the octane of white lightnin' with the inhibitions of Screaming Jay Hawkins. Pitman etches sophisticated guitar solos while Cecka cavorts on bass... if the world were a cooler place, these guys would be big."
Andy Garrigue, Style Weekly

"Sure they're doing Sinatra, so did Nancy Reagan. The Useless Playboys are Richmond's answer to what would have happend had Louis Jordan dropped acid with Jack Keroac."
Barry Gottlieb, Nitelife Magazine

"...their shiftless, hopped-up, juke-joint style...on stage antics make them irresistible to even the worst dancers and temperate teetotalers. Swinging music for swinging lovers."
Wes Coddington, Throttle Magazine

Above: A sample tour press release & bio.

Press

The press are the people and publications that will write about you and your music. In most markets that you play there will be a daily paper, a weekly paper, a college paper and a fanzine. Always check with the club to see what papers are the best to contact, and get names and phone numbers of who to talk to. You need to ask who is the pop music writer/critic/editor, who does the calendar listings, who does live reviews and who does show previews. If you give a newspaper information far enough in advance you can usually get at least a mention somewhere.

Daily papers tend to be pretty mainstream and unless you have a great angle for a story or one of the staff writers is an overwhelming fanatic for you, coverage in a daily paper may be limited. The best you can probably do is get a calendar listing which means they will list the band name, date of the show and name of the club.

Weekly papers are usually a little more open to covering indie bands because the focus for most of these papers is bringing attention to entertainment and popular culture. Again you need to find out who the music editor is, the listings editor and any pop music writers. As a rule, weekly papers come out every Wednesday or Thursday — their deadline for calendar listings and show previews is about 2 to 3 weeks before the street date. Weekly papers are also more apt to run photos of bands.

College papers can be open to interviewing unknown bands and plugging a live show. Again, get all the information to the editor or music editor of the paper.

Fanzines often have erratic publication schedules but they are important to contact and keep in touch with. They usually will not do concert listings, but most do live show reviews. Invite any writers for a local fanzine down to your show. Hopefully they will like what they hear and write about you and start talking about you.

Radio

For the past ten years or so, college radio has been the source of new music, scenes and trends. It stands out as a forum which is open to changes, experiments and the beauty of loud fuzzy guitars.

If you have a single or a demo tape or a CD be sure to send your material to the college radio station in the city you want to play, if you haven't already. Let them know what date you're playing, ask them to play your music and see if the club works with the station to do any kind of giveaways. Call the station and see if you can go on the air for an interview or to give away copies of your record or tickets to the show. Most stations will do this, some won't. It's always worth a try.

Record Stores

As a rule, the cool, independently owned record store in any city is run by people who know music. People who have all the Simple Machines *Working Holiday* singles or love The Grifters or own everything on the Estrus label or can tell you about the first time they saw The Replacements in some divey bar with only ten other people in the audience.

Even if you don't have anything for them to sell, make contact with the store. People who work at record stores are music enthusiasts who pride themselves in knowing what is going on before anyone else does. Tell them what your band is about, send them flyers, stickers and bring t-shirts (as a rule, you should give a little bit of band propaganda to everyone you meet — there's nothing quite like blatant self-promotion for people to remember you by). Of course invite them to the gig, and if you do have records leave a few with them to sell on consignment or see if they'll buy some from you flat out.

Things do overlap and quite often the kid behind the counter is also the show promoter and his best friend is the deejay at the college radio station who has the demo-listening show!

Keep in mind that for every person that you send something to, whether it's a club or college deejay or pop music writer or record store clerk, follow-up with a phone call to make sure that whatever was sent was received. Follow-through is crucial and it not only keeps the relationship going but also keeps you aware of what's going on. Maybe your band will actually get a preview in the weekly paper or maybe the promoter needs more posters. If you think you're calling too much, you probably are but still keep trying until you get some kind of response. Also keep in mind that a certain amount of common sense has to play into all this so when I say to keep calling, that does not mean every day, three times a day, it just means to be persistent and follow-up with everything.

BUDGETING YOUR TOUR

Most likely, you'll be funding this tour on your own, or on whatever money the band has made on local shows. Before you consider a tour feasible, you'll have to account for all your expenses. This is what you need to plan for financially:

Per Diems

★ The per diem is the allowance that everyone gets per day for personal expenses and food. Depending on what the band finances are, it should range from $5.00 to $15.00.

For per diems, (also known as PD's) multiply the number of band members to the dollar amount that you are allotting — that will be the daily per diem total.
5 band members
$7.00 per diem
5 band members multiplied by $7.00 per person = $35.00 a day
$35.00 a day multiplied by 7 days = $245.00 a week.

If you don't want to structure this and have to deal with the responsibility of someone handing out the money, just have a band fund that will cover all your group expenses, everything from meals to gas to guitar strings. There should always be one person though who is responsible for keeping track of the money (more on that later).

Gas Money

★ Here's a formula to help figure out how much money will be needed for gas.
Determine the distance you need to travel: **100 miles**
Estimate what your van gets per mile: **20 miles per gallon**
Divide the distance you have to go by the miles per gallon: **100 miles divided by 20 gallons equals 5 gallons**
Estimate the cost of gas per gallon: **$1.40**
Multiply gas cost by number of gallons: $1.40 x 5 gallons = **$7.00**

So, to go a 100 miles it would cost the band $7.00. If you're traveling 300 miles you'll need at least $21.00 for gas. It's also good to figure in oil and any other van mishaps, repairs or needs that may occur. If it's possible, it helps if there is at least one credit card and a AAA card that can be used.

Phone bill

★ travel with a calling card, but also be aware that at the end of the tour you may end up with a hefty phone bill.

Accommodations

★ More often than not, there will be a friendly soul who will offer you a floor to sleep on after the show. Remember your manners when staying with strangers and act the way your mother would want you to. Also know that a "touring band" sleeping at someone's place sometimes turns into an all-night party where the band is the center of attention and is expected to entertain the hosts with witty, humorous anecdotes about life on the road. This is all great, unless you're exhausted and have a ten-hour drive the next morning.

If you are getting hotel rooms, check with the club you're playing at first and see if they have any kind of deal established with the local Motel 6 where bands can get a discount on the room rate. Again, if you have an Automobile Club card, you can tell them the city you're in and the price range you want to spend and they can usually find you a hotel.

Merchandising

The two main functions of merchandising are to make some extra money and to get your name out there. It costs some money up front but it sure is helpful to have good looking t-shirts to sell. The cost of one-color t-shirt can average about $4.00 to $6.00 and can be sold between $8.00 and $12.00. Or, go to a thrift store and buy a bunch of cheap permanent press button-down shirts and just silk-screen on them. Be creative and resourceful! Other good merchandise to sell and give away are stickers, postcards and even matchbooks. All this stuff helps people remember you and helps the band earn some extra coin.

BAND RESPONSIBILITIES

The best way to run a tour is to divide responsibilities amongst everyone in the band. Booking the actual tour can be a full-time, nerve-wracking effort so all of the other jobs should be delegated.

Here's a list of stuff that needs to be done or kept in mind when pursuing a well-crafted juggernaut of a tour:

Tour manager: The tour manager usually ends up being the person who booked the tour since they have made the initial contacts. Their job can include:

★ Advancing the show a few days prior to the date, which means checking in with the club and confirming load-in and soundcheck times. Even though this was done when the show was first confirmed you should always double-check.

★ Getting precise, clear directions to the destination.

★ Identifying yourself to the promoter, club owner, bartender and/or sound persons as soon as you get to the club. Establish that you are the person that will collect the money at the end of the show. Again, with promoters and clubs, there are good ones that will be encouraging and supportive when they hand you the cash and there will be those that grumble and hand over the money begrudgingly and say, "You know, I lost money on this show."

★ Always counting the money — as soon as you get it — and having whatever contract you have in hand in case there is any kind of dispute or discrepancy over the amount paid.

Merchandise: Someone to be in charge of whatever merchandise you are selling, including t-shirts, singles and cassettes. This person will have to keep track of what is sold and given away and how much money comes in from sales. This person can also be in charge of starting a mailing list. Make postcards with the band's address on the back for people to fill out and either send in or give to you at the show. Start an address book so the next time you play that town again you can let the people who were there the first time know about your next show. Also, always have some sort of xeroxed catalog to give to people on the road, even if you only have one cassette released.

Money: This can either be a separate job from the tour manager or it can be another facet of it. This person will be responsible for all the money that is coming in as well as going out, and should keep a log in a notebook of daily per diems given and money made at each show. Keep track of every bit of money that goes out: gas money, food, repairs, etc. Save all your receipts too!

Promotion: This person should send out postcards, press releases or any material pertaining to the show to press, radio and retail. Their job also entails following-up with phone calls, and seeing if any kind of interview or coverage can happen.

Van stuff: Checking the oil, making sure the vehicle keeps running, keeping it filled with gas; keep the windows clean and keep the van clean.

Load-in: This means making sure that all the equipment gets loaded in the van, and that nothing is left behind.

These are all jobs that everyone can take part in — it shouldn't be one person's responsibility to cleanup after everyone in the van — it just helps to have each person aware of their one main job.

REALITY CHECKS

★ Money. Be prepared. Have some personal cash, access to a credit card, or a generous, understanding girlfriend/boyfriend/parent who will answer the phone at 3 AM when you're stranded between home and who-knows-where in need of a new radiator. The fact is, there is no guarantee that you will make money while you are on the road, so be sure to have some cash in pocket or at least close at hand in case of an emergency.

★ Keep the van clean. Throw out excessive/all trash whenever you stop. The living experience in the van is tight and claustrophobic enough without it being a storage space for every daily newspaper purchased, every flyer saved or empty bottle to accumulate. The van becomes your little world — so keep the environment safe, sane and clean!

★ When you get to the club, befriend the bartenders, doormen, and soundperson — these are the people who will be telling their friends about you and wearing your t-shirts long after you're gone.

★ Make sure there is a variety of tapes, magazines, books, even games to kill time. Bring a deck of cards. Do crossword puzzles. Keep a journal.

★ If a band member meets someone at a gig and they take off, make sure they have the phone # of where the rest of the band will be and someone in the band has their phone number. No one wants to seem like a nagging mom when you're out having fun but then again, no one wants to lose a band member in Kalamazoo, Michigan because the drummer met a temporary significant other and can't be located.

★ Be respectful of each other's space. There will be times when that highway is slipping beneath you, the stereo is blasting the latest Guided By Voices record and the jokes and conversation will seem witty, charming, hell, even engaging and interesting! The camaraderie will let you feel and believe that there isn't anywhere else you'd rather be... And, there will be times when the thought of spending another 15 minutes

— let alone another six-hour drive — with the same four people you've been with the last 3 weeks makes you sick to your stomach. The van becomes your world — and there isn't any room for head-trips, mind-fucks or psychotic reactions. If you need to get away, wait 'til after sound check: take a walk, check out a movie (if you have time) write in a journal, call home, shop at a thrift store or go have a cup of coffee. Be respectful and sensitive to the fact that everyone needs their space.

★ If you're going to be gone for a lengthy period, try to have someone at home to take care of your bills, feed your cats and do any business that needs to be done. The tour mindset is pretty simple: how to get from point A to point B and what the scenery looks like from the van window fills your head. You get into the rhythm of the road; you have a destination, you're meeting people — it's easy to forget about paying your phone bill or your boss at work or even what's happening in world events. Make sure the important stuff is taken care of as much as possible — it makes it easier when you're coming off the road.

★ Bring a sleeping bag. You never really know *where* you'll be sleeping.

VAN-O-RAMA

Things To Look For When Buying A Used Van

From John Murphy, Ford Mechanic to the Stars.

★ 3/4 Ton or 1 Ton for heavier loads, 1/2 Ton for lighter loads.

★ Always go for the lowest mileage possible, always!

★ Make sure it's driving straight, and that it hasn't been in any accidents.

★ Listen for any engine knocks.

★ Go for electronic ignition over points.

★ Cruise control is always a plus on those ten-hour drives through Kansas.

★ Do a compression test before you buy.

★ Make sure it can pass the smog check (where applicable).

★ If at all possible, when you go to buy a van bring a friend along who is a mechanic, or at least knows something about vans.

John Murphy's Pick: Ford Econoline E250 Extended Cab, with a 7.5 liter (460ci) V8 and C6 transmission.

YOUR VAN SUCKS!

However, that Beauville, Sportsman, Econoline or whatever, is all that comes between the world and the musical seeds you want to sow. And without a loft your van is only pulling half-duty. Several thousand miles of touring have shown my band(s) that there are three crucial benefits to the loft way-of-life: Security—keeping your equipment out of sight keeps it yours. Sleep—the platform provides a comfortable alternative to sleeping sitting up. Safety—the loft ends the guitar, bass and drums avalanches that result from quick stops.

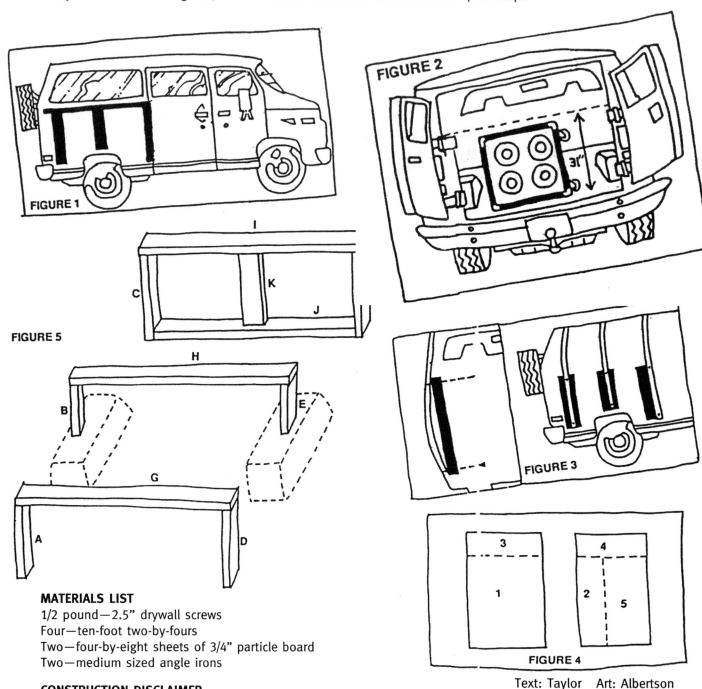

FIGURE 1

FIGURE 2

FIGURE 3

FIGURE 4

FIGURE 5

MATERIALS LIST
1/2 pound—2.5" drywall screws
Four—ten-foot two-by-fours
Two—four-by-eight sheets of 3/4" particle board
Two—medium sized angle irons

Text: Taylor   Art: Albertson

CONSTRUCTION DISCLAIMER
These directions are for building the cheapest, most bare-bones loft you can. Sure, you could listen to your carpenter friend and frame the platform like you would the floor of a house, but it just isn't necessary. Overbuilding your loft just costs more money and usually leaves you with less storage space than this method.

Building Your Loft, by Mercy Rule

Dimensions

Basically, the loft is just a big locker to store your Marshalls and Stratocasters in when you are not around. How much equipment your band has determines its size, but I like them to extend roughly from the back doors to where the side door starts (about six feet) and from the floor to the bottom of the side windows (about 31 inches). (See figure 1.) Your dimensions depend on how you stack the gear and what kind of van you have. These illustrations and measurements are based on a full-size Chevy van. For example, a Marshall 4x12 cabinet is about 30 inches wide, so if you place it on its side and it's the tallest part of your pile, make your frame no shorter than 31 inches tall. I add an inch or so extra in case it sags. (See figure 2.) Regardless of the loft size, the trick is to have no equipment visible from the outside, while providing a usable sleeping space above it all. Make sure to leave enough space so that with a futon or some sleeping bags on it, you can still roll over.

Frame

The 2x4 frame is just six uprights (three on a side) and three beams spanning the width of the van. Most vans have an internal steel frame or skeleton, and it is important that you screw your uprights to it, NOT TO THE SHEET METAL SIDES OF YOUR VAN. (See figure 3.) If you have interior siding covering up the frame, rip it out. The van sides and frame are curved, so your posts can only be screwed at the top and bottom. (See figure 3.) After attaching the four corner posts, (A,C,D,F of figure 5) run a 2x4 across the tops of A and C and measure from the bottom of the board to the top of the wheel well to give you the length of posts B and E. After the six posts are in, measure across the width of the van to give you the lengths of pieces G,H and I. Then screw them to the tops of the posts. Nothing is really "square" in a van, so your three beams will probably all be different lengths. A fourth beam, J, must be installed on the floor of the van between the two most forward posts, C and F. Screw it to the posts and use angle irons to attach it to the floor. CHECKING UNDER THE VAN FIRST, so you won't drill into your muffler or fuel line. This board takes most of the shock when equipment slams into it during load-ins and quick stops. A final upright, K, should be screwed between the floor beam, J, and the 2x4 directly above it, I.

Top

The top of the loft is really what holds this thing together, so don't mess it up. I recommend three-quarter inch particle board (two 4x8 sheets is enough) because the plywood edges that you'll be climbing over tend to splinter. The trick here is to cut your platform pieces so you have enough wood left over to close in the inner wall of the frame. If you make the platform two pieces, you should have three 24-inch-wide wall pieces left. (See figure 4.) Square your first platform piece, 1, to the inner most beam, I, and you'll see how the van tapers in towards the back. After some creative trimming, the board should fit flush to both the side of the van frame and to the 2x4 frame. Once the first piece fits, measure the remaining space and cut piece 2 from your second 4x8 sheet. (See figure 4.) Trim it until it falls into place. Screw both pieces down, making sure to countersink the screw holes so your sleeping bags, etc, don't get caught on the screw heads. Use the remaining particle board, parts 3, 4, and 5 to close in the compartment.

Tips

Now that your valuables are safely hidden away, don't blow your cover by spray painting your band name on the side of the van or by covering the back doors with musical gear stickers. The more the vehicle looks like mom and dad's family truckster, the safer your stuff will be. Curtains further hamper thugs from eyeing your stinky clothes, cameras, etc. Finally, if you are as cramped for space as we are, put your spare tire on a rack that fits on the back doors. Also, install a hasp and padlock on the rear doors—you'll sleep better at night—no matter how hard the floor or how loud the rest area.

Our band was in Chicago recently to finish making a record. We got there the night before we were to start and decided to visit some friends at a bar. Since we weren't playing that night, we kind of felt nervous about leaving a van full of gear unattended, but we found a good spot just across the street,—and hey!—it was even under a street lamp. Throughout the evening, I periodically looked out a window to check on the van. Returning to the van a couple of hours later, we were shocked to find the driver's side vent window smashed and most of the contents of the van in disarray. Our 24-track master tapes were strewn about, but undamaged, and most of our clothes and personal belongings, including $400 worth of tools were gone. The bad guys even moved the back seat during their frantic search, but could only guess at what treasures lay behind the mysterious, impenetrable wall that faced them.

Had they stolen the whole van the bad guys would have scored all of our gear, including a few vintage guitars we hauled along just for the recording session. But because the entire rear portion of the van was totally enclosed, the band was able to avoid a paralyzing blow that would have left us emotionally and financially crippled.

Vans OF THE STARS!

ZUZU'S PETALS

Make: 1979 Chevy van
Color: Aqua
Van's Name: Betty
Purchase price: Under 2 G's
Mileage at Purchase: 80,000
Current Mileage: 180,000
The van runs on: fumes usually
The band runs on: Coke and Motrin 800's
Miles per gallon: 6
Number of people who tour in it: 3.5
Stereo: Wacked out Radio Shack Deluxe
Favorite thing to listen to: $4.99 truck stop tapes (i.e. Bad Boyz of the 70s)
Coolest thing about our van: It still runs
The coolest thing we did to our van was: Hang up Eric's velvet Elvis
The suckiest thing about our van: We can't get out
Is there anybody's van you'd trade it for? The Cows van or the Oscar Meyer Weenie truck.
Other: It looks like Barbie's dream van after Ken dumped her and she ended up on Ice.

PHOTO: BRIAN GARRITY

OVERWHELMING COLORFAST

Make: 1975 Dodge Sportsman
Color: Metallic Pea
Purchase Price: One Grand
Mileage at Purchase: 83,000
Current Mileage: 90,000
Number of people who tour in it: 6
Miles per gallon: 5-8
The van runs on: Methane
The band runs on: Taco Bell, Sentences
Stereo: "One Sony piece of shit cassette with three inch speakers"
Favorite thing to listen to: Robin Harris, "Bebe's Kids"
Coolest thing about our van: No brakes. Naugahyde upholstery. Earth tones.
The coolest thing we do with our van is: "Rear-end others."
The suckiest thing about our van: "Smells like Roz (a hippie)."
Is there anybody's van you'd trade it for? "Rocket from the Crypt's Special Ed bus"
Other: "Yeah right. Right?"

Vans OF THE STARS!

FIREHOSE

Make: Ford Econoline 250
Color: White
Purchase Price: $12.5 K
Mileage at Purchase: 2,300
Current Mileage: 120,000
Miles per gallon: 11
Number of people who tour in it: 4.5
The van runs on: gasoline (90 octane or higher)
The band runs on: mota and chow
Type of sound system: Toshiba dash cassette (20 w/ch)
Favorite thing to listen to: madonna, mingus, richard hell, roky erickson
Coolest thing about our van: brahma bull stickers on each front door
The coolest thing we did to our van was: weld a safe to the floor.
The suckiest thing about our van: it ain't a toyota
Is there anybody's van you'd trade it for? nope—karma wails!

wise up:
dump the chevys + gmc's
d.boon was killed in a
dodge ram.
go for the heaviest suspension
available (1 ton).
no 6 cylinders for
freeway!
no windows to
let people see
what you have
to donate —
spray paint
them white
on the inside
(Caution!
don't attempt
this on the
windshield)

BUFFALO TOM

Make: 1988 Dodge Ram
Color: Blue
Purchase Price: Approx. 12,000 (used)
Mileage at Purchase: 20,000
Current Mileage: Approx. 100,000
Number of People who tour in it: up to 7 with U-Haul attached
Miles per gallon: 10
The van runs on: unleaded
The band runs on: "Just coffee, lately."
Stereo: AM/FM cassette bought in North Carolina
Favorite thing to listen to: We've been listening to a lot of recorded books lately, but it's hard to get people to shut up.
Last book listened to: *Heart of Darkness* by Joseph Conrad
Coolest thing about our van: "Our mascot. We've got someone who sleeps in it... but... well... I guess I won't go into that."
The grossest thing we've done to our van: "Tom threw up in it once."
The suckiest thing about our van: "Looks like we're the Amherst College Swim Team. Plus, for a while it used about two quarts of oil every 300 miles, but we got it fixed."
Anybody's van you'd trade it for: "Ideally, we would each get our own car to drive."
Other: "Once you get it going, it'll go like, 70, 90 miles per hour, but it's hard to stop. It's dangerous."

STATE-BY-STATE DIRECTORY

What follows is over 2,500 contacts across the continental United States, and a few Canadian contacts as well. We've organized the states alphabetically, the cities are alphabetical within each state, and the contacts are alphabetical within each category. We've added comments if we think contacts are particularly notable, and in some cases we've included info. on what to do and where to eat and sleep in a given city. These comments are purely subjective; what we like you may hate and vice-versa. After a few tours, you'll have created your own custom list of contacts reflecting your own likes and dislikes.

When musical styles are listed, we frequently use the word "Alternative," that's right, the big industry buzz word attached to the likes of Pearl Jam, Cracker, and Fugazi alike. We don't know what the hip new word in your town is (experimental, cutting-edge, punk, pop-core, pop-punk, disco, acid jazz or whatever) so we have decided to just stick with "alternative." Other musical styles are listed where applicable, but nothing is set in stone. If you're a country band and you can't find a show in a particular city, try the rock clubs, you never know. Record stores listed are ones that will buy or consign records, tapes and CDs from independent bands or labels.

While we have made every effort to make sure that these listings are correct, things do change. Please make sure to verify the correct address and information of anyone you talk to.

ALABAMA
Birmingham
Venues

Five Points South Music Hall
1016 20th St S
Birmingham AL 35205
205-322-2207
Capacity: 1000

Louie Louie
2001 Highland Ave
S Birmingham AL 35205
Capacity: 900
Rock, jazz, blues

The Nick
2514 10th Ave. S.
Birmingham, AL. 35205
205-252-3831
Capacity: 250
All styles

The Underground
691 Vine St
Monteballo AL 35115
205-665-0908
Capacity:300
All styles

Zydeco
2001 15th S
Birmingham AL 35205
205-933-1032
Capacity: 600
Alternative, rock, blues

Press

Birmingham News
Shawn Ryan
2200 4th Ave. N.
Birmingham, AL. 35203
205-325-2222
Daily paper

Black & White
P.O. Box 13215
Birmingham AL 35202
205-933-0460
Alternative monthly

Record Stores

Charlemagne
1924 1/2 11th Ave.
Birmingham AL 35205
205-322-5349
CD, LP, CA

Music Stores

Highland Music
2917 Highland Ave.
Birmingham AL 35205
205-254-3288
Sales, rentals, guitar and amp repairs.

Music Alley
113 Lorna Brook Village
Birmingham AL 35216
205-988-3688
Sales, rentals, repairs.

Mobile
Venues

Culture Shock
659 Holcombe Ave
Mobile AL 36606
334-471-9940
Capacity: 200-300

GT Henry's
462 Dauphin St.
Mobile AL 36602
334-432-0300
Capacity: 300 inside; 1,280 outside
All Styles

The Lumberyard
2617 Dauphin St
Mobile AL 36607
334-476-4609
Capacity: 500
All Styles

McNasty's
462 Dauphin St
Mobile AL 36602
334-4321835
Capacity: 300 inside, 1280 outside
All Styles

The Original Poor Richard's
5955 Old Shell Rd.
Mobile AL 36689
334-341-5051
Capacity: 165
Alternative, All styles

Press

The Bayside Loafer
563 Holcombe Ave.
Mobile AL 36606
334-478-6100
Weekly entertainment paper

The Harbinger
PO Box U-980
Mobile AL 36688
334-476-0430
Biweekly newspaper

Radio

WOWW 107.3
PO Box 2788
Pensacola FL 32513
904-434-7388

WTOH 105.9
Spring Hill College
4000 Dauphin St.
Mobile AL 36608
334-380-3848
College alternative

Record Stores

Satori Sound Records
5460 Old Shell Rd.
Mobile AL 36608
334-343-6677
CD, CA, LP

Music Stores

M&S Music
180 N. Beltline Hwy
Mobile AL 36607
334-476-1303
Most instruments; repairs and rentals

Food

Dauphin St. downtown is the main area of Mobile for hanging out. There aren't too many good restaurants open late, but you may want to check out **Crystal's All Night**. Otherwise you will be stuck going to the Waffle House or something. Across the bay in Daffney, **Papa's Place** is a fine Italian restaurant that's not too expensive.

Shelter

There are the typical Motel 6-type chains downtown; try those located on Government St.

Etc.

Not a whole lot to check out in the area, but there is a brewery downtown. According to our friend Charles, the number one pastime in Mobile is to go over to Biloxi, Mississippi for gambling. Mobile is also close to some beaches. Since there is not too much happening out by the colleges, it's best to stick near downtown.

Other places to play in Alabama:

Tip Top Cafe
Lance Church
123 Maple Ave. NW
Huntsville, AL. 35801
205-534-9185
Capacity: 200
All Styles

The Chucker
Ludovic Goubet
2121 6th Street
Tuscaloosa, AL. 35401
205-391-0708
Capacity: 160
All Styles

Egans
1229 University
Tuscaloosa AL 35401
205-391-0708
Capacity: 50

Ivory Tusk
1215 University Blvd
Tuscaloosa AL 35401
205-752-3435
Capacity: 800
All Styles

ARIZONA
Mesa
Venues

Hollywood Alley
2610 W. Baseline Rd.
Mesa AZ 85202
602-820-7117
Capacity: 300
Alternative, All Styles

The Nile Theater
105 W Main St.
Mesa AZ
602-649-2766
Capacity: 1,300
All-ages with a bar
Punk, alternative, rock
Usually booked through Adams Agency out of nearby Phoenix.

Press
(Also see Phoenix press info.)

Grind Magazine
PO Box 2830
Mesa AZ 85214
602-624-3567
An occasional fanzine that features local and national indie bands.

Blast
2404 W. Huntington Dr.
Tempe AZ 85282
602-438-8042
Fax: 602-438-7854
Biweekly magazine

Record Stores

Fugitive Records
1055 N Mesa Dr.
Mesa AZ 85201
602-644-0650
CD, CA, LP, 7"

Rockaway Records
1310 W Southern, #3
Mesa AZ 85202
602-964-6301
CD, CA, LP

Stinkweed's Record Exchange
1940 W Baseline Rd., Ste 1
Mesa AZ 85202
602-897-7109
CD, CA, LP
This is a great store with a good selection of vinyl and 7"s.

Music Stores

Musician's Discount
1911 W Broadway, #17
Mesa AZ 85202
602-827-1725
Guitars and drums; most repairs; no rentals.

Food
Los Dos Molinos on S. Alma School in Mesa is a good Mexican food place.

Shelter
Best Western at 1666 S. Dobson Rd. (602-831-7000)

Etc.
Savers on W. Broadway Rd. is a cool thrift store.

Phoenix
Venues

Boston's Nightclub
910 N McClintock Dr.
Tempe AZ
602-921-7343
Capacity: 250
All-ages
Rock, punk, alternative

Char's Has the Blues
4631 N 7th Ave.
Phoenix AZ 85013
602-230-0205
Capacity: 150
Blues

Gibson's
410 S Mill Ave.
Tempe AZ
602-967-1234
Capacity: 500
21 and up
Alternative

Long Wong's
701 S Mill Ave.
Tempe AZ 85281
602-966-3147
Capacity: 120
Alternative

The Mason Jar
2303 E. Indian School Rd.
Phoenix AZ 85016
602-954-0455
Capacity: 200
Rock, alternative, punk, metal

The Roxy
2110 E Highland
Phoenix AZ
602-912-9566
Capacity: 680

Promoters

Adams Agency
63 E Main St. Ste 701
Mesa AZ
602-649-9224
Cory

Suckerpunch Presents
902 S 28th Ave. #2
Phoenix AZ
602-352-1370
Noah

Press

Buzzkill
World Enterprises
PO Box 43950
Phoenix AZ 85050
Magazine

Country Spirit Magazine
PO Box 3174
Tempe AZ 85280
602-966-6236
Monthly country music magazine

New Times Weekly
PO Box 2510
Phoenix AZ 85002
602-271-0040
Weekly newspaper
Has a concert calendar and two music review sections. Send material c/o Peter Gilstrap.

ADVICE FROM THE ROAD

TEN SIGNS THAT YOU ARE HEADED FOR TROUBLE AT THE SHOW

(in no particular order)

From Fogboy of Foreskin 500.

1. Promoterhead leaves to take shower right before doors open.

2. Soundman has a freshie (small ponytail located on back of head).

3. Club you are playing turns out to be local band's practice space.

4. One electrical outlet for whole club.

5. Pizza.

6. Bartender says people don't show up until late.

7. All you can drink at bar (sounds good at first, but in the long run can be very detrimental - unless you are Ed Hall).

8. Security has 6 "D" Maglights.

9. Band in next room is doing country version of "Cocaine."

10. Promoterhead wants you to do quick set so he can get the reggae dance party started.

Planet Magazine
1000 E Apache Ste 206
Tempe AZ 85281
602-804-1679
Monthly music magazine
They cover local and national
indie bands.

State Press Magazine
Arizona State University
15 Matthews Ctr.
Tempe AZ 85287-1502
602-965-1695
Daily newspaper

Zia Zine
c/o Chud Graphics
910 S. Hohokum #120
Tempe AZ 85281
Reviews, interviews, concert
listings.

Radio

KASR 680am
Arizona State University
Tempe AZ 85287-1305
602-965-4163
College alternative

KUPD 97.9
1900 W Carmen St.
Tempe AZ 85283
602-345-5921
Commercial, alternative rock

Record Stores

Eastside Records
217 W University
Tempe AZ
602-968-2011
CD, CA, LP
Specializing in independents,
imports and special orders. They
still carry new vinyl and have a
large selection of blues and jazz.
"This is one of the best stores -
period." The store even has a
great aquarium stocked with
exotic, salt-water fish. Ask for
Ben, Mike or Geoff.

Zia Records
105 W University
Tempe AZ 85282
602-829-1967
CD, LP, CA, video

Music Stores

Bass Place
1438 N Scottsdale Rd.
Tempe AZ
602-423-1161
This is the place to come for
your bass.

Bizarre Guitar and Drum
749 W Camelback
Phoenix AZ 85013
602-248-9297
Guitars and drums; minor
repairs; no rentals

D.J.'s Rock and Roll Music
2801 E McDowell
Phoenix AZ 85008
602-275-0654
Most instruments; no guitar
repairs; PA rentals

Guitar and Keyboard City
1945 E Indian School Rd.
Phoenix AZ 85016
602-230-2206
Most instruments; guitar repairs;
PA, guitar and keyboard rentals

The Guitar Shop
6830 5th Ave., Ste 101
Scottsdale AZ 85251
602-994-8749
Most instruments; guitar repairs;
no rentals

Guitar Specialty Services
930 W Broadway Rd.
Tempe AZ
602-829-9630
Instrument repairs

Musician's Electronic Exchange
2434 E Thomas Rd.
Phoenix AZ 85016
602-955-3750
Guitar and amp sales and
repairs

Precision Guitar
4442 N 7th Ave. Ste 6
Phoenix AZ
602-265-7760
Guitar repairs

Synthony Music
3939 E Campbell
Phoenix AZ 85018
602-955-3590
Electronic instrument sales and
repairs; no rentals

Food

May West on University and **Two Pesos** Mexican Cafe on Southern Ave. are both good 24-hour restaurants in Tempe. **Rosita's Place** on McDowell in Phoenix is another good Mexican food place. **Gentle Strength Co-op** on W. University in Tempe is a good vegetarian place. **Big Wong** on W. Indian School Rd. in Phoenix is a Chinese restaurant with a most gratifying name.

Shelter

Motel 6 at 513 W Broadway Rd. in Tempe (602-967-8696) **Travelodge** at 1005 E Apache Blvd. in Tempe (602-968-7871)

Etc.

The **Salvation Army** on N. Scotsdale Rd. in Tempe is a thrift store with the clothing for you. If not, try the **Disabled American Veterans** on E. Apache Blvd. in Tempe. **Java Road** on E. 7th St. in Tempe is a hip hangout/coffee shop. Some sightseeing locations include Arcosanti, Oak Creek Canyon/ Sedona, Papago Park in Phoenix, Montezuma's Castle, and Jerome.

Tucson

According to the advice from the sage **Blacky Ranchette**, a man of sound mind who has spent his share of time in the desert, falling into Tucson is like being caught in a whirling vortex. Basically, once you're in the rhythm of the swirl it's hard to get out — that is, if you want to. Playing a show in Tucson, hanging out at **Club Congress** and being in the desert is a getaway that every band should try to do. There is always the potential for it to be one of the more pleasurable performing and mind-clearing experiences.

Venues

Club Congress
(inside the Hotel Congress)
Dan Vinick
311 E. Congress
Tucson, AZ 85701
520-622-8848
Hotel Congress, located in downtown, is the center of the Tucson vortex Not only can this hotel boast being the oldest, but it offers the best cowboy bar around (The Tap Room, complete with vinyl jukebox) and a restaurant that stays open late (The Cup) and the newly refurbished Club Congress all under one roof. The Club Congress has played center stager to Tucson's credible/creative local music scene that includes Giant Sand, Friends OF Dean Martin, Rainer, Al Perry and The Cattlemen, Naked Prey and Dog & Pony Show. If you're a band playing at the Congress you are usually guaranteed a stay in one of their hotel rooms, a space that would make any fan of Charles Bukowski or Jack Kerouac feel right at home.

Downtown Performance Center (DPC)
Steve Eye
31 E. Toole
Tucson, AZ. 85701
520-628-1650
All ages
Big warehouse space that usually books some art events as well as music in the vein of good loud punk rock. Longtime promoter Steve Eye is a skateboarding aficionado and can point you to the best places to skate.

The Rock
136 N. Park
Tuscon AZ 85702
520-629-9211

Press

Tucson Weekly
Mike Metzger
2616 1/2 E. 6th Street
Tucson, AZ 85716

Record Stores

Toxic Shock
424 E. 6th Street.
Tucson, AZ 85705
520-623-2008
New, used CDS and lots of vinyl; specializing in indie labels, punk stuff and local music. Ask if you can sell your single there on consignment.

Music Stores

The Chicago Store
130 E. Congress
Tucson, AZ 85701
If you need anything from guitar strings to an accordion to a used Les Paul to a stand-up bass or cello this place offers deals and encourages its customers to haggle on both new and used instruments.

Food

The Cup (see under Club Congress) A great place for coffee drinking; try their soups of the day and Hotel Salad and pasta dishes and desserts! Always satisfying. **Maya Quetzal** on 429 N. 4th Ave. has quality Guatemalan food, lots of vegetarian choices. **El Minuto Cafe** at 354 S. Main Ave. serves traditional Mexican food, and is open 'til 3am.

Etc.

Of course in Tucson, you have the desert and lots of it. If you have the time take off on Speedway and drive until you reach the Saguaro Desert -- towering cactus as far as the eye can see! Along 4th Ave., a leisure afternoon can be spent nosing around all the thrift stores, finding deals at the **Value Village**, stocking up on vitamins at the neighborhood co-op, hanging out at **Toxic Ranch** or getting an ice cream at one of the few surviving **Dairy Queens**.

ARKANSAS
Little Rock
Venues

Bad Bob's
2204 E Harding
Pine Bluff AR 71611
501-534-9515
Capacity: 1200
Country

BJ's Starstudded Honkytonk
8323 New Benton Hwy
Little Rock AR 72209
501-562-6000
Capacity:
Country

Blue Mesa
1719 Merrill Dr.
Little Rock AR 72211
501-221-7777
Capacity: 120
Alternative, All Styles
Great Restaurant

Juanita's Cantina Ballroom
1300 S Main St.
Little Rock AR 72202
501-374-3660
Capacity: 400
Alternative
Great Mexican food; voted best in Arkansas for food and music eight straight years; promoter has deals with hotels.

Vino's
7th and Chester St.
Little Rock AR 72201
501-375-8466
Live alternative music; sometimes they do poetry readings

Promoters

Mark Abernathy
501-221-7777

Bennie Turner
501-374-3660

Press

Arkansas Democrat-Gazette
PO Box 2221
Little Rock AR 72203
501-378-3400
Daily newspaper

Little Rock Freepress
824 W Seventh St.
Little Rock AR 72201
501-372-4719
Biweekly alternative newspaper

Nightflying
PO Box 250276
Little Rock AR 72225
501-664-5099
Monthly newspaper

Radio

KUCA 91.3
University of Central Arkansas
Conway AR 72032
501-450-5555
Folk, Jazz

KHDX 93.1
Hendrix College
Conway AR 72032
501-450-1339
Fax: 501-450-1200
Alternative

KABF 88.3
1501 Arch St.
Little Rock AR 72202
501-372-6119
All Styles

KMJX 105.1
11101 Anderson Dr.
Little Rock AR 72212
501-224-6500
Fax: 501-224-6598
Classic Rock

Record Stores

Arkansas Record and CD Exchange
4212 MacArthur Dr.
North Little Rock AR 72118
501-753-7877
CD, CA, LP

Been Around Records
1216 S University
Little Rock AR 72204
501-663-8767
CD, CA, LP

Discount Records
3400 S University
Little Rock AR 72204
501-565-9848
CD, CA, LP

Electric Moo
301 W Main
Russleville AR 72801
501-968-3337
CD, CA

Peaches
4808 JFK Blvd.
North Little Rock AR 72116
501-771-0055
CD, CA, LP

Music Stores

Boyd Music Center
5702 W 12th St.
Little Rock AR 72204
501-664-3614
Sales, repairs, rentals

Music Makers
1121 N Rodney Parkham Rd.
Little Rock AR 72212
501-224-0606
Most instruments; guitar and electronic repairs; no rentals

CALIFORNIA
Fresno
Venues

Bisla's
50 E. Herndon
Fresno CA 93720
206-436-8703
Capacity: 360
Alternative, hip-hop, rock.

Club Fred
1426 N Van Ness Ave.
Fresno CA 93728
209-233-3733
Capacity: 210
Rock, Blues, Alternative

The Fulton
1243 Fulton Mall
Fresno CA 93721
209-486-2582
Capacity: 120
Alternative, rock, variety.

Press

Fresno Bee
1626 E St.
Fresno CA 93786
209-441-6111
Daily newspaper

Konfuzed
5201 N Maple Ave.
Fresno CA 93740-0046
209-278-6982,278-2598
Monthly music guide

Metro News
Box 11964
Fresno CA 93776
209-445-4131
Weekly newspaper

Radio

KKDJ 105.9
1525 E Shaw Ave., Ste 200
Fresno CA 93710
209-266-5800
Rock

KRZR 103.7
1765 N Fine St.
Fresno CA 93727
209-252-8994
Rock, Metal

KFSR 90.7
5201 N Maple Ave.
Fresno CA 93740-0046
209-278-4500
fax 209-278-6985
All Styles

Record Stores

Danny's Records
432 E Bullard Ave
Fresno CA 93710
209-447-5447

Ragin Records
729 E Olive St.
Fresno CA 93728
209-485-9926
CD, CA, LP
Call Paul
Ragin' Records will promote shows for indie or punk rock bands.

Tower Records
5611 N Blackstone Ave.
Fresno CA 93703
209-431-4700
CD, CA

Music Stores

Archer Music
855 E Fern Ave.
Fresno VA 93728
209-264-0908
Most instruments; repairs and rentals

Sound Stage
1649 N Blackstone Ave.
Fresno CA 93703
209-233-6531
Most instruments; guitar and amp repairs; no rentals

Food

Cafe Intermezzo in the Tower District, the only place that has cafes.

Shelter

Motels on the 99 and 41 tend to be pretty cheap. **Ragin' Records** will help find places to stay at people's houses for the bands

Los Angeles Orange County Riverside

Venues

Alligator Lounge
3321 Pico Blvd.
Santa Monica, CA 90405
310-449-1844
Lots of blues, rootsy/folk stuff, some alternative nights
Capacity: 300

Al's Bar
305 S Hewitt St.
Los Angeles CA 90013
213-687-3558
Capacity: 174
Alternative

Amazon Bar and Grill
14649 Ventura Blvd.
Sherman Oaks CA 91403
818-986-7502
Capacity: 400
Acoustic, Mellow Alternative

The Barn
UC Riverside
900 University Ave
Riverside CA 92521
909-787-5729
Capacity: 500
Alternative, punk

The Blue Saloon
4657 Lankershim Blvd.
North Hollywood CA 91601
818-766-4644
Capacity: 150
Rockabilly, Blues

The Coach House
33157 Camino Capistrano
San Juan Capistrano CA 92675
714-496-8930
Capacity: 480
All Styles

Coconut Teaszer
8117 Sunset Blvd.
Hollywood CA 90046
213-654-4773
Capacity: 285
Rock, Alternative

The Crazy Horse
1580 Brookhollow Dr.
Santa Ana CA 92075
714-549-1512
Capacity: 300
Country

The Dragonfly
6510 Santa Monica Blvd.
Hollywood, CA 90028
213-466-6111
Alternative

FM Station Live
11700 Victory Blvd.
N Hollywood CA 91606
818-769-2221
Capacity: 500
Rock

The Foothill Club
1922 Cherry St.
Signal Hill CA 90806
310-494-5196
310-434-8988, for booking

Frogs
16714 Hawthorne Blvd.
Lawndale CA 90260
310-371-2257
Capacity: 280
Rock, R&B

Hell's Gate
6423 Yucca Street
Hollywood, CA
213-463-9661
or mail stuff to:
Larry Mann
445 N. Gardner Street
Hollywood, CA 90028
Alternative, variety.

Jabberjaw
5711 W Pico Blvd.
Los Angeles CA 90019
213-732-3463
Capacity: 250
Alternative
All-ages
In its five-year history Jabberjaw has become an important part of historical indie-rock culture. The all-ages spot was originally just a cool hang-out coffee house with a lots of 70s kitsch. Fast forward to today and it is the spot for any young band to play. Sure, the sound system needs some work and on the nights when Jon Spencer Blues

TOURING IS BULLSHIT

by Cole Coonce of Braindead Sound Machine

It is a common misconception among artists, labels, and agents that touring is necessary to promote your typical recording act. This is bullshit.

Touring is a tool designed by the record companies to keep the artist financially subservient in a most dehumanizing vassal/fiefdom type relationship. Consider it contemporary sharecropping. Forty acres and an Econoline.

Check your recording contract for the part marked "Recoupables." This is a euphemism for "Artists' Profit Margin Or Lack Thereof." One must understand that a small label is willing to shell out $5-10,000 clams for a two month traveling nose-dive and a major will finance up to 100 G's for a six-month traveling jail sentence. But here comes the weird part: they want it back.

So tally up Tour Support with the other record label negative-cashflow-brainfarts-that-seemed-like-a-good-idea-at-the-time: Exorbitant Recording Costs (due to tracking and mixing at a ludicrously overpriced hopelessly trite "drum ing Video Budgets (for arty promotional clip MTV, dude," but will more Uber Studio famous for a sound") and Bank Break- a hopelessly banal, quasi- that is "sure to get on likely see limited airplay on public access).

Record Companies are modeled after such paradigms of financial oppression as the Bank of America, the Federal Reserve and Lucifer hisself-i.e., credit institutions whose best "interests" (pun accepted) are not served by ever allowing their loan recipients, a.k.a. the artist, to "recoup" or pay back their loans.

What I'm saying, kids, is if your dad owes the B. of A. some serious coin, they will take his house; if you owe Coyote God Records a ton of dough, they will take your career. The U.S. Treasury Department owes over 3 trillion dead presidents to the Federal Reserve, who are making obscene profits off the interest itself. Bomb Throwing Fag owes Anti-Christ Records six-figures in recoupables, who is making a tidy profit even though B.T.F. never "recouped."

Two months of meager per-diem, assholic club techies, and a claustrophobic van saturated in the roadies' buttfunk is hardly worth the acute financial hit (and is of extremely dubious promotional value).

If you're going to sell your soul to the devil, keep your overhead low.

Cole Coonce has dropped out of music and now writes for Full Throttle News *and* Dragster Illustrated, *and attends only NHRA events.*

Explosion or Rocket From The Crypt played there was hardly enough air to breathe but that's all secondary compared to the friendly supportive atmosphere the place has. And it is to the credit of club proprietors Gary Dent and Michelle Carr who support the indie-rock community and all artists who may be doing just a little something different. Jabberjaw has been there in the beginning with Hole, Helmet and The Melvins and they continue to attract the best of the underground: Low, Unwound, Tattle Tale, Kicking Giant and Nectarine. Beside their musical pedigree, Jabberjaw is a place that treats bands with respect and gives the kids a place to go (that means you!) Complete with a back patio and wandering cats.

John Bull Pub
958 S Fair Oaks
Pasadena CA 91105
818-441-4353
Capacity: 250
Blues, Funk, R&B, Rock

Luna Park
665 N. Robertson
W. Hollywood, CA 90069
310-652-0611
Luna Park is a split-level restaurant/performance space that combines class and kitsch. The upstairs room is usually reserved for bigger names and the intimate downstairs room is for small theatre groups or comics before the music starts. The music choice and clientele for Luna Park is eclectic, on any given night the upstairs room can have respected singer-songwriters followed by art-rockers like Billy Wisdom or Extra Fancy while downstairs you can have a mix of roots rock, alternative/jazz/swing and an ex-punk rocker fronting a country band.

The Marquee
7000 Garden Grove Blvd.
Westminster CA 92683
714-891-1181
Capacity: 500
Rock, Dude

The Mint
6010 W. Pico Blvd.
Los Angeles, CA 90042
213-937-9630
Small, intimate venue with red leather booths. Lots of blues and singer/songwriter stuff.

Molly Malone's
575 S Fairfax Blvd.
Los Angeles CA 90036
213-935-2707
Capacity: 200
Acoustic

The Natural Fudge Company
5224 Fountain Ave.
Hollywood CA 90029
213-669-8003
Capacity: 100
All ages
Rock, Alternative, hippie stuff

The Palomino
6907 Lankershim Blvd.
N Hollywood CA 91605
818-764-4010
Capacity: 300
Country, Blues, Rock
All-ages

The Roxy
9009 Sunset Blvd.
W Hollywood CA 90069
310-276-2229
Capacity: 500
Alternative, All Styles

Showcase Theatre
683 S Main St 91720
Corona CA
Capacity: 500
Alternative, punk, ska, grindcore

Spaceland
1717 Silverlake Blvd.
mail stuff to:
Mitchell Frank
373 N. La Cienega Blvd.
Los Angeles, CA 90048
310-652-9002
Normally a Latino sports bar with some leftover disco decor, Spaceland operates on Wednesday, Thursday, Friday and Saturday nights and some Saturday afternoons. You are almost guaranteed a friendly audience of music fans/supporters on any given night.

Troubadour
9081 Santa Monica Blvd.
W Hollywood CA 90069
310-276-6168
Capacity:
Rock, Metal, Blues, Alternative

The Viper Room
8852 Sunset Blvd.
W Hollywood CA 90069
310-358-1880
Capacity: 100
Alternative, Rock, Metal
All the stories are true and then some . . . Thursday night is "martini night" with lounge and swing music, the rest of the week is anything goes. The Viper does not make a career helping young bands and definitely opts for those surprise performances from The Black Crows and Pearl Jam instead. If you have the need, go by the place but chances are you won't be able to afford the $15 cover charge if you are on tour. Spend your money down the street at Tower Records or Book Soup.

Whiskey-A-Go-Go
8901 Sunset Blvd.
W Hollywood CA 90069
310-652-4205
Capacity: 450
Rock, Alternative

Press

The Angry Thoreauan
PO Box 2246
Anaheim CA 92814
714-740-3063
Quarterly magazine

BAM
6767 Forest Lawn Dr., Ste 110
Los Angeles CA 90068
213-851-8600
Biweekly music magazine

Ben Is Dead
PO Box 3166
Hollywood CA 90028
213-960-7674
Bimonthly fanzine

Flipside
PO Box 60790
Pasadena CA 91116
818-585-0395
Bimonthly fanzine

LA Weekly
6715 Sunset Blvd
Los Angeles CA 90027
213-465-4414
Weekly entertainment
newspaper

Los Angeles Reader
5550 Wilshire Blvd.
Los Angeles CA 90036-3389
213-965-7430
Weekly entertainment
newspaper

Los Angeles Times
Attn: Calendar Section
Times-Mirror Square
Los Angeles CA 90053
213-237-5324
fax 213-237-7630
Attn: Lori Pike
Daily newspaper

Mean Street
2061 3rd St., Ste G
Riverside CA 92507
714-684-7184
Monthly music magazine

Music Connection
6640 Sunset Blvd. #120
Hollywood CA 90028
213-462-5772
Biweekly music magazine

Pasadena Weekly
50 S Delancey Ave., Ste 200
Pasadena CA 91105
818-584-1500
Weekly entertainment
newspaper

Shred
1057 E Imperial Hwy, Ste 264
Placentia CA 92670
714-572-2565
Monthly music magazine

Stool
625 E 4th St., Ste 261
Long Beach CA 90802
Alternative fanzine

URB Magazine
1680 N Vine St. Ste 1012
Hollywood CA 90028
213-993-0291
Monthly music magazine

Village View
Bob Remstein
2342 Sawtelle Blvd.
Los Angeles, CA 90048
213-664-1972
Weekly

Radio

KLOS 95.5
3321 S La Cienaga
Los Angeles CA 90016
310-840-4800
Commercial Rock

KLA 99.9 Cafm, 530 am cc
UCLA
2400 Ackerman Union
Los Angeles CA 90024
310-825-9104, 825-9105
Fax: 310-206-0906
All Styles

KXLU 88.9 fm
Loyola Marymount University
7101 W 80th St.
Los Angeles CA 90045
310-338-2866
Alternative, Reggae, Hip-Hop,
Classical
On-air performances and inter-
views, night-time specialty
shows

KSCR 98.3 cafm
USC
404 Student Union
Los Angeles CA 90089
213-740-5727, 310-740-1853
All Styles

KMBU 98.3 cafm
Pepperdine University
Malibu CA 90265
310-456-4132
Fax: 310-456-7751

KCRW 88.9 fm
Santa Monica College
1900 Pico Blvd.
Santa Monica CA 90405
310-450-5183
All Styles

KLBC 91.1 cafm
Long Beach City College
4901 E Carson
Long Beach CA 90808
310-420-4312
Rock, Rap, Dance, Alternative

KLON 88.1 fm
CSULB
1288 Bellflower Blvd.
Long Beach CA 90815
310-985-5566
Jazz

KPCC 89.3 fm
Pasadena City College
1570 E Colorado Blvd.
Pasadena CA 91106
818-585-7000
Fax: 818-585-7916
Jazz, Blues, Country

KCLU 101.5 cafm
California Lutheran University
60 W Olsen Rd.
Thousand Oaks CA 91360
805-493-3474

KROQ 106.7 fm
PO Box 10670
Burbank CA 91505
818-567-1067
Fax: 818-520-1329
Commercial Alternative

KPFK 90.7 fm
PO Box 8092
Universal City CA 91608
818-985-2711
Alternative, Jazz, Classical

KUCR 88.3 fm
UC Riverside
Riverside CA 92521
909-787-3421
All styles

Record Stores

Aron's
1150 N Highland Ave.
Los Angeles CA 90038
213-469-4700
CD, CA, LP

Alternative Groove
200 Pier Ave.
Hermosa Beach CA 90254
310-379-3137
CD, CA, LP, a cool store that
also runs a record label.

Barton's Records
4018 Buckingham Rd.
Los Angeles CA 90008
213-298-9338
CD, CA
reggae

Bionic Records
9549 Valley View
Cypress CA 90630
714-828-4225
CD, CA, LP

Bleecker Bob's
7454 Melrose Ave.
Hollywood CA 90046
213-951-9111
CD, CA, LP

CD Warehouse
125 Tustin Ave.
Orange CA 92667
714-771-6646
CD, CA

Cheap Guy Music
10265 Arlington Ave
Riverside CA 92503
909-688-3050
CD, CA, LP, lots of punk, ska

Green Hell
6655 #7 Hollywood Blvd.
Los Angeles CA 90028
213-962-3570
CD, CA, LP

Kulcha Beat
2232 E Seventh St.
Long Beach CA 90804
310-439-4334
CD, CA, LP
Reggae, Ska, Rocksteady

Mad Platter
10117 Hole Ave
Riverside CA 92503
CD, CA, LP

Peer Records
2301 W Balboa Blvd.
Newport Beach CA 92663
714-675-4057
CD, CA

Poo-Bah Records
1101 E Walnut Ave.
Pasadena CA 91106
818-449-3359
CD, CA

Record Rover
12204 Venice Blvd.
Los Angeles CA 90066
310-390-3132

Rhino Records
1720 Westwood Blvd.
Los Angeles CA 90024
310-474-8685
CD, CA, LP

Rockaway Records
2395 N Glendale Blvd.
Los Angeles CA 90039
213-664-3232
CD, CA, LP

Street Sounds
7751 Melrose Ave.
Hollywood CA 90046
213-651-0630
CD, CA, LP

Tower Records
1028 Westwood Blvd.
Los Angeles CA 90024
310-208-3061
CD, CA

Vinyl Fetish
7305 Melrose
Hollywood CA 90046
213-935-1300
CD, CA, LP

Zed Records
1940 Lakewood Blvd.
Long Beach CA 90815
310-498-2757
CD, CA, LP

Music Stores

ABC Music
4114 W Burbank
Burbank CA 91505
818-842-8196
Most instruments; electronic and guitar repairs; no rentals

Goodman Music
3501 Cahuenga Blvd. W
Universal City CA 90068
213-845-1145
Keyboards, synthesizers, samplers, amps; no repairs or rentals

Guitar Center
7425 Sunset Blvd.
Hollywood CA 90046
213-874-1060
Most instruments; no repairs or rentals

Guitar Guitar
14270 Ventura Blvd.
Sherman Oaks CA 91423
818-789-1706
Most instruments; guitar, electronics and amp repairs; guitar and electronics rentals

Guitar Row
9 or 10 music stores along Sunset between La Brea and Fairfax

Lier's Music
452 N "E" St.
San Bernardino CA 92401
909-884-8815
Most instruments; guitar and electronics repair; no rentals

Musictek Services
12041 Burbank Blvd.
N Hollywood CA 91607
818-506-4055
Most amp-type equipment; specializing in vintage amp and synthesizer repairs (emergency service available); no rentals

Nadine's Music
6251 Santa Monica Blvd.
Hollywood CA 90038
213-464-7550
Amps, keyboards, recording equipment; guitar repairs; most rentals

Performance Guitar
6301 1/2 Yucca St.
Hollywood CA 90028
213-462-7004
Custom guitars and amps; most repairs; no rentals

Spitzer Music
6305 Laurel Canyon Blvd.
N Hollywood CA 91606
818-763-3383
Most instruments; guitar, electronic and drum repairs; no rentals

Westwood Musical Instruments
10936 Santa Monica Blvd.
Los Angeles CA 90025
310-478-4251
Most instruments; guitar and electronic repairs; most rentals

Food

El Coyote on Beverly Blvd. near La Brea; cheap Mexican food, closes at 10 or 11pm. **Ship's** at La Cienega and Olympic; all-night diner, you can make your own toast at the table. **Canter's** on Fairfax south of Melrose; an expensive but decent diner open all night. **Millies** on Sunset near Marathon in Silver Lake; good, cheap, vegetarian. **Spaghetti Factory** on Sunset between Argyle and Western; cheap pasta and a cheap full bar. **Mani's**, a no sugar bakery/coffee shop open late! **The Source** on Sunset, vegetarian, **Leanor's** in the valley; veggie-Mex, **Orion** on Vine; fast-food vegetarian, **Beechwood Cafe** in Hollywood special veggie plate, cheap breakfast. **Joseph's Cafe** on Ivar and Yucca, a little pricey, but this place has the ultimate Tsatziki. **Cafe Noura** in W. Hollywood is all Middle Eastern with everything from Hummus to Turkish salads. Lots of late night Thai food at the East end of Hollywood Bl.

Shelter

Try to stay at somebody's house. The hotels, especially in Hollywood, are to be avoided. They'll rip you off, won't let you party, and make you check out by 11 am.

Etc.

There's good thrift stores on Fairfax near Olympic, **Jet Rag** on La Brea near Willoughby has good cheap used clothes. Also, check out the whole Vermont shopping area north of Sunset: **Y Que, Mondo Video, Amok Books, X-Girl,** and the **Onyx Coffeehouse. Dog Park** at Laurel Canyon's Mulholland Dr.

Oakland Berkeley
Venues

The Afterworld Lounge at Blakes
2367 Telegraph Ave.
Berkeley CA 94704
510-848-0886
Capacity: 250
Alternative, Experimental

Berkeley Square
1333 University Ave.
Berkeley CA 94702
510-841-6555
Capacity: 450
Alternative, Funk, Reggae

Bison Brewery
2598 Telegraph
Berkeley CA 94704
510-841-7734
Capacity: 250 94704
510-841-7734
Alternative, folk, blue

Blakes
2367 Telegraph
Berkeley CA 94704
510-848-0886
Capacity: 250
510-547-4862
All styles

Cadillac Ranch
1655 B Willow Paths Rd
Concord CA 94520
510-686-6809
Capacity: 385
Country

Denim and Diamonds
2203 Mariner Circle Loop
Alameda CA 94501
510-521-9200
Capacity: 500
Country

Freight and Salvage Coffee House
1111 Addison St.
Berkeley CA 94702
510-548-7603
Capacity: 220
Folk, Jazz, Blues, Bluegrass

Gilman Street
924 Gilman
Berkeley CA 94701
510-525-9926
Capacity: 250
Indie bands only

Merchant's Bar
401 Second St.
Oakland CA 94607
510-465-8032
Capacity: 150
Rock, Alternative

Starry Plough
3101 Shattuck Ave.
Berkeley CA 94705
510-841-2082
Capacity: 200
Alternative, Funk, Folk, Psychedelic

Press

BAM
(see San Francisco)

The Bay Guardian
(see San Francisco)

The Daily Californian
2150 Dwight Way
Berkeley CA 94704
510-548-8300
Daily Newspaper (free)

East Bay Express
PO Box 3198
Berkeley CA 94703
510-540-7400
Weekly newspaper

Radio

KALX 90.7 fm
UC Berkeley
2311 Bowditch St.
Berkeley CA 94720
510-642-1111
All styles

KJAZ 92.7 fm
1131 Harbor Bay Pkwy
Alameda CA 94501
510-769-4800
Jazz

KPFA
1929 Martin Luther King Jr Way
Berkeley CA 94704
510-848-6767
All styles

KSMC 88.9/89.5 fm
St. Mary's College
PO Box 223
Moraga CA 94575
510-376-1242

KSUH
CSU Hayward
Hayward CA 94542
510-885-3588

KVHS 90.5 fm
Clayton Valley High School
1101 Alberta Way
Concord CA 94521
510-682-5847
Metal, Top 40

Record Stores

Amoeba Music
2455 Telegraph Ave.
Berkeley CA 94704
510-549-1125
CD, CA, LP

Leopold's Records
2518 Durant
Berkeley CA 94704
510-848-2015
CD, CA, LP

Mod Lang
2136 University Ave.
Berkeley CA 94704
510-486-1880
CD, LP

Rasputin's Records
2350 Telegraph Ave.
Berkeley CA 94704
510-848-9005
CD, CA, LP

Music Stores

Studio Resource Centers
10566 San Pablo Ave.
El Cerrito CA 94530
510-559-8618
Sales, repairs, rentals

Subway Guitars
1800 Cedar St.
Berkeley CA 94703
510-841-4105
Used guitar, amp sales, repairs

Food

Betty's in Berkeley, you may spot stars such as Robin Williams. Good, medium priced vegetarian and carnivorian cuisine.

Shelter

Stay out of downtown Oakland with your equipment; in fact, you may want to keep your whole body out of downtown Oakland at night.

Sacramento Davis

Venues

The Boardwalk
9426 Greenback Ln
Orangevale CA 95662
916-988-9247
Capacity: 460
Rock, Metal

The Cattle Club
7042 Folson Blvd.
Sacramento CA 95826
916-448-2582
Capacity: 300
Alternative

Old Ironsides
1901 10th St.
Sacramento CA 95814
916-443-9751
Capacity: 175
21 and up
Alternative, jazz

The Palms Playhouse
726 Drummond Ave.
Davis CA 95616
916-756-8502
Capacity: 150
Folk, Blues, Jazz

Sudwerk
2001 Second St.
Davis CA 95616
916-758-8700
Jazz, Blues, Rock.

Press

The California Aggie
UC Davis
25 Lower Freeborn Hall
Davis CA 95616
916-752-0208
Daily newspaper

The Magpie Weekly
2322 J St.
PO Box 160248
Sacramento CA 95816
916-448-2235
Weekly entertainment paper

Sac This Week
P.O. Box 160248
Sacramento CA 95816
916-448-2235
Weekly

Sacramento News and Review
2210 21 St.
Sacramento CA 95818
916-737-1234
Weekly news and entertainment

Valley Music News
2740 Auburn Bl.
Sacramento CA 95821
916-484-7575
Bi-monthly

Radio

KCBL 88.7 cafm
4623 T St.
Sacramento CA 95819

KDVS 90.3 fm
UC Davis
14 Lower Freeborn Hall
Davis CA 95616
916-752-9903
All styles
Best station in the area

KEDG 530 am cc
CSU Sacramento
6000 J St.
Sacramento CA 95819
916-278-5882
All Styles

KRXQ 93.7 fm
5345 Madison Ave., Ste 100
Sacramento CA 95841
916-334-7777
Commercial Rock

KWOD 106.5 fm
801 K St. 27th Fl
Sacramento CA 95814
916-448-5000
Commercial Alternative

KXJZ 90.9 fm
3416 American River Dr, Ste B
Sacramento CA 95864
916-485-5977
Jazz

Record Stores

Barney's
15 West Main St.
Woodland CA 95695
916-662-6376

The Beat Records
1700 J Street
Sacramento CA 95814
916-446-4402
CD, CA, LP

Dimple Records
1701 Santa Clara Dr
Roseville CA 95661
916-781-2800
CD, CA

Recycle Records
205 F St.
Davis CA 95616
916-756-4943
CD, CA, LP

Spirit Records
2246 Sunrise Blvd. #2
Rancho Cordova CA 95670
916-638-0158
CD, CA, LP

Tower Records
2514 Watt Ave.
Sacramento CA 95821
916-482-9191
CD, CA, LP

Music Stores

Davis Music
615 2nd St.
Davis CA 95616
916-758-4010
Sales, repairs, rentals

Skip's Music
2740 Auburn Blvd.
Sacramento CA 95821
916-484-7575
Most sales, repairs and rentals

Drum and Guitar City
7324 B Folsom Blvd.
Sacramento CA 95826
916-383-2489
Drum, guitar, and bass sales
and rentals

Food

Spaghetti Factory on 'J' St. and
railroad tracks, good cheap
Italian, tons of food and bread.
Beatniks, a Vegan Juice Bar in
Sacramento.

Shelter

There are a bunch of cheap
hotels off the freeways.

★ A few hours north of Sacramento is the college town of
Chico, home of Launch Vomit to
any of you who may remember.
Cheap beer, good thrift stores
and lots of nice scenery. A good
venue there is:

Juanita's
Syb
PO Box 3605
Chico, CA 95927
916-893-4215
Alternative

San Diego
Venues

The Belly Up Tavern
143 S Cedros Ave.
Solana Beach CA 92075
619-481-8140
Capacity: 600
All Styles
If you like to play loud, this is
not the club for you. They have
a decibel meter right in front of
the stage. Mostly blues, rock,
alternative

Blind Melons
710 Garnet Ave.
Pacific Beach CA 92109
619-483-7844
Capacity: 150
R&B, Reggae, rock

Bodie's
528 F St.
San Diego CA 92101
619-236-8988
Capacity: 200
Blues, Rock, Alternative, Industrial
Try to play with a large drawing
local band. It is a cool place to
play, and in a cool part of
downtown, the Gaslamp District.

The Casbah
2501 Kettner Bl.
San Diego CA 92101
619-232-HELL
Capacity: 250
Alternative, Rockabilly, other.
This is probably the most
desirable club in the area to
play if you are a touring indie
band.

Dream Street
2228 Bacon St.
San Diego CA 92107
619-222-8131
Capacity: 285
Rock, Alternative

Granny's
2516 University Ave.
San Diego CA 92104
619-298-9089
Capacity: 100
All styles, good beer, no cover.

Megalopolis Bar & Grill
4321 Fairmount Ave.
San Diego CA 92105
619-584-7900
Capacity: 100
All styles except punk and metal
Once a very cool club for louder
bands, this place has acquired
more of a folky, quiet atmosphere, so don't bring those
Marshall half stacks in here.

The New Bacchanal
8022 Claremont Mesa Blvd.
San Diego CA 92111
619-277-7326
Capacity: 1,000
Rock, country, oldies

Soma
5305 Metro St.
San Diego CA 92110
619-239-7662
Capacity: 1,500
Alternative, punk, metal, ska.

Soul Kitchen
168 E. Main Street
El Cajon, CA
619-579-3627 (leave message)
All ages. Coffeehouse. Punk,
Alternative.

The Spirit
1130 Buenos Ave.
San Diego CA 92110
619-276-3993
Capacity: 350
All Styles, mostly rock

Velvet
2812 Kettner Bl.
San Diego CA 92101
619-692-1080
Capacity: 100
This is the building where the
Casbah used to be. Mostly
Alternative music, local and
touring bands.

Press

360
PO Box 81623
San Diego CA 92138-1623
Monthly music fanzine

The Daily Aztec
SDSU, PFSA Bldg, Rm 361
San Diego CA 92182-9114
619-594-6975
Daily college newspaper

Genetic Disorder
P.O. Box 151362
San Diego CA 92175
Punk fanzine, monthly.

HYPNO Magazine
624 Broadway 3rd Fl
San Diego CA 92101
619-239-9746, 696-0662

San Diego Reader
PO Box 85803
San Diego CA 92168-5803
619-235-3000
Weekly alternative newspaper.
THE concert listings for S.D.

UCSD Guardian
9500 Gilman Dr, 0316
La Jolla CA 92093
619-534-6583
Fax: 619-534-7691
College newspaper
Send material to the A&E
section

THE POSIES

Make: 1989 Ford XLT

Color: Grey and Maroon

Mileage at Purchase: ?

Current Mileage: ?

Number of people who tour in it: 6 + Ed Fotheringham

Miles per gallon: about 2 GPM (Gallons Per Mile)

The van runs on: Gravity. We start our tours in Denver.

The band runs on: Everybody else (in the world) smokes pot but me. I think its Stoopid.

Stereo: Auto-reverse cassette that eats tapes when it turns over.

Favorite thing to listen to: I make mix tapes that I like, but everyone else calls them "annoying." There's a great college radio station in Bozeman, MT.

Coolest thing avout our van: We rent it to other bands for big $ and make them vacuum it. Suckers include: Mudhoney, Gnome, Fastbacks.

The coolest thing we did to our van was: Tried to sell it to Mudhoney for $13,000. Almost worked.

The suckiest thing about our van: The trailer hitch that we always forget abour when parallel parking... we hit our legs on it too.

Is there anybody's van you'd trade it for? Flop's — it has individual captains chairs and 2 TVs.

"The van runs on gravity. All our tours start in Denver."

USD Vista
5998 Alcala Park
San Diego CA 92110-2492
619-260-4584
College newspaper

Radio

KGCR 540 am cc
Grossmont College
8800 Grossmont College Dr
El Cajon CA 92020
619-465-1700
All Styles

KSDT 95.7 cafm
UCSD B015
La Jolla CA 92093
619-534-4225
Alternative

KKSM
Palomar College
1140 W Mission Rd.
San Marcos CA 92069
619-744-1150

KCR 98.9 cafm
SDSU
San Diego CA 92182
619-594-6982
All Styles

XHRM 92.5 fm
2434 South Port Way, Ste A
National City CA 91950
619-336-4900
80's retro, Alternative

KLOZ 102.1 fm
5735 Kearney Villa Rd., Ste G
San Diego CA 92123
619-560-5464
Rock, Alternative

XTRA 91.1
4891 Pacific Hwy
San Diego CA 92110
619-291-9191
Commercial Alternative

Record Stores

Blue Meanie Records
916 Broadway
El Cajon CA 92021
619-442-2212
CD, CA, LP

Lou's Records
434 N Hwy 101
Encinitas CA 92024
619-632-5959
CD, CA, LP

Music Trader
6663 El Cajon Blvd.
San Diego CA 92115
619-462-2274
CD, CA

Off The Record
3849 5th Ave.
San Diego CA 92103
619-298-4755
CD, CA, LP

Taang!-West Records and Threads
978 Garnet Ave.
Pacific Beach CA 92109
619-270-4905
CD, CA, LP

Tower Records
6405 El Cajon Blvd.
San Diego CA 92115
619-287-1420
CD, CA, LP

Music Stores

Blue Guitar
1020 Garnet Ave.
Pacific Beach CA 92109
619-272-2171

Freedom Guitar
1053 8th Ave.
San Diego CA 92101
619-235-6664

Guitar Center
6533 El Cajon Blvd.
San Diego CA 92115
619-583-9751
Fax: 619-583-0209

Guitar Trader
7120 Clairemont Mesa Blvd.
San Diego CA 92111
619-565-8814
Fax: 619-565-8490

Moze Guitars
4701 College Ave.
San Diego CA 92115
619-583-2182

Music Mart
5040 Convoy St.
San Diego CA
619-565-4414

New World Music and Sound
5620 Kearny Mesa Rd.
San Diego CA 92111
619-569-1944
Fax: 619-569-2040

Top Gear Guitar Pro Shop
7293 University Ave.
La Mesa CA 91941
619-464-4969
Guitar and amp repairs

Food

Pick one of the hundreds of taco shops and indulge, but you must wait until after load-out. After drinking all night the food will be the best you've ever had at 3 am. **The Big Kitchen** in Golden Hill at 30th and Grape has some of the best breakfast food in San Diego.

Etc.

The Gaslamp Quarter downtown has many nightime restaurants and bars. **The Live Wire** on El Cajon Bl. and Alabama in Hillcrest is a great bar with an excellent jukebox. Go to the beach.

San Francisco
Venues

The Blue Lamp
561 Geary Blvd.
San Francisco CA 94102
415-885-1464
(Becky) 415-431-4552
Blues and Jazz; Rock on weekends

The Bottom of the Hill
1233 17th St.
San Francisco CA 94107
415-626-4455
Capacity: 250
Alternative, Rock, Blues
21 and up
This is a great place to play, they treat bands very well and are open to booking up-and-

coming indie touring bands. On Sunday afternoons, they have the $2 barbeque. It is an all-you-can-eat extravaganza with live music, good food and plenty of cheap beer. It is a great time if you happen to be in the city on a Sunday night, and even better if you get to play.

Brave New World
1751 Fulton St.
San Francisco CA 94117
415-441-1751, 563-7288
Capacity: 500
Alternative
21 and up
This bar is divided into two sections; the front is a locals only neighborhood bar. The folks are friendly, but they all seem to have known each other for about 25 years. In the rear is where the bands play. It can be a cool place to play, but the quality of music is rather inconsistent. It is definitely worth a try, at least for the experience.

The Chameleon
853 Valencia
San Francisco CA 94110
415-821-1891
Capacity: 99
Alternative, some jazz

Club Boomerang
1840 Haight St.
San Francisco CA 94117-2712
415-387-2996
Capacity: 300
Rock, Blues, Alternative

Cocodrie's
1024 Kearny St.
San Francisco CA 94133
415-986-6678
Capacity: 250
Rock, Alternative
18 and up

The Covered Wagon Saloon
Stacy
917 Folsom
San Francisco CA 94107
415-974-1585
Mostly acoustic

DNA Lounge
375 11th St.
San Francisco CA 94103
415-626-1409
Capacity: 600
Alternative, Hip-Hop, Funk
This large venue in the SOMA district does occasional shows, but it is not likely that your band will be booked here; they do mostly established touring bands.

Elbo Room
647 Valencia St.
San Francisco CA 94110
415-552-7788
Capacity: 325
Alternative, jazz.

El Rio
3158 Mission St
San Francisco CA 94110
415-282-3325
Alternative, salsa

The Great American Music Hall
859 O'Farrell
San Francisco CA 94109
415-885-0750
Capacity: 500
All styles

Hotel Utah
500 4th St.
San Francisco CA 94107
415-421-8308
Capacity: 200
Rock, Alternative

Kilowatt
3160 16th St
San Francisco CA 94103
415-861-2595
Capacity: 250
Alternative

Last Day Saloon
406 Clement St.
San Francisco CA 94118
415-387-6343
Capacity: 300
All styles

Nightbreak
1821 Haight St
San Francisco CA 94117
415-221-9008
Capacity: 300
Alternative, various styles
This club is located in the Haight, near Golden Gate Park.

On Sunday nights they have Sushi Sunday; a sushi chef comes in and makes cheap ($3-$5) six-piece sushi dinners. There are also five or six bands playing. This is definitely a cool place to play and hang out.

Paradise Lounge
1501 Folsom St.
San Francisco CA 94103
415-621-1912
Capacity: 450
All Styles
This club features a lot of local bands, and a few well-known out-of-towners.

The Purple Onion
140 Columbus Ave.
San Francisco CA 94133
415-398-8415
Capacity: 200
Garage Rock, Alternative
This is definitely a cool place to play, especially for the North Beach area, but you have to deal with some fairly steep stairs loading down into the club. The atmosphere is that of a dive, and the owner/manager/booker is cool, but has his crazy, unpredictable moments. He may get up on stage and politely ask you to leave if he doesn't like you.

Slim's
333 11th St
San Francisco CA 94103
415-235-0333
Capacity: 430
Blues, alternative, reggae

Trocadero Transfer
520 4th St.
San Francisco CA 9410
415-995-4600
Capacity: 800
The Troc does an occasional show, but mostly big bands. This club is usually a dance place.

Press
(It is known fact among record publicists that San Francisco is the hardest town to get press in, unless you're the Counting Crows or Green Day.)

The American Music Press
41 Octavia St. #10
San Francisco CA 94102
415-255-9452
Monthly music magazine

BAM
3470 Buskirk Ave.
Pleasant Hill CA 94523
510-934-3700
Biweekly music magazine

Bananafish
PO Box 424762
San Francisco CA 94142
Semiannual fanzine

The S.F. Bay Guardian
520 Hampshire St.
San Francisco CA 94110
415-255-3100
Weekly alternative newspaper

The Bomb Hip-Hop Magazine
4104 24th St., Ste 105
San Francisco CA 94114
415-826-9479
Monthly Hip-Hop magazine

Maximum Rock'N'Roll
PO Box 460760
San Francisco CA 94146
415-648-3561
Monthly fanzine

San Francisco Weekly
425 Brannan St.
San Francisco CA 94107
415-541-0700
Weekly art newspaper

Thrasher
1303 Underwood Ave.
San Francisco CA 94124
415-822-3083

Radio

KCSF 90.9 cafm
City College of San Francisco
50 Phelan Ave.
San Francisco CA 94112
415-239-3444
Alternative, Hip-Hop, Metal

KSFS 100.7 cafm
San Francisco State University
1600 Holloway Ave.
San Francisco CA 94132
415-338-2428
Alternative, Experimental

KUSF 90.3 fm
University of San Francisco
2130 Fulton St.
San Francisco CA 94117
415-386-5873
Blues, Rap, Jazz, Country

KFOG 104.5 fm
55 Hawthorne St., #11
San Francisco CA 94105
415-543-1045
Commercial Alternative, Rock, Blues

KITS 105.3
730 Harrison St.
San Francisco CA 94107
415-512-1053
Commercial Alternative

Record Stores

Aquarius Records
3961 24th St.
San Francisco CA 94114
415-647-2272
CD, CA, LP

Epicenter
475 Valencia 2nd Floor
San Francisco CA 94103
415-431-2725
LP, 7"

Neurotic Records
1100 Folsom St.
San Francisco CA 94103
415-552-8069
CD, CA, LP

Reckless Records
1401 Haight St.
San Francisco CA 94117
415-431-3434
CD, CA, LP

Record Finder
258 Noe St.
San Francisco CA 94114
415-431-4443
CD, CA, LP

Rough Trade
1529 Haight St.
San Francisco CA 94117
415-621-5121
CD, CA, LP

Streetlight Records
3979 24th St.
San Francisco CA 94114
415-282-3550
CD, CA, LP

Music Stores

Black Market Music
1016 Howard St.
San Francisco CA 94103
415-252-1055

Guitar Center
1321 Mission St.
San Francisco CA 94103
415-626-7655
Most instruments; no repairs or rentals

Haight Ashbury Music Center
1540 Haight St.
San Francisco CA 94117
415-863-7327
Most instruments; guitar, electronic and drum repairs; most rentals

Food

A burrito at one of the many Mexican Food joints in the Mission is a must and cheap. Try **Panchita's**, there are three in the Mission, one right on the corner of 16th and Mission in la corazón de la michon. The **Crescent City Cafe** on Haight and Masonic, New Orleans style creole, get them red beans and rice! **Spaghetti Western** in the lower Haight is a good breakfast place, **All You Knead**, in the heart of Haight, has a large selection of food, beer, vegetarian. **Holey Bagle**, there is one in Noe Valley on 24th and Sanchez, and one on Masonic and Haight. Try the vegetable schmear on the poppy seed bagle. Get your "cheap, hangover breakfast" of home fries, bacon and eggs at **New Dawn** on 16th and Valencia.

Shelter

Your best bet is to either drive out of the city or stay with an acquaintance. Parking is a bear, and not really all that safe, especially in the areas where you will find cheap motels. Find a new friend, quick!

Etc.

San Francisco is a tourist's haven. There are a million things to see, some touristy, some not. The museums in Golden Gate Park and the park in general is very cool if it is not crowded. Go thrift shopping in either the Mission district, or the Haight. North Beach has great old bars where the likes of Kerouac and Ginsberg once frequented. Go to **Vesuvio** and read the mural on the wall next to the entrance. **City Lights**, started by writer Lawrence Ferlenghetti, is a great bookstore with lots of small press titles. China Town is always nice for a great cheap meal, culture and possibly a dirty fortune cookie. Take the ferry or go over the bridge to Marin, there are great hiking trails and I believe Jerry Garcia lives up in that area somewhere, along with a few other rock guys who have made more money than all of us combined. **The Chameleon** on Friday nights has a great happy hour, is a good place to hang out and is host to mellow music. In the **Fairmont Hotel** on California and Mason near Chinatown, is **The Tonga Room**. This is an amazing place. Don't eat there, but definitely go for the happy hour. The room is dark, has a waterfall and lagoon, and a boat floating on the water. The decor is very cheesy '60s with big red lamps and big drinks.

San Jose
Venues

Cactus Club
417 S First St.
San Jose CA 95113
408-986-0866
Capacity: 300
Alternative, Rock, Reggae
It may be difficult to get a slot here if you are completely unknown, but this is the place in San Jose for indie bands.

Club Oasis
200 N First St.
San Jose CA 95111
408-292-3346
Capacity: 800
All styles
This club usually does more well-known bands, but you may be booked as an opener.

FX The Club
400 S First St.
San Jose CA 95113
408-298-9796
Capacity: 650
Alternative
This club features some of the more well-known alternative touring bands, but rarely books lesser-known indie bands. Try the Cactus Club first.

The Saddle Rack
1310 Auzerais Ave.
San Jose CA 95126
408-286-3393
Capacity: 1400
Country

Toons
52 E Santa Clara
San Jose CA 95112
408-292-7464
Capacity: 200
Rock, Motown, R&B, Jazz

Press

Metro
550 S First St.
San Jose CA 95113
408-298-8000
Weekly entertainment newspaper

San Jose Mercury News
750 Ridder Park Dr.
San Jose CA 95190
Daily newspaper

South Bay Music Review
1421 Sanborn
San Jose CA 95110-3621
Weekly

Radio

KJCC 104.1 fm
San Jose City College
2100 Moorpark Ave.
San Jose CA 95128
408-298-2181
Alternative, Hip-Hop

KSCU 103.3 fm
Santa Clara University
500 El Camino Real
PO Box 3207
Santa Clara CA 95053
408-554-4907
Rap, Reggae, Dance, Jazz, Alternative

KSJS 90.7 fm
San Jose State University
Hugh Gillis Hall #100
San Jose CA 95192
408-924-4547
Alternative, Jazz, Reggae, Rap

KZSU 90.1 fm
Stanford University
PO Box B
Stanford CA 94309
415-723-4839
Alternative

KOME 98.5 fm
3031 Tisch Way, Ste 3
San Jose CA 95128
408-985-9800
Commercial Rock

KRTY 95.3 fm
PO Box 995
San Jose CA 95108
408-293-8030
Country

Record Stores

AB Compact Disc Exchange
109 E Santa Clara St.
San Jose CA 95113
408-294-0345
CD

Streetlight Records
980 S Bascom Ave.
San Jose CA 95128
408-292-1404
CD, CA, LP

Music Stores

Guitar Showcase
3090 S Bascom Ave.
San Jose CA 95124
408-377-5864
Most guitars and amps; electronic and guitar repairs; PA, guitar, and amp rentals

Pro-Audio Marketplace
467 Saratoga Ave. #440M
San Jose CA 95129-1326
408-247-5250
Fax: 408-984-1030

Santa Cruz
Venues

The Catalyst
10011 Pacific Ave
Santa Cruz CA 95060
408-423-1336
Capacity: 900
All styles. Main venue in town. 2 stages.

Kuumba Jazz Center
320-2 Cedar St
Santa Cruz CA 95060
408-427-2227
Capacity: 200
Jazz, folk, world music. Nonprofit

Live Soup & Brewery Cafe
1602 Ocean St
Santa Cruz CA 95060
408-458-3461
Capacity: 200
All styles

Palookaville
1133 Pacific Ave
Santa Cruz CA 95060
408-454-0660
Capacity:650
All styles

The Redroom
1001 Center St
Santa Cruz CA 95060
408-426-2994
Capacity: 400
Punk, alternative

Press

Good Times
PO Box 1885
Santa Cruz CA 95061
408-458-1100
Weekly news and entertainment

The Metro
111 Union St
Santa Cruz Ca 95060
408-457-9000
Weekly news, arts

The Santa Cruz Co Sentinel
207 Church
Santa Cruz CA 95060
408-423-4242
Daily news

Radio

KAZU 90.3 fm
PO Box 210
Pacific Grove CA 93950
408-375-7275
All styles public radio.

Record Stores

Cymbaline
435 Front St
Santa Cruz CA 95060
408-423-3949
also
475-41st Ave, Capitola CA
498 Alvarado, Monterey CA

Etc.
Don't miss the **Big Dipper** roller coaster on the Boardwalk. Also **Zachary's Basic Breakfast**, a great deal and good for you.

★ Arcata, California is a stopping point that could break up the drives between Northern California and Oregon or Washington. The market is on its way to becoming decent with a built-in audience of Humboldt University students who probably don't get as many young touring bands coming through their town as other places. Unfortunately we don't have all the other helpful hints but chances are you won't be hard pressed to find a good vegetarian restaurant in Arcata.

This promoter puts on all-ages alternative shows. Send your stuff to:

Irie Water Works
PO Box 5169
Arcata, CA 95521

TOURING WITH A BABY

By Nancy McCoy of Downy Mildew

Touring with a baby is certainly possible, but it's expensive and very difficult for everybody present. Downy Mildew toured for 4 weeks when my daughter Isabel was 2 1/2 months old. I didn't feel ready to tour yet, but there wasn't much choice if I wanted to stay in the band. We had just released an album, now we needed to tour. I was fortunate that my husband Iain was also our soundman, so we were able to help each other with everything.

The first 2 weeks of the tour were on the East Coast, beginning with the New Music Seminar in NYC. For our first night, I had to hire a baby sitter to come to our hotel room and sit for about 5 hours (at $11/hour plus cab fare home, the NYC going rate). It was the longest I had ever been away from Isabel, and I was stressed out for the whole evening - soundcheck through the show. I was worried that Isabel was back at the hotel crying for me. This type of stress never went away, even after four weeks on the road.

For the rest of the tour, we brought along a friend, Heidi, to be a nanny. She would stay at the hotel with Isabel while we did soundcheck and the show. She was wonderful with Isabel, but it was hard for both of them, as Isabel was still breast feeding, and definitely wasn't too thrilled with the bottles she was given when I wasn't there. Meanwhile, I was at the show with my breasts becoming more and more engorged, thinking with their own minds that it was time to feed Isabel. I lived in fear that they would leak during our set, but fortunately it never happened. By the time I would get back to the hotel room, Isabel was usually asleep, so I would go to bed with extremely full breasts, and when I would wake up in the morning, they would be rock-hard. Isabel woke up every morning at 6:00 AM, not especially caring what time I had gone to bed. Heidi was great about getting up with her, but since I was breast feeding, I had to get up as well.

All was going well for a while, at least I thought so, until Jenny let me know that the rest of the band thought I was too distracted and was making too many mistakes. It was true. It was also very hard on them as far as space was concerned. Not only was there a baby in the hotel room and in the van, there was also a nanny (whom they all liked, but space is space), a car seat with Isabel, a portable crib, a stroller, and extra luggage.

For the second two weeks, we decided to try it with us in a separate car to create more space. It was on the West Coast, so the drives were longer and it would be harder for everybody to have a cramped van with a crying baby in the car seat. That part got even worse. The long drives were too much for Isabel. We had 4-12 hour drives, and she couldn't sit in her car seat for that long. We would pull over as often as we could, but we were always late for a soundcheck or an interview. Isabel would scream and scream, and a couple of times when we were too late to pull over, we took her out of the seat while we drove. Not only is that very dangerous, but it's also illegal. That's when I realized that this was not going to work. It wasn't worth the risk we were taking.

So I traded in my rock'n'roll shoes for lots of mornings with Barney and Big Bird.

Nancy McCoy, mother of 2, now works in the Music Video Department at Warner Brothers.

COLORADO
Boulder
Venues

Caffe Mars
1425 Pearl St
Boulder CO 80302
303-938-1750
Capacity: 80
Folk, jazz, R&B

Club 156
Room 156 UMC
Boulder CO 80309
303-492-7704
Capacity: 157
Alternative
This is an all-ages club that serves alcohol on the University of Colorado campus. It is said to be the place for smaller sized punk bands to play

The Dark Horse
2922 Baseline Rd.
Boulder CO 80303
303-442-8162
Capacity: 400
Blues, Rock, Reggae

Fox Theatre and Cafe
1135 13th St.
Boulder CO 80302
303-447-0095
Capacity: 650
21 and up, some all-ages shows. All styles. Recommended for just about anything.

The Marquee Club
1109 Walnut St.
Boulder CO 80301
303-447-1803
Capacity: 800
Primarily Techno; some larger alternative shows, like the Reverend Horton Heat, but not too much indie stuff

Tulagi's
1129 Boulder CO 80302
303-442-1369
Capacity: 500
Anything but Metal

Press

Boulder Beat
PO Box X
Boulder CO 90306-000X

Boulder Daily Camera
PO Box 591
Boulder CO 80306
303-442-1202
Daily newspaper

Boulder Weekly
1320 Pearl St., Ste 295
Boulder CO 80302
303-494-5511
Weekly alternative newspaper

Colorado Daily
839 Pearl St.
Boulder CO 80302
303-443-6272
Daily Newspaper

Radio

KBCO 97.3 fm
4840 River Bend Rd.
Boulder CO 80301
303-444-5600
Alternative, Blues, Rock

KGNU 88.5 fm
PO Box 885
Boulder CO 80306
303-449-4885
Classical, Jazz, Bluegrass, Folk

KUCB 530 am/104 cafm
University Of Colorado
UC Campus Box 207
Boulder CO 80307
303-492-5031
Fax: 303-492-5105
Alternative
The best station in town.

Record Stores

Albums on the Hill
1128 13th St.
Boulder CO 80302
303-447-0159
CD, CA, LP
Recommended

Wax Trax
1143 13th St.
Boulder CO 80302
303-444-9829
CD, CA, LP
Recommended

Music Stores

Pro Sound
1638 Pearl St.
Boulder CO 80302
303-444-1731
Most instruments; minor repairs; PA and amp rentals; an excellent drum shop

Robb's Music
1580 Canyon Blvd.
Boulder CO 80302
303-443-8448
Most instruments; guitar, keyboard and electronic repairs; PA, guitar and amp rentals
The recommended place for gear

Food

There are no 24-hour places in Boulder. **The Harvest** on Pearl has a good selection of veggie food. **Healthy Habits** on Baseline is another good vegetarian place, breakfast and all.

Shelter

The Highlander Inn on 28th St.
Skyland Motel, next to the Highlander

Denver
Venues

Bluebird Theater
3317 E Colfax Ave
Denver CO 80206
303-333-7749
Capacity:500
All Styles

El Chapultepec
1962 Market St.
Denver CO 80202
303-295-9126
Capacity: 75
Jazz

Cricket on the Hill
1209 E 13th Ave.
Denver CO 80218
303-830-9020
Capacity: 200
Rock, Blues, Funk, Country

Herman's Hideaway
1578 S Broadway
Denver CO 80210
303-777-2535
Capacity: 500
All styles

Jimmy's Grille
320 S Birch
Denver CO 80222
303-322-5334
Capacity: 500
Reggae, Blues

Lion's Lair
2022 E Colfax Ave.
Denver CO 80206
303-320-9200
Capacity: 100
Alternative, Rap
A small venue but they will have
unsigned touring bands play,
one of the two or three recommended stops for indie bands

The Little Bear Saloon
Main St., Hwy 74
Evergreen CO 80439
303-674-5355
Capacity: 375
Rock, R&B, Country, Reggae

Mercury Cafe
2199 California St.
Denver CO 80205
303-294-9258
Capacity: 400
some all-ages
All Styles
Vegetarian food, performance art
Will book indie bands, a very
eclectic atmosphere and opened
to just about everything

The Ogden Theater
Nobody in Particular Presents
935 E Colfax Ave.
Denver CO 80218
303-830-2525
Capacity: 1,100
Not for new bands

Seven South
7 S Broadway
Denver CO 80209
303-744-0513
Capacity: 157
Alternative, Rap
A recommended club for indie
touring bands

The Skyline Cafe
777 W 29th Ave.
Denver CO 80216
303-296-3232
Capacity: 300
Blues, R&B, Jazz, Alternative
not recommended for indie
touring bands

Ziggy's
4923 W 38th St
Denver CO 80212
303-455-9930
Capacity: 115
Blues

Press

Colorado Music Magazine
2785 N Speer Blvd., Ste 240
Denver CO 80211

Denver Post
1560 Broadway
Denver CO 80202
303-820-1365
Daily newspaper

The Hooligan
PO Box 18907
Denver, CO 80218
303-363-6155
Music reviews, "Sassy" commen-
tary, fanzine.

Rocky Mountain News
400 W Colfax
Denver CO 80204
303-892-2562
Daily newspaper

Westword
PO Box 5970
Denver CO 80217
303-296-7744
Weekly newspaper

Radio

KBPI 106.7 fm
1380 Lawrence St., Ste 1300
Denver CO 80204
303-893-3699
Commercial Rock

KPKE 96.5
7075 W Hampton
Denver CO 80227
303-989-1340
Alternative

KRCX 590 am
Regis University
3333 Regis Blvd.
Denver CO 80221
303-458-4140
Alternative
A small station but probably the
one that will play your records

KTCL 93.3
1611 South College, Ste 211
Fort Collins CO 80525
303-484-5449
Commercial Alternative

KUVO 89.3
PO Box 11111
Denver Co 80211
303-480-9272
Jazz

Record Stores

Jerry's Record Exchange
312 E Colfax
Denver CO 80203
303-830-2336
CD, CA, LP

Pirate Records
2139 S Sheridan Blvd.
Denver CO 80227
303-763-8773
CD, CA

Recycle Records
6739 W Colfax
Lakewood CO 80214
303-238-4289
CD, CA, LP

Twist & Shout
724 Pearl St.
Denver CO 80209
303-722-1943
CD, CA

Wax Trax
638 E 13th Ave.
Denver CO 80203
303-831-7246
CD, CA, LP
In the downtown area; they still sell new vinyl; this is the best record store to find independent label product.

Music Stores

Crescendo Music
5682 S Cedar
Littleton CO 80120
303-798-2681
Most instruments; guitar repairs; PA, guitar, and amp rentals

First Bass
222 S Broadway
Denver CO 80209-1510
303-698-2277
Sales, repairs. A great place for bass players

The Guitar Merchants
18 S Broadway
Denver CO 80207
303-744-9664
Guitars and amps; guitar repairs; guitar and amp rentals. A reputable repair shop.

Pro Sound
7405 E Iliff Ave.
Denver CO 80231
303-751-7575
Sales, repairs and rentals

Rupp's Drum Shop
2160 S Holly
Denver CO 80222
303-756-5777
Drum sales, repairs, and rentals
A great place for drums

Food

Jerusalem Cafe on Evans, vegetarian food in the Middle Eastern style, open 24 hours. **Alexander's** on Colfaz and Grant, this is an excellent hole in the wall for pizza. **City Spirit** downtown, a little yuppy, but they do have good vegetarian food.

Shelter

On I-25 you may find a few cheap motels.

CONNECTICUT
Danbury

Venues

Arch St
PO Box 1203
Greenwich CT 06830
203-629-5744
Capacity: 544

The Globe Theater
71 Wall St
Norwalk Ct 06850
203-866-2999
Capacity: 1100
All Styles

Shenanigans
80 Washington St
South Norwalk CT 06854
203-853-0142
Capacity: 400
Classic Rock, R&B

TK's American Cafe
255 White St.
Danbury CT 06810
203-730-1776
Capacity: 130
21 and up
Sunday night is "punk rock night."

Tuxedo Junction
2 Ives St
Danbury CT 06810
203-748-2561
Capacity: 503
All Styles

Promoters

Poison Dwarf Productions
Debbie or Greg
15 Osbourne St.
Danbury CT 06810
203-744-0813

Press

Chairs Missing
PO Box 522
Stratford CT 06497-0522
Fanzine

Connecticut Post
410 State St
Bridgeport CT 06604
203-330-6355
Daily Newspaper

Danbury News Times
333 Main St.
Danbury CT 06810

Fairfield Connecticut Weekly
Band Box c/o the Weekly
180 Post Road East, Ste 8
Westport CT 06880

Frogbelly Local
PO Box 1372
Glastonbury CT 06033
203-586-7035
Monthly magazine

Mixx Magazine
324 Main Ave
Box 287
Norwalk CT 06851
205-854-9294
Monthly magazine

Radio

WPKN 89.5
244 University Ave
Bridgeport CT 06601
203-576-4895
All Styles

WXCI 91.7 fm
W. Connecticut State University
181 White St.
Danbury CT 06810
203-837-8387
Alternative, All styles
Occasional acoustic performances if contacted two weeks in advance

Record Stores

Trash American Style
12 Mill Plain Rd.
Danbury CT 06810
203-792-1630

Volt Music
28 Backus Ave.
Danbury CT 06810
203-730-2204

Music Stores

Eastcoast Music Mall
25 Hayestown Rd.
Danbury CT 06811
203-748-2799
Most instruments; repairs and rentals

Eddie Kanes Music
2 Granville Ave.
Danbury CT 06810
203-748-4923
Band instruments; guitar, drum, amp, (and some keyboard) sales, repairs, and rentals

The Music Guild
276 Main St.
Danbury CT 06810
203-792-6761
Most instruments sales and repairs; rentals for everything except drums

Joe does guitar repairs. He lives in nearby Newtown. He specializes in vintage guitars. He comes highly recommended by the Monsterland guitar virtuoso Greg Vegas. 203-426-0580

Food

Sesame Seed Restaurant, a vegetarian place at 68 West Wooster. **Tortilla Flats**, a Mexican place on E. Pembroke Rd. **New Englander Diner** at Ives St. and R.R. Place.

Shelter

Try the **Super 8 Motel** on Mill Plain Rd. in Danbury.

Etc.

Check out the two story **Salvation Army** on Main St., it is HUGE! The Goodwill on White St. is also nice. If you have a day off, the **Bethel Cinema** shows cool "indie" movies. The **Seattle Espresso** Coffee Shop on Main St. and the **Dr. Java** Coffee Shop in Downtown Bethel are very nice places to relax and have a double espresso.

Hartford
Venues

880 Club
880 Maple Ave.
Hartford CT 06114
203-956-2428
Capacity: 107
Jazz

The Blue Star
26 Trumbull
Hartford CT 06095
203-527-4557
Capacity: 120
Jazz

Cahoots
639 Main St.
E Hartford CT 06108
203-528-2488
Capacity: 120
Acoustic

The Cellar
1 Civic Center Pl.
Hartford CT 06103
203-549-6788
Capacity: 185
Jazz

City's Edge
482 Farmington Ave
Hartford CT 06105
203-232-2260
Capacity: 300
Strictly jazz

Mad Murphy's, Inc.
22 Union Station
Hartford CT 06103
203-549-1722
Capacity: 330
Oldies Rock'N'Roll

The Municipal Cafe/Down Under
485 Main St.
Hartford CT 06103-3004
203-278-4844
Capacity: Municipal Cafe is 200; Down Under is 300
R&B, Blues, Cajun, Rock

Oh! Riley's
35 Oak St.
Manchester CT 06040
203-649-2811
Capacity: 175
Rock, Acoustic, Zydeco

The Russian Lady
191 Ann St.
Hartford CT 06103
203-525-3003
Capacity: 500
Reggae, Rock
3 Story club, stage is on the top, (hope you brought small amps)

Scarlett O'Hara's
59 Pratt St.
Hartford CT 06103
203-728-8290
Capacity: 200
Alternative, Experimental

South City Cafe
768 Maple Ave.
Hartford CT 06114
203-278-6723
Capacity: 160
Alternative

Sports Palace+
16 Broad St
New Britain CT
203-229-3344
Capacity: 900
Hardcore funk, ska, and any other underground music

The Sting
677 W Main St.
New Britain CT 06053
203-229-0880
Capacity: 1,200
All Styles

Press

Creativity
PO Box 2564
New Britain CT 06050
203-231-2302

The Hartford Advocate
30 Arbor St.
Hartford CT 06106
203-548-9300
Weekly newspaper

Hartford Courant
285 Broad St.
Hartford CT 06115
203-241-6200
Daily newspaper

Radio

WESU 88.1
Wesleyan University
Wesleyan Station
Middletown CT 06457
203-347-0050
Alternative, Metal, Jazz, Rap

WFCS 107.7 fm
Connecticut State University
1615 Stanley St.
New Britain CT 06050
203-832-3750
All styles

WHCN 105.9 fm
1039 Asylum Ave.
Hartford CT 06105
203-247-1060
Commercial Rock

WHUS 91.7 fm
University of Connecticut
2110 Hillside Rd., Box U8R
Storrs CT 06268
203-486-2960
Fax: 203-486-2955
Rock, Jazz, Alternative, Metal

WMXC CLC
Middlesex Community College
100 Training Hill Rd.
Middletown CT 06457
203-343-5795
All Styles

WRTC 89.3 fm
Trinity College
300 Summit St.
Hartford CT 06106
203-297-2450
Jazz, Metal

WSAM 610 am cc
University of Hartford
200 Bloomfield Ave.
West Hartford CT 06117
203-768-4238
Alternative

WWUH 91.3
University of Hartford
200 Bloomfield Ave
West Hartford CT 06117
203-768-4725
Alternative, blues, rock

Record Stores

Al Franklin's
1 Civic Center
Hartford CT 06103
203-527-2157
CD, CA, LP

Brass City Records
489 Meadow St.
Waterbury CT 06702
203-574-7805
CD, CA, LP

Phoenix Records
384 Stillson Rd.
Waterbury CT 06705
203-756-1617
CD, CA, LP

Record Breaker
2453 Berlin Turnpike
Newington CT 06111
203-666-0696
CD

Record Express
71 Pratt St.
Hartford CT 06103
203-522-8060
CD, CA

Music Stores

Beller's Music
50 Purnell Pl.
Manchester CT 06040
203-649-2036
Most instruments; guitar repairs;
PA rentals

CP Sound
PO Box 406
Waterford CT 06385
203-848-0411
Amp rentals

Creative Music
506 Silas Dean Hwy
Wethersfield CT 06109
203-563-1098
Drums and drum repairs

Daddy's Junky Music
593 Hartford Rd.
New Britain CT 06053
203-224-4648
Most instruments; some rentals

Don's Music
785 Terryville Ave.
Bristol CT 06010
203-582-7557
Most instruments; guitar repairs
and rentals

LaSalle Music
993 Main St.
E Hartford CT 06108
203-298-3500
Most instruments; guitar repairs;
most rentals

Melody Music
474 Prospect Ave.
W Hartford CT 06105
203-233-4997
Most instruments; repairs and
rentals

The Music Shop
229 Queen St.
Southington CT 06489
203-628-7878
Most instruments and rentals;
guitar and amp repairs

New Haven
Venues

Durty McDuff's Public House
37 N Rd.
E Windsor CT 06088
203-292-6772
Capacity: 250
Rock

El 'N' Gee
86 Golden St.
New London CT 06320
203-437-3800
Capacity: inside 300; outside
160
Alternative, Reggae

Malcolm's Jazz and Dance Club
71 Whitney Ave.
New Haven CT 06511
203-772-4773
Capacity: 175
Jazz

Shenanigans
80 Washington St.
South Norwalk CT 06854
203-853-0142
Capacity: 400
Rock, R&B

The Shoebox Theatre Co.
8 Svea Ave
Branford CT
06405-3724
203-483-7188
Capacity: 52
Mostly acoustic rock, folk,and
classical

Toad's Place
300 York St.
New Haven CT 06511
203-562-5694
Capacity: 750

Tune Inn
29 Center St.
New Haven CT 06511
203-772-4310
Capacity: 500
Alternative
All-ages

Promoters

Fernando Pinto
99 Howe St.
New Haven CT 06511
203-497-9831

Press

New Haven Advocate
1 Long Wharf Dr
New Haven CT 06511
203-789-0010
Weekly newspaper

New Haven Register
40 Sargeant Dr
New Haven CT 06511
203-789-0010
Weekly Newspaper

Radio

WNHU 88.7 fm
300 Orange Ave.
West Haven CT 06516
203-934-8888
Alternative, Rock, Jazz
This is the hip station, according
to top secret local sources.

WPKN 89.5 fm
244 University Ave.
Bridgeport CT 06601
203-576-4895
All Styles

WPLR
1191 Dixwell
New Haven CT 06514
203-287-9070
All Styles

WQAQ 88.3 fm
Quinnipiac College
555 New Rd.
Hamden CT 06518
203-288-5251 x8355

WYBC 94.3 fm
Yale University
Box WYBC Yale Station
New Haven CT 06520
203-432-4127
All styles

Record Stores

Cutler's Compact Disc
33 Broadway
New Haven CT 06511
203-777-6271
CD, CA, LP

Elevator Music Shop
29 Center St.
New Haven CT 06506
This is the store to check out.

Macaw Music
1391 Boston Post Rd.
Old Saybrook CT 06475
203-388-4662
CD, LP, CA, 7"

Music Stores

Sam Ash Music
95 Amity Rd.
New Haven CT 06525
203-389-0500
Most instruments; electronic and
guitar repairs; no rentals. Highly
recommended.

Goldy Libro
756 Chapel St.
New Haven CT 06510
203-562-5133
Most instrument sales and
rentals

JC Music
523 W Main St.
Meriden CT 06451
203-630-2496
Sales, guitar, amp, and keyboard repairs, most rentals.

Music Center of Westport
1460 Post Rd. E
Westport CT 06880
203-259-7615
Most instrument sales and
repairs; PA and amp rentals

Total Music
2458 Boston Post Rd.
Guilford CT 06437
203-458-8844
Most repairs and rentals

Food

Mamouns on Howe St. in New
Haven is probably a safe bet, if
you'd rather gamble then eat at
McDonald's.

Shelter

Try the **Days Inn** in Milford if
you cannot locate floor space.

Etc.

Go to **East & West Rock** in New
Haven and let us know what it's
all about.

DELAWARE
Newark
Wilmington
Venues

Barn Door
845 Tatnall St.
Wilmington DE 19801
302-655-7749
Capacity: 100
Alternative, Rock

Buggy Tavern
1705 Marsh Rd.
Wilmington DE 19810
302-478-7559
Capacity: 150
Blues, Rock

Coda Tavern
519 E Basin Rd
New Castle DE 19720
Capacity: 350
All Styles

Del Haven Cafe
925 Orange St.
Wilmington DE 19801
302-656-9381
Capacity: 200
Alternative

Kelly's Logan House
1701 Delaware Ave.
Trolley Square
Wilmington DE 19806
302-655-6426
Capacity: 400
Blues, Rock

Knucklehead Saloon
1208 Washington St.
Wilmington DE 19801
302-429-0749
Capacity: 113
Alternative, Rock

Stone Balloon
University of Delaware
115 E Main St.
Newark DE 19711
302-368-2001
Capacity: 1,000
All styles
21 and up

The Warehouse Pub
953 W Pulaski Hwy
Elkton MD 21921
410-398-0249
Capacity: 255
Rock, Alternative, Acoustic

Press

Big Shout
1120 West St.
Wilmington DE 19801
302-888-2929
Monthly arts newspaper

The Bob
PO Box 7223
Wilmington DE 19803
302-477-1248
Cool music monthly

Wilmington News Journal
PO Box 15505
Wilmington DE 19850
302-324-2886
Daily newspaper

Radio

WVUD 91.3 fm
University of Delaware
Perkins Student Center
Newark DE 19716
302-831-2701
All styles

Record Stores

Bert's
2501 Concord Pike
Wilmington DE 19803
302-478-3724
CD, CA

Jeramiah's
246 Philadelphia Pike
Wilmington DE 19809
302-762-2155
CD, CA, LP

Planet of Sound
1606 Delaware Ave.
Wilmington DE 19806
302-655-4013
CD, CA

Rainbow Records
3654 Concord Pike
Wilmington DE 19803
302-479-7738
CD, CA

Wonderland
110 W Main St.
Newark DE 19711
302-738-6856
CD, CA, 7"

Music Stores

Accent Music
5810 Kirkwood Hwy
Wilmington DE 19808
302-999-9939
Most instruments; repairs and rentals

Mid Atlantic Music
1702 Kirkwood Hwy
Wilmington DE 19805
302-995-7170
Most instrument sales and repairs; no rentals

FLORIDA
Gainesville
Venues

Covered Dish
210 SW 2nd Ave.
Gainesville FL 32601
904-377-3334
Capacity: 450
Alternative.

The Edge
845 N University Blvd
Jacksonville FL 32211
904-745-1511
Capacity: 1500
All Styles

Florida Theater
233 W University Ave
Gainesville FL 32601
904-375-7361
Capacity: 1,100
All Styles

Hard Back Cafe
232 SE 1st St.
Gainesville FL 32601
904-338-8389
Capacity: 200
Alternative

Richenbachers
104 S. Main
Gainesville FL 32601
904-375-5363
Capacity: 250
Rock

Press

Gainesville Sun
P.O. Box 147147
Gainesville FL 32614
904-374-5000
Daily

Moon Magazine
14 E. University Ave #206
Gainesville FL 32601
904-377-5374
Bi-weekly

Radio

WRUF
P.O. Box 14444
Gainesville FL 32604
904-392-0771
Rock

Record Stores

Bubaloo's Records
1634 NW First Ave
Gainesville FL 32602
904-371-6310
CD, CA, LP

Hyde & Zeke
1620 W. University
Gainesville FL 32603
904-376-1687
Indie label, LP, CD

Schoolkids
1632 W. University Ave.
Gainesville FL 32601
904-377-9245
CD, used, indie.

Shaft Records
804 W. University
Gainesville FL
904-371-2980
CD, indies, LP

Music Stores

Lipham Music
3427 W. University
Gainesville FL 32607
904-372-5353
Sales, repairs

Pro Frets
619 S. Main St #J
Gainesville FL 32601
904-373-1839

Sim's Music
4908 NW 34th #15
Gainesville FL 32605
904-377-8986

Etc.

El Indio, hidden in the Gainesville Shopping Center (Main St.), has good, inexpensive Mexican food. **Burrito Brothers** on W. University has fine burritos and t-shirts! Salty Dogs on W. University has spicy food and cold beer. Try the **Lucky 7** for thrift store shopping. Go tube riding at **Fresh Water Springs** — great to cool off if you're touring in the summer!

Melbourne Orlando
Venues

The Asylum
1717 Wickham Rd.
Melbourne FL 32935
407-259-2450
Alternative, rock, blues, reggae

The Edge
100 W Livington St
Orlando FL 32801
407-426-9165
Capacity: 1600
All Styles

The Junkyard
436 Halbranch Rd.
Casselberry FL 32707
407-678-YARD
Rock, jazz, blues

Sapphire Supper Club
54 N. Orange Ave.
Orlando FL 32801
407-246-1419
Jazz, blues.

Press

Central Florida Future/Axis
University of Central Florida
PO Box 25000
Orlando FL 32816
407-823-6397
Biweekly newspaper

Florida Today
Gannet Plaza
Melbourne FL 32902
407-242-3500
Daily newspaper

Ink Nineteen
PO Box 1947
Melbourne FL 32902
407-253-0290
Monthly music magazine

STAY HOME

by Charlie Popdefect

I'd suggest you stay home if you don't really know the people you are about to share practically every moment with for the duration of a tour. Things as trivial as sitting in the front seat of the van, who gets to shower last or even a slice of bread can be the opening volley in some of the most evil, dragged-out battles I've ever encountered. We've found that bringing someone along to sell merchandise helps to keep the rest of us from going at each other's throats, but make sure they're a neutral party, i.e. no boyfriends, girlfriends, mothers, so as not to upset the delicate balance of power in the band.

There's not much point in leaving your jobs, beds and loved ones if you haven't set up your tour before you leave. Try to start planning your trip 3 or 4 months before you go. Make sure a record will be out a month before you leave so there's plenty of time for it to sit in the music director's box at the local college station. Also, get together T-shirts, hats, other bands' records, anything that you can get your hands on that can be sold, hopefully with your name on it. T-shirts have more than once made what would have been a losing money tour, a break-even money tour. Don't leave home without them. But the main reason to start so early is to deal with your promo kits before the booking agents. Make calling the clubs and then call to see if they made it there. Also find out when the booker will have had a chance to listen to your shit, and when they will be able to accept calls. Phone bills are one of the biggest expenses on tour so try to make the conversations brief and to the point. Don't put all of your eggs into one basket either. Try to contact more than one club for a date if you can, and never rest on a "pencilled you in" date. I've had a booking agent drag me along for months with that line only to have the date pulled for a trained seal act. I'm not joking! Once you do get a confirmed date, notify the local radio, newspapers and record stores, and tell them when you will be there. We try to send post-cards with our schedule on them and whatever promo we can spare. Even now, with the help of our label, we rarely get all these things done on time. Something eventually will fuck up so be prepared to improvise. The more of this that does come together, the more enjoyable your trip will be.

Make sure your transportation will get you where you are going. Popdefect has mainly depended on 1970s American vans, they're easy to work on and parts are relatively cheap and available. If you don't have a mechanic in the band, get one, or at least learn some basics. Our drummer taught himself and has saved us a lot of money and missed shows. Also make sure your van is secure, and if you're in a bad area have someone sleep with the gear.

When you're on tour it's very easy to get pissed at one another. Just try to remember that club owners and booking agents have been exploiting bands a long time, and that you shouldn't blame the unfortunate band member who has to deal with doing your booking for a lousy show. Give each other some space and time alone whenever possible. And most of all, don't forget why your doing this in the first place.

Do's, Do Not's, Maybe's, Maybe Not's, etc., etc., etc.

1. Push starting the van. Our first, no, make that our second van was a 3 speed, 6 cylinder Ford Econoline 150, $800. That's not so important really but hey, it had a clutch! (in other words, yes, you could push start it. This is something we did for months, until learning that with a clean battery cable, it could start with just the turn of a key).

2. When cruising down the highways and interstates of this world, it's always a great idea for someone to know how much fuel is in the gas tank. Breakdowns may still happen from time to time (flat tires, too much moisture from a foggy night in the mountains etc.), but with a little effort, running out of gas can easily be avoided. Good luck buying gas in North Dakota in the middle of the night.

3. 1st Ave. and the 7th St. Entry in Minneapolis. Consistently the finest club in the U.S. to play and see shows.

4. An oil change is a relatively simple, easy and painless process. If your touring vehicle hasn't had one in a while you may be rather impressed by how much more efficiently it will function.

5. Asking the promoter for travel directions. What a truly great way to save time en route to the venue you plan to perform in (a novel concept as well).

6. Some type of car stereo in your touring vehicle is a must. Preferably one with a cassette player that works.

7. In May of '94, after playing a show at Thurston's in Chicago, we met a photographer by the name of Chris Andrus. It seems that this guy's current mission in life is to be in the *Guiness Book of World Records* under the title of "Most Bands Shot By A Photographer In A Single Year." He tells us that he's out there every night of the week going from club to club throughout the greater Chicago metropolitan area, shooting countless live shots, portraits (you name it) of every band he can. He's for real! He's even got a power generator and a lighting rig in the back of his jeep (we saw this) so as to be able to be ready for any occasion. If you're in Chicago, don't be surprised when you meet him, you probably will.

8. If you have a day off on tour:

Beware of the little old lady working behind the information desk of the Niagra Falls Visitation Center in Upstate New York. Be careful not to smile at her as she will most certainly notify security of your whereabouts, who will in turn soon decide that some criminal activity is brewing. Please remember that if you do leave for a couple of hours and then return to view the falls at night that this action will force security to notify the police who will in turn be compelled to harass you for quite some time and possibly attempt to arrest you for tourism!

Quote en quote, sightseeing is usually a lame thing to do anyway.

9. If touring the northern U.S. or Canada during the winter there's a fair chance of driving through a blizzard or heavy snowstorm. If you're familiar with this kind of thing, it's fairly easy to deal with.

Otherwise: Slip, slide, enjoy the ride. As you wind up in the ditch at the roadside.

Popdefect continues to tour. In fact, they're probably on the road as you read this.

In Print
University of Central Florida
2704 Hunt Club Lane
Orlando FL 32826
407-381-2522
fax 407-679-1621

JAM Magazine
PO Box 151720
Altamonte FL 32715
407-767-8377
Biweekly music magazine

Orlando Sentinel
633 N. Orange
Orlando FL 32801
407-420-5000
Daily

Soul Power
P.O. Box 1909
Orlando FL 32801
407-246-0072

Radio

WFIT 89.5 fm
Florida Institute of Technology
150 W. University Bl.
Melbourne FL 32901
All styles

WUCF 89.9 fm
University of Central Florida
4000 Central Florida Bl.
Orlando FL 32816
407-823-2664
All styles

Record Stores

East West
4895 S. Orange Ave.
Orlando FL 32806
407-859-8991
CD, CA

Groove Tube
980 N Hwy A1A
Indialantic FL 32903
407-723-5267

Play It Again
3148 W. New Haven
Melbourne FL 32904
407-724-5685
CD, CA. LP

Wax tree records
3092 Aloma Ave
Winter Park FL 32792
407-677-8897

Music Stores

Guitar Factory
2816 Edgewater Dr.
Orlando FL 32804
407-425-1070

Guitar Haven
936 E. New Haven Ave.
Melbourne FL 32901
407-676-3948

Pensacola
Venues

Sluggo's
PO Box 174
Pensacola FL 32591
904-435-0543

Press

Pensacola News Journal
P.O. Box 12710
Pensacola FL 32574
Daily newspaper

Radio

WFSR 87.7 cafm
University of West Florida
Bldg 22, Rm 219A
Pensacola FL 32514
904-474-2691
All styles, Alternative

Tallahassee
Venues

Club Down Under
Florida State University
Student Campus Entertainment
Tallahassee FL 32306
904-644-6710
Capacity: 350
All styles, a good place for indie
bands to try.

Cow Haus
836 Lake Bradford Rd.
Tallahassee FL 3230
904-574-2697
18 and Up
Another good venue for indie
bands to try.

Late Night Library
809 Gay St.
Tallahassee FL 32304
904-224-2429
Capacity: 700
Various styles

Waterworks
104 1/2 S Monroe
Tallahassee FL 32301
904-224-1887
Very receptive to touring indie
bands.

Press

Florida Flambeau
PO Box 20287
Tallahassee FL 32316
904-681-6692
Weekly newspaper

Tallahassee Democrat
PO Box 990
Tallahassee FL 32302
904-599-2149
Daily newspaper

Radio

WRZK 106.1 fm
120 E Lafayette St., Ste 203
Tallahassee FL 32301
904-942-4100
Commercial Rock

WVFS 89.7 fm
Florida State University
420 Diffenbaugh R61
Tallahassee FL 32306
904-644-1879
All Styles

Record Stores

Vinyl Fever
2033 W Pensacola St.
Tallahassee FL 32304
904-576-4314
CD, CA, LP

Music Stores

Main Street Music
1114 N Monroe St.
Tallahassee FL 32303
904-224-6158
Most instrument sales and
rentals

Scott Tennyson Guitar Service
1304 N Monroe St.
Tallahassee FL 32303
904-224-3361
Most instrument sales, repairs,
and rentals

Food

The **New Leaf Cafe** is a good
vegetarian place. **Cabo's** is a
decent Mexican place. If you are
looking for a hip part of town
with restaurants and shops etc.,
we were told that no such
animal yet exists.

Shelter

Try either the **Travel Lodge** on
Tennessee St. (if renovation is
complete) or the **Tallahassee
Motor Lodge.**

Tampa
St. Petersburg
Venues

Blue Chair Music
1625 E. 7th Ave.
Tampa FL 33605
813-247-1300
Capacity: 150
Record store/club, all styles.

Brass Mug
1441 E. Fletcher Ave.
Tampa FL 33612
813-972-8152
Capacity: 150

Club Detroit / Jannus Landing
16 Second St. North
St. Petersburg FL 33701
813-896-1244
Capacity: 1500
Alternative, rock, reggae

Iron Horse MAcoustic Cafe
160 E. Tarpon Ave.
Tarpon Springs FL 34689
813-943-8016
Capacity: 100

Skipper's Smokehouse
910 Skipper Rd.
Tampa FL 33613
813-971-0666
Capacity: 850
Blues, reggae

Stone Lounge
14609 N. Nebraska Ave.
Tampa FL 33613
813-971-0078
Capacity: 350
Original

Press

Chew
P.O. Box 77008
Tampa FL 33607
813-229-0323
Monthly

Moe
P.O. Box 320753
Tampa FL 33679
813-254-4858
Quarterly fanzine

Tampa Tribune
202 S. Parker St.
Tampa FL 33606
813-272-7566

Weekly Planet
402 Reo St. #218
Tampa FL 33609
813-286-1600
Weekly

Radio

WMNF 88.5
1210 East MLK Bl.
Tampa FL 33603
813-238-8001
All styles

WUSF
University of South Florida
4202 Fowler Ave.
Tampa FL 33620
813-974-4890
NPR

Record Stores

Ace's Records
1518 E Fowler Ave
Tampa FL 33612
813-978-9655
CD, LP, Tape

The Alternative Record Store
11900 N. Nebraska Ave.
Tampa FL 33613
813-977-6383
CD, LP, Indie label

Asylum Records
6566 Central Ave
St Petersburg Fl 33707
813-384-1221
CD, Tape

Daddy Kool
5900 S Tamiami Trail Ste K
Sarasota FL 34231
813-921-7271
CD, Tape, Video

Music Revolution
4055 Dalemabry Hwy
Tampa FL 33611
813-831-8889
CD, LP, Tape, Video

Record Exchange
6702 Central Ave
St Petersburg Fl 33707
813-343-5845
CD, LP, Tape, Video

Vinyl Fever
2307 S Dale Mabry Hwy
Tampa FL 33629
813-251-8399
CD, LP, Tape, Video

Vinyl Museum
2000 Gulf-to-Bay Blvd
Clearwater FL 34625
813-442-4655
CD, LP, Video, Tape

Music Stores

Bringe Music
2129 1st Ave. N
St. Petersburg FL 33713
813-822-3460
Sales, repairs, rentals

Paragon Music
2119 W. Hillsborough Ave.
Tampa FL 33603
813-876-3459
Sales, repairs, rentals

Other places to play in Florida

Einstein A Go-Go
327 N. 1st St.
Jacksonville Beach FL 32250
904-246-4073
Capacity: 250
This highly reccomended club books all styles of alternative music.

GEORGIA
Athens
Venues

The Atomic Music Hall
140 E washington St
Athens GA 30601
706-543-7114
Capacity: 400
Mainly strong local punk and alternative bands

40 Watt
285 W Washington St.
Athens GA 30601
706-549-7871
Capacity: 1,000
Alternative
This is the hip alternative venue to play, they treat you like you're important (but always remember that you're not).

City Bar
220 College Ave.
Athens GA 30601
706-546-7612
Jazz, Blues, Rock, Folk
A very classy bar, the booking agent there says that anyone with talent can come and play.

Club 155 at W.A. Coopers
155 Whit Davis Rd.
Athens Ga 30605
706-543-0470
Capacity: 250
R&B, Jazz, Rock, Country

Compadres
320 E Clayton St.
Athens GA 30601
706-546-0190
Capacity: 450
Jazz, Blues, Acoustic

David's
2180 W Broad St.
Athens GA 30605
706-354-1711
Capacity:
Country Rock

DT's Down Under
140 E Clayton St.
Athens GA 30601
706-543-9276
Capacity: 100
Acoustic

The Georgia Theatre
215 N Lumpkin St.
Athens GA 30601
706-353-3405
Capacity: 1,000
Alternative

Hi-Hat Club
321 E Clayton St.
Athens GA 30601
706-549-5508
Capacity: 300
All Styles

Half Moon Pub
301 E Clayton St.
Athens GA 30601
706-208-9712
Capacity: 250
Jazz, Blues, Folk, Acoustic
Poetry readings

Press

Athens Banner Herald
525 Calhoun Dr.
Athens GA 30601
Daily newspaper

Athens Daily News Star
P.O. Box 912
Athens GA 30603
Daily newspaper

The Athens Observer
P.O. Box 112
Athens GA 30603
706-353-9300
Weekly newspaper

Flagpole Magazine
PO Box 1027
Athens GA 30603
706-549-9523
Weekly magazine

Red & Black
University of Georgia
123 N Jackson St.
Athens GA 30601
706-543-1809
Daily newspaper

Radio

WPUP 103.7 fm
255 S Miledge Ave.
Athens GA 30605
706-549-6222
Commercial Alternative

WUOG 90.5 fm
University of Georgia
Box 2065 Memorial Hall
Athens GA 30602
706-542-7100
Alternative, Blues, Country, Rap, Reggae
Call about doing an interview or on-air performance

Record Stores

Big Shot
128 College Ave.
Athens GA 30601
706-543-6666
CD, CA

Wuxtry
197 E Clayton St.
Athens GA 30601
706-369-9428
CD, CA

Music Stores

Athens Music
480 E Broad St., #002
Athens GA 30601
706-549-0677
Vintage guitars; PA rentals; no repairs

Chick Piano
240 W Clayton St.
Athens GA 30601
706-543-4348
Most instruments; amp and guitar repairs; no rentals

Draisen-Edwards Music
447 E Clayton St.
Athens GA 30601
706-548-7233
Most instruments; guitar and amp repairs; PA rentals

Music Exchange
124 Alps Rd.
Athens GA 30606
706-549-6199
Most instruments; guitar repairs; PA and instrument rentals

New'd Sound
855 W Broad St.
Athens GA 30601
706-548-8544
Most instrument sales, repairs, and rentals

Food

Guaranteed at 167 E Broad St. has a juice bar and vegetarian menu. Michael Stipe owns the building. **Jittery Joe's** is "the coolest coffee shop in town!" It is located at 243 W. Washington St.

Shelter

You may want to try one of the following: **Classic Inn** - 230 N Finley St., 706-543-6511, **Scottish Inns** - 410 Macon Hwy, 706-546-8161, **Hi-Way Host** - 525 Macon Hwy, 706-549-0697.

Etc.

Here is a list of some cool stores to check out: **Stovepipe Books** - 243 W Washington, 706-369-0202, **Potter's House** - 450 Prince Ave., 706-353-6741, **Rockethead** - in front of the 40 Watt, **Oracle** - 228 E Clayton St., **Salvation Army** - 470 Oconee St., 706-549-8094; and 393 N Finley St., 706-548-7850, **Thrift House** of Emanuel Episcopal Church - 414 N Thomas, 706-543-7047.

Atlanta
Venues

Blind Willie's
828 N Highland
Atlanta GA 30306
404-873-2583
Capacity: 100
Blues, Cajun, Zydeco, Folk

Caffeinds
3095 Peachtree Rd
Atlanta GA 30305
404-262-7774
Capacity: 150
Jazz, acoustic

The Chameleon Club
3179 Peachtree Rd.
Atlanta GA 30305
404-261-8004
Capacity: 450
Alternative, Blues, Rock

The Dark Horse Tavern
816 N Highland Ave.
Atlanta GA 30306
404-873-3607
Capacity: 250
Alternative, Blues, Dance

Eddie's Attic
515-B N Mcdonugh St.
Decatur GA 30030
404-377-4976
Capacity: 225
Acoustic Music

Homage Cafe
255 Trinity Ave.
Atlanta GA 30303
404-681-2662
Capacity: 200
Jazz, Folk, Alternative

The Masquerade
695 North Ave. NE
Atlanta GA 30308
404-577-8178
Capacity: 1,200
Alternative, Rock

Mid-Town Music Hall
931 Monroe Dr
Atlanta GA 30308
404-872-0060
Capacity: 350
Alternative, Rock

The Point
420 Moreland Ave.
Atlanta GA 30307
404-659-3522
Capacity: 300
Alternative, Rock

Smith's Olde Bar
1578 Piedmont Ave
Atlanta GA 30324
404-875-1522
Capacity: 250
All Styles

Somber Reptile
842 Marietta St.
Atlanta GA 30307
404-881-9701
Capacity: 350
Alternative, Rock, Ska

The Star Bar
437 Moreland Ave.
Atlanta GA 30307
404-681-9018
Capacity: 200
Rock, Folk, R&B, Alternative

Variety Playhouse
1099 Euclid Ave
Atlanta GA 30307
404-521-1786
Capacity: 800-1000
All styles

The Wreck Room
800 Marietta St.
Atlanta GA 30318
404-874-8544
Capacity: 500 indoor and
outdoor
Various styles

Press

The Atlanta Journal/Constitution
PO Box 4689
Altanta GA 30302
404-526-5151
Daily Newspaper

baby sue music review
PO Box 1111
Decatur GA 30031-1111
404-875-8951

Creative Loafing
750 Willoughby Way NE
Atlanta GA 30312
404-688-5623
Weekly alternative newspaper

High Point Magazine
1133-C Euclid Ave.
Atlanta GA 30307
Biweekly alternative newspaper

The Technique
Georgia Tech
Mail Code 0290
Atlanta GA 30332
404-894-2830
Weekly college newspaper

Radio

WCHZ 95.1 fm
PO Box 14689
Augusta GA 30919
706-650-1122
Commercial Alternative

WCLK 91.9 fm
Clark/Atlanta University
111 James P. Brawley Sr SW
Atlanta GA 30314
404-880-8273
Jazz, Blues, Reggae, R&B

WKLS 96.1 fm
1800 Century Blvd., #1200
Atlanta GA 30345
404-325-0960
Commercial Rock, Alternative

WMRE 530 am cc
Emory University
PO Box 21114
Atlanta GA 30322
404-727-9672
All styles

WRAS 88.5 fm
Georgia State University
University Center Box 1813
Atlanta GA 30303
404-651-2240
Rap, Alternative, Reggae, Rock

WREK 91.1 fm
Georgia Tech
Atlanta GA 30332
404-894-2468
All Styles

WRFG 89.3 fm
1083 Austin Ave.
Atlanta GA 30307
404-523-3471
Blues, Jazz, Reggae, World Beat

Record Stores

Eat More Records
2185 Briarcliff Rd.
Atlanta GA 30329
404-634-3000
CD, CA, LP

Rainy Day Records
3005 N Druid Hills Rd.
Atlanta GA 30329
404-636-6166
CD, CA, LP

Tower Records
3400 Wooddale Dr
Atlanta GA 30326
404-264-1217
CD, CA, LP

Wax 'N' Facts
432 Moreland Ave. NE
Atlanta GA 30307
404-525-2275
CD, CA, LP

Wuxtry
2096 N Decatur Rd
Decatur GA 30033
404-329-0020
CD, LP, Tape, Video

Music Stores

Atlanta Discount Music
3701 Clarmont Rd. NE
Atlanta Ga 30341
404-457-3400
Most instruments; guitar and
keyboard repairs; no rentals

Atlanta Pro Percussion
2520 Spring Rd.
Smyrna GA 30080
404-436-3786
Drums and percussion sales,
repairs, and rentals

Clark Music
470 Ponce de Leon Ave.
Atlanta GA 30308
404-876-0011
Most instruments; guitar repairs;
PA rentals

Echeverria Guitars
676-B N Highland Ave.
Atlanta GA 30306
404-876-5358
Guitar sales and repairs

Wizard Electronics
1438 Tullie Rd.
Atlanta GA 30329
404-325-4891

IDAHO

Don't know much about Idaho, except if you get a show here it helps break up those long stretches of northern driving going east and west. Oh yea, it's the "potato state" too, get 'em mashed.

Venues

Bogie's
1124 Front St
Boise ID 83702
208-342-9663
Capacity: 500
All Styles

Dreamwalker
1015 Main St.
Boise ID 83702
208-343-4196
Capacity: 300
Folk, reggae, alternative.

Grainey's Basement
107 S 6th St
Boise ID 83702
208-345-2955
Capacity: 178
All Styles

John's Alley
PO Box 8992
Moscow ID 83843
208-882-7531
Capacity: 125
All Styles

Mardi Gras
615 S 9th
Boise ID 83702
208-342-5553
Capacity: 800
Country rock and ballroom acts

Neurolox
Alan Ireland
113 N. 11th Street
Boise, ID. 83702

Press

The Arbiter
Boise State University
1910 University Dr
Boise ID 83725
208-345-8204
Weekly newspaper

The Argonaut
University of Idaho
301 Student Media
Student Union
Moscow ID 83844-4271
208-885-7825
Biweekly newspaper

Idaho Statesman
Michael Deeds
PO Box 40
Boise, ID 83707
Daily

Boise Weekly
PO Box 1657
Boise, ID 83701
Weekly

Radio

KBSU 90.3
Boise State University
1910 University Dr
Boise ID 83725
208-385-3663
All Styles

KUOI 89.3
University of Idaho
Student Union Bldg, 3rd Floor
moscow, ID 83845
208-885-6433
All Styles

Record Stores

Back Track Records/RPM
312 S Main
Moscow ID 83843
208-883 1464
CD, LP, 7"

Record Exchange
1105 W. Idaho
Boise ID
208-344-8010
CDs, vinyl, indie stuff

CD Merchant
580 Main St.
Boise ID 83702
208-331-1200
CDs, vinyl, used

Etc.

Brick Oven Beanery at 801 Main St. has some vegetarian items, soups, salads, meat & potatoes. **Twin Dragon** at 2200 Fairview for Chinese.

ILLINOIS
Chicago
Venues

Abby Pub
3420 W Grace at Elston
Chicago, IL 60618
312-478-4408
Capacity: 300+
Acoustic, folk, Irish Music

The Avalon
959 W Belmont
Chicago IL 60657
312-472-3020
Capacity: 500
Alternative, Jazz, Rock
A good place for indie bands to get a show, probably an opening slot for a well known act.

Beat Kitchen
2100 W Belmont
Chicago IL 60618
312-281-4444
Capacity: 350
Rock, Folk, Alternative

Biddy Mulligan's
7644 N Sheridan Rd.
Chicago IL 60626
312-761-6532
Capacity: 550
Reggae, Blues, Alternative, Rock

Buddy Guy's Legends
754 S Wabash
Chicago IL 60605
312-427-1190
Capacity: 400
Blues, R&B, Zydeco

The Bulls
1916 N Lincoln Park W
Chicago IL 60614
312-337-3000
Capacity: 130
Jazz

Cabaret Metro/Smart Bar
3730 N Clark
Chicago IL 60613
312-549-4140, 549-0203
Capacity: 1,000
Alternative
Send tape or CD at least two months in advance. This club does indie bands, but usually bands that are quite established with a guaranteed draw.

The Cubby Bear
1059 W Addison
Chicago IL 60613
312-327-1662
Capacity: 800
Blues, Rock, Jazz, Country, Folk,
Alternative

Czar Bar
1814 W Division
Chicago IL 60622
312-772-5453
Capacity: 500
Alternative

Double Door
1572 N. Milwaukee Ave.
Chicago, IL
312-489-3160
Capacity: 500
Owned by Joe Shanahan, owner
of Cabaret Metro. Mostly
alternative, try to get an opening slot here.

The Elbo Room
2871 N Lincoln Ave.
Chicago IL 60657
312-549-5549, 549-7700
Capacity: 200
Various styles

Empty Bottle
21035 N Western
Chicago, IL. 60622
312-276-3600
Alternative touring bands

Fitzgerald's
6615 Roosevelt Rd.
Berwyn IL 60402
708-788-2118
Capacity: 350
Alternative

The Green Mill
4802 N Broadway
Chicago IL 60640
312-878-5552
Capacity: 100
Jazz

The Hot House
1565 N Milwaukee Ave.
Chicago IL 60622
312-235-2334
Capacity: 250
Alternative, Jazz, Afro/Latin
Caribbean. All-ages

Lincoln Tap Room
3010 N Lincoln Ave.
Chicago IL 60657
312-868-0060
Capacity: 300
Rock, Alternative

Lounge Ax
2438 N Lincoln Ave.
Chicago IL 60614
312-525-6620
Capacity: 400
Alternative
This is a great place for indie
bands to play, but it is sometimes difficult to get a show
here because of the "hip" factor.

Morseland
1218 W Morse
Chicago IL 60626
312-743-5955
Capacity: 150
Alternative, Jazz

Phyllis' Musical Inn
1800 W Division St.
Chicago IL 60622
312-486-9862
Capacity: 100
Alternative, Rock, Blues, Jazz-
fusion

Schuba's
3159 N Southport
Chicago IL 60657
312-525-2508
Capacity: 175
All styles

Synergy
243 W Roosevelt Rd
West Chicago IL 60185
708-231-6000
Capacity:750+
All Styles

The Thirsty Whale
8800 W Grand Ave.
River Grove IL 60171
708-456-2414
Capacity: 700
Rock, Alternative

Thurston's
1248 W George
Chicago IL 60657
312-472-6900
Capacity: 200
Alternative. Ask for the spaghetti
dinner.

The Wild Hare
3530 N Clark St.
Chicago IL 60657
312-327-4273, 327-0800
Capacity: 100
Reggae, World Beat

Press

Butt Rag
PO Box 14724
Chicago IL 60622
312-292-1899
Quarterly fanzine

Chicago Reader
11 East Illinois
Chicago IL 60611
312-828-0350
Weekly newspaper
The Reader will print pictures
that they think look cool and
everyone in Chicago picks up a
Reader.

Chicago Sun-Times
401 N Wabash
Chicago IL 60611
312-321-3000
Daily newspaper

Chicago Tribune
435 N Michigan
Chicago IL 60611
312-222-3650
Daily newspaper

New City
770 N Halstead, Ste 208
Chicago IL 60622
312-243-8786
Weekly alternative newspaper
This paper focuses on "hep"
local stuff.

Oil the Music Magazine
PO Box 412
Moline IL 61266-0412
309-764-0451
Monthly Music Magazine

Pure Magazine
PO Box 25665
Chicago IL 60625
312 -772-5570
Quarterly art and entertainment
magazine

Speedkills
PO Box 14561
Chicago IL 60614
Quarterly fanzine

Tail Spins
c/o Brent Ritzeo
PO Box 5467
Evanson IL 60204
708-866-9544
The Editor says, "I publish
anything."

Radio

WBEZ 91.5
105 W Adams St, 39th Fl
Chicago IL 60603
312-460-9150
Jazz, World Music, Latin, Folk

WCBR 92.7 fm
120 W University Dr
Arlington Heights IL 60004
708-255-5800
Commercial Alternative

WCRX 88.1 fm
Columbia College
600 S Michigan Ave.
Chicago IL 60605
312-663-1693
Fax: 312-663-1707
Dance, Rap, Alternative, Hip-Hop

WHPK 88.5 fm
University of Chicago
5706 S University Ave.
Chicago IL 60637
312-702-8289
Alternative, Blues, Rock, Reggae,
Jazz. This station plays indie
rock at night & early mornings.

WKQX 101.1 fm
PO Box 3404
Chicago IL 60654
312-527-8348
Commercial Alternative

WLUP 100 am
875 N Michigan Ave., Ste 3750
Chicago IL 60611
312-440-5270
Commercial Rock

WNUR 89.3 fm
Northwestern University
1905 Sheridan Rd.
Evanston IL 60201
708-491-7101
Alternative, Jazz and Rap
This station plays good indie
stuff especially during school.
They are a little less reliable
during the summer. If you are in
a "hip" band and have a record

Vans of the STARS!

FLOP

Make: 1984 Ford Econoline XL

Color: Brown (Taupe and Poop)

Purchase Price: $3,500

Van's Name: The Good Times Estate!

Mileage at Purchase: 100,000

Current Mileage: 120,000

Average number of people who tour in it: 4.5

Miles per gallon: 90

The van runs on: Tires on the road

The band runs on: Liquor mixed with Snapple and
Double Tall Lattes with some gooooood tastin' wine!
Yeah.

Type of sound system: AM/FM, cassette, electric style
with speakers (4)

Favorite thing to listen to: Oldies and snuff tapes.

Coolest thing about our van: Captain's seats, blinds, fold
out bed, 3.2 cubic foot loft (and engine) cruise control.

The coolest thing we did to our van was: Totalled it.

The suckiest thing about our van: It's dead. RIP Good
Times Estate.

Is there anybody's van you'd trade it for? The Posies.
It runs.

out, they may have your band on for a interview and on-air performance.

WOUI 88.9 fm
Illinois Institute of Technology
3300 S Federal St.
Chicago IL 60616
312-567-3087
Fax: 312-567-5180
Alternative

WRDP 630 am cc
DePaul University
2345 N Clifton Ave.
Chicago IL 60614
312-325-7340

WXAV 88.3 fm
St. Xavier University
3700 W 103rd St.
Chicago IL 60655
312-779-9858
Fax: 312-779-9061
All styles

WXRT 93.1 fm
4949 W Belmont
Chicago IL 60641
312-777-1700
Commercial Rock and Alternative

WZRD 88.3 fm
Northeastern Illinois University
5500 N St. Louis
Chicago IL 60625
312-794-2861
Alternative, Jazz, Reggae

Record Stores

Ajax Records
2156 W Chicago Ave
Chicago IL 60622
312-772-4783

Blackout Records
3729 N Southport
Chicago IL 60613
312-296-0744
CD, CA, LP

Evil Clown Compact Discs
3418 N Halstead
Chicago IL 60657
312-472-4761
CD only, this is a recommended store.

Reckless Records
3157 N Broadway
Chicago IL 60657
312-404-5080

Record Swap
18061 Dixie Highway
Homewood IL 60430
708-798-0222
CD, CA, LP

Vintage Vinyl
925 Davis St.
Evanston IL 60201
708-328-2899
CD, CA, LP

Waxtrax Records
1653 N Damen
Chicago IL 60647
312-862-2121
CD, CA, LP

Music Stores

Great Lakes Guitar
2333 North Avenue
Chicago IL 60622
312-432-9388
Has a small shop with weird guitars, strings and picks (normal)

Flynn Guitars and Music
821 Noyes St.
Evanston IL 60201
708-491-0500
Guitar, bass, and amp sales and repairs

Guitar Center
3228 N Clark
Chicago IL 60657
312-327-5687
Most instrument sales

Minstrel Music
8041 Milwaukee Ave.
Niles IL 60714
708-965-2550
Guitar, amp, and PA sales, rentals and repairs

Music Crib
9753 Southwest Hwy
Oak Lawn IL 60453
708-363-5545
Guitar and bass sales; guitar and some drum repairs; PA rentals

Musician's Network
5505 N Clark
Chicago IL 60640
312-728-2929
Most instruments, new and vintage; amp repairs, especially tube amps; PA and instrument rentals.
This place "has nice guys who can fix things over night."

Park Ave. Music, Inc
3 S Park Ave.
Lombard IL 60148
708-691-8535
Most instruments; guitar and amp repairs; no rentals

Food

Candeche is a 24 hour Mexican food place. **Chicago Diner** is a vegetarian place. **Winer's Circus** is a 24-hour hotdog stand. **Jim's Grill** at 1429 W. Irving Park has "Kick Ass Korean!" The food is really great and really cheap. If you try the Be Bim Bop or the vegetable pancakes you are guaranteed satisfaction. They also have posters on the walls of such stars as Smashing Pumpkins (big bonus).

Shelter

"Find some friends quick; there are no cheap hotels in Chicago." But you can try the **Days Inn** on Diversey Parkway.

Etc.

In Chicago there is a thrift store on every corner. But **Village Thrift** at 2100 W. Roscoe is very good. **Rag Stock** on Belmont and the **Belmont Thrift Store** are also stocked fairly well.

Champaign

About 3 hours south of Chicago is Champaign -- home of Poster Children and Hum. The only venue in town is:

The Blind Pig
Ward Gollings
6 Taylor
Champaign, IL. 61820
217-351-7444

INDIANA
Bloomington
Venues

Bear's Place
1316 E Third
Bloomington IN 47401
812-339-3460
Capacity: 100+
Acoustic, Folk, Jazz

The Bluebird
216 N Walnut St
Bloomington IN 47404
812-336-3984
Capacity: 500
All styles

Rhino's
325 S Walnut St
Bloomington IN 47404
812-333-3430
Capacity:500
Hip-hop, Funk, Alternative

2nd Story
201 S College
Bloomington IN 47401
812- 336-2582
Alternative

Press

Bloomington Herald Times
PO Box 909
Bloomington, IN 47402
Daily paper
812-332-4401

Bloomington Voice
3902 B South Old State Road 37
Bloomington, IN 47401
Weekly
812-331-0963

Radio

WIUS 95.1 fm, 1570 am
Indiana University/Bloomington
815 East 8th Street
Bloomington IN 47401
812-855-6552
Alternative

WQAX
Indiana University/Bloomington
P.O. Box 2593
Bloomington IN 47401
812-332-9415
Alternative

WTTS 92.3 fm
400 One City Center
Bloomington IN 47404
812-332-3366
Rock, Alternative

Record Stores

Karma Records
116 S Indiana Ave
Bloomington IN 47408
812-323-0551
CD, LP, Tape, Video

Streetside Records
421 E Kirkwood Ave
Bloomington IN 47408
812-323-0551
CD, LP, Tape, Video

Tracks
415 E Kirkwood Ave
Bloomington, IN 47408
812-332-3576
CD, Tape

Indianapolis
Venues

C.T. Peppers
6283 N College Ave.
Indianapolis IN 46220
317-257-6277
Capacity: 300
Blues, Rock

The Slippery Noodle
372 S Meridian St.
Indianapolis IN 46225
317-631-6968, 631-6974
Capacity: 200
Blues

Vogue
6259 College Ave.
Indianapolis IN 46220
317-259-7029
Capacity: 900
Alternative, Blues, Reggae

Press

**Indianapolis Star and
Indianapolis News**
307 N. Pennsylvania St.
Indianapolis IN 46204
Daily newspapers
317-633-1240

NUVO
811 E Westfield Blvd.
Indianapolis IN 46220
317-254-2400
Weekly newspaper

Radio

WRZX 103.3
6161 Fall Creek Rd
Indianapolis IN 46220
317-257-7565
New Rock, Alternative

Record Stores

Rick's Records
5605 N Keystone Ave.
Indianapolis IN 46220
317-259-4087
CD, CA, LP, 7"

Tracks
5485 82 St.
Indianapolis IN 46250
317-576-0404
CD, CA

Music Stores

Guitarworks
1675 W Smith Valley Rd.
Greenwood IN 46142
317-885-1510
Most instruments; guitar, amp
and bass repairs; no rentals

IRC Music
5911 E 82 St.
Indianapolis IN 46250
317-849-7965
Sales and repairs; PA, amp and
keyboard rentals

IRC Music South
8811 Hardegan St.
Target County Line Mall
317-881-8252
Most instruments; guitar repairs;
PA, amp and keyboard rentals

IOWA
Des Moines
Venues

2nd Ave. Foundry
200B SW 2nd Ave.
Des Moines, IA 50309
515-244-5657

Press

Des Moines Register
PO Box 957
Des Moines, IA 50304
515-284-8000
Daily

City View
100 4th St.
Des Moines, IA 50309
515-288-3336
Weekly

Iowa City
Venues

Big Dogs
1202 1/2 Third St. SE
Cedar Rapids IA 52401
319-365-6141
Capacity: 800
Country, Blues, Rock

Chantilly Lace
1712 Second Ave.
Rock Island IL 61201
309-793-4088
Capacity: 1,000
Blues, Rock, Reggae

Gabe's Oasis
330 E Washington St.
Iowa City IA 52240
319-354-4788
Capacity: 250
Various styles
"Will do any style as long as it is cool." This is the best known club in the area.

O'Leary's Pub
202 6th Ave. S
Clinton IA 52732
319-242-1995
Capacity: 170
Blues

The Rock Island Brewing Co.
1815 Second Ave.
Rock Island IL 61201
309-793-0085
Capacity: 300 inside; 3,000 outside
Various styles

Stick Man's
1510 N Harrison
Davenport IA 52803
319-322-7724
Capacity: 250
All styles

Union Bar
121 E College St.
Iowa City IA 52240
319-339-7713
Alternative, "Only big shows here, if you are just starting out don't waste your time."

Promoters

S.C.O.P.E.
This is the student concert committee at the University of Iowa. They do a variety of venues both large and small. Some semesters they do a lot of shows, some hardly any. To find out their schedule call the main switchboard at the University, 319-335-3500, and ask for the current number.

Press

Daily Iowan
University of Iowa
201 N Communications Ctr
Iowa City IA 52242
319-335-5851
Daily newspaper
"If you can get a story in the DI, you will most certainly have a successful show."

Iowa City Magazine
111 Wright St.
Iowa City IA 52240
319-351-0466
Monthly magazine

Icon
PO Box 3002
Iowa City IA 52244-3002
319-351-1531
Biweekly free newspaper

Oil the Music Tabloid
PO Box 412
Moline IL 61266-0412
309-764-0451
Biweekly music magazine

The Press Citizen
1725 N Dodge St.
Iowa City IA 52245
319-337-3181
Daily newspaper

Quad City Times
500 E 3rd St
Davenport IA 52801
319-383-2200
Daily Newspaper

River Cities Reader
110 W Third St.
Davenport IA 52801
319-324-0049
Monthly arts and entertainment paper

Slowfish
2895 9th Ave
Rock Island IL 61202
309-793-4333
Biweekly free news and arts paper

Radio

KALA 88.5 and 105.5 fm
St. Ambrose University
518 W Locust St.
Davenport IA 52803
319-383-8907
All styles

KCLN 97.7 fm
1853 442nd Ave.
Clinton IA 52732
319-243-5256
Commercial Adult Contemporary

KRNA 94.1 fm
2105 ACT Circle
Iowa City IA 52245-9636
319-351-9300
Commercial Alternative

KRUI 89.7 fm
University of Iowa
897 S Quad
Iowa City IA 52242
319-335-9525, 335-8970
All styles

KUNI 90.9 fm
University of Northern Iowa
Cedar Falls IA 52242
319-273-6400
Alternative

Record Stores

Apollo
13 S Linn
Iowa City IA 52240
319-354-9341
CD, CA, LP

BJ Records
6 1/2 S Dubuque St.
Iowa City IA 52240
319-338-8251
CD, CA

Co-op Records
119 Washington St.
Iowa City IA 52240
319-339-0211
CD, CA, LP

Real Records
130 E Washington St.
Iowa City IA 52240
319-354-0158
CD, CA

The Record Collector
4 1/2 Linn St.
Iowa City IA 52240
319-337-5029
CD, CA, LP

Music Stores

G&O Music
415 14th St.
Moline IL 61265
309-764-6649
Most instruments, except
keyboards; guitar and amp
repairs; PA rentals

Gilbert Street Pawn
319 S Gilbert
Iowa City IA
319-354-7910

Guitar Foundation
323 E Market St.
Iowa City IA 52245
319-351-0932
Guitar and PA sales; guitar
repairs; PA and amp rentals

Music Loft
1445 First Ave. SE
Cedar Rapids IA 52402
Most instrument sales, repairs,
and rentals

Music Mart
1818 18th Ave.
E Moline IA 61244
309-762-9147
Most instrument sales and
repairs

West Music
1705 First Ave.
Iowa City IA 52240
319-351-9111
Most instruments; PA repairs
and rentals

Food

Hamburg Inn at 214 N. Linn,
337-5512, **New Pioneer Co-op**, a
fresh food market at 22 S. Van
Buren, **Country Kitchen** at 1402
S. Gilbert and 2208 N. Dodge,
Givannis at 109 E. College St.,
"the best place to eat in Iowa
City, not too expensive."

Shelter

Days Inn on I-80 at Exit 242 in
Coralville, 319-351-6600, **Motel
6** at 810 1st Ave. in Coralville,
319-354-0030, **Mar-kee Motel** at
707 1st Ave. in Coralville, 319-
351-6131.

Etc.

Ragstock, 207 E. Washington
St., 319-338-0553, **Salvation
Army** Store: 1213 Gilbert Ct.,
Goodwill Store: 1410 S. 1st
Ave., **Herbert Hoover's Presiden-
tial Museum** - West Branch,
University of Iowa Art Museum.
Prairie Lights Bookstore should
not be missed.

KANSAS
Lawrence
Venues

The Bottleneck
737 New Hampshire
Lawrence KS 66044
913-841-5483
Capacity: 450
Alternative, Reggae, Blues
The last place left to play in the
area if you are an indie alternative type band; everything else
is being closed down by the
wicked government.

Full Moon Cafe
803 Massachusetts Ave.
Lawrence KS 66044-2680
913-832-0444
Capacity: 50
Various styles, folky, acoustic.
A good place to eat, vegetarian
food at reasonable prices, and if
you play there, a free meal.

The Getaway Inn
1023 W 6th St.
Topeka KS 66606
913-232-1161
Capacity: 150
R&B, Rock, Reggae

The Granada
1020 Massachusetts
Lawrence KS 66044
913-842-1390
Capacity: 600
Various styles
An old theater where bands may
be able to play, but this is a
pretty large venue for the area.

Mulligan's
1016 Massachusetts St.
Lawrence KS 66044
913-865-4055
Capacity: 209
Jazz, R&B, Rock, Acoustic,
Reggae
Kind of the college/fraternity
scene hangs out in this club.

The Jazzhaus
926 1/2 Massachusetts
Lawrence KS 66044
913-749-3320
Capacity: 214
Jazz, R&B, Alternative

KU Ballroom
5th Fl, Kansas Union
University of Kansas
Lawrence KS 66045
913-864-3477
Capacity: 800
Alternative
Big bands like Dinosaur Jr. and Nirvana have played here. This is not the venue for relatively unknown bands.

Press

Lawrence Journal
609 New Hampshire
Lawrence KS 66044
Daily paper

The New Times
13010 Beverly
Overland Park KS 66209
Entertainment weekly

The Note
735 1/2 New Hampshire
Lawrence KS 66044
913-843-6561
Fax: 913-843-1189
Monthly newspaper

Ooga Booga
Carrie Jo
PO Box 442334
Lawrence KS 66044
913-832-9154
This fanzine will cover the record and do live reviews for indie touring bands.

Radio

KANU 91.5 fm
University of Kansas
Broadcasting Hall
Lawrence KS 66045
913-864-4530
Classical, Jazz

KJHK 90.7 fm
University of Kansas
200 Stauffer-Flint Hall
Lawrence KS 66045
913-864-5483
Alternative
This station has a more open format, so it's pretty likely that they'll play your material.

KLZR 105.9 fm
3035 Iowa
Lawrence KS 6604
913-843-1320
Commercial Alternative
This is more of a mainstream station, less likely to play your stuff, but there is a possibility.

KRZZ The New 96.3
2402 E 37th St N
Wichita KS 67219
316-832-9600
Alternative

Record Stores

Alley Cat
717 Massachusetts St.
Lawrence KS 66044
913-865-0122
CD, CA, LP

Hastings
2000 W 23rd
Lawrence KS 66046
913-832-0817
CD, CA, LP

Kief's
2429 Iowa St.
Lawrence KS 66046
913-842-1544
CD, CA, LP

Junior's Farm Records
924 1/2 Massachusetts St.
Lawrence KS 66044
c/o Cody and Mark
This is the best record store for consignment type stuff with indie bands and they will do in-store performances and promotion.

Love Garden
936 1/2 Massachusetts St.
Lawrence KS 66044
913-843-1551
CD, CA, LP
A very highly recommended store

Recycled Sounds
622 W 12th St
Lawrence KS 66044
913-841-9475
CD, LP, Tape

Streetside
1403 W 23rd St.
Lawrence KS 66046
913-842-7173
CD, CA

Music Stores

Harmonic Arts
841 New Hampshire
Lawrence KS 66044
913-842-3321
Most instrument sales and repairs; PA, amp and used gear rentals
Recommended

Haye's House of Music
2011 W 6th St.
Topeka KS 66606
913-234-4472
Most instruments; guitar and bass repairs

Mass St. Music
1347 Massachusetts St.
Lawrence KS 66044
913-843-3535
Most instrument sales and repairs; PA rentals

Midwestern Music Company
5911 Dearborn
Mission KS 66202
913-262-8877
Used gear; most repairs and rentals

Richard's
716 1/2 Massachusetts
Lawrence KS 66044
913-842-0021
New and vintage instruments; guitar, amp and drum repairs; PA rentals. A good place for repairs.

Food

All of these restaurants are on **Massachusetts Street**, which is pretty much the hub of the cultural world of Lawrence. **Full Moon Cafe**, good vegetarian, **Free State Brewery** has good food and beer, **Papa Keno's** is a really good pizza place, **Herbivore's** is a good vegetarian place.

Shelter

People in Lawrence are all so nice that there will never be a problem finding someone to stay with.

Etc.

The third album by Urge Overkill was called *Stul*, referring to **Stul**, Kansas which is located 10 miles outside Lawrence and is supposedly a gateway to hell; there is a special graveyard in Stul. Go swimming in **Lone Star Lake**, 15 miles outside Lawrence. Look for **William S. Burroughs**, he hangs out in the **Town Crier** and other magazine and book stores on Massachusetts Street.

KENTUCKY
Lexington
Venues

Cheapside Bar & Grill
131 Cheapside
Lexington KY 40507
606-254-0046
Capacity: 175
All Styles

Lynagh's
388 Woodland Ave.
Lexington, KY 40508
606-255-1292

Millenium
156 W Main St
Lexington KY 40507
606-225-9194
Capacity: 500
All Styles

Radio

WKQQ 98.1
PO Box 100
Lexington KY 40590
606-252-6694
Classic Rock

WRFL
University Of Kentucky
Box 777 University Station
Lexington KY 40506
606-257-1557

Louisville
Venues

The Brewery
426 Baxter Ave.
Louisville KY 40204
502-583-3420
Capacity: 1500
All styles.

Buckhead Bar & Grill
215 Hurstbourne Pkwy.
Louisville KY 40222
502-429-6650
Capacity: 250
All styles, mostly acoustic.

Butchertown Pub
1335 Story Ave.
Louisville KY 40206
502-583-2242
Capacity: 880
Alternative, Rock, R&B

Cherokee Blues Club
1047 Bardstown Rd.
Louisville KY 40204
502-456-2580
Capacity: 350
Alternative, Rock, Reggae
This place has a vegetarian restaurant/coffee shop in the front and all-ages club in the back. This is pretty much the place to play in Louisville.

Dutch's
3922 Frankfort Ave.
Louisville KY 40207
502-895-9004
Capacity: 100
Alternative, Rock, Blues

Jim Porter's Good Time Emporium
2345 Lexington Rd.
Louisville KY 40206
502-452-9531
Capacity: 300
Oldies, Country

Kentucky Center for the Arts
5 Riverfront Plaza
Louisville KY 40202
502-562-0100
Capacity: 600-2,400
All styles

Phoenix Hill Tavern
644 Baxter Ave.
Louisville KY 40204
502-589-4957
Capacity: 1,000
Rock, Alternative
I was here once. There was a cover band rehearsing for their "gig" that night. They played some Green Day song about 25 times and then went into Foreigner. You be the judge.

Red Barn / Multipurpose Room
University of Louisville
Louisville KY 40292
502-852-6691
Capacity: 425-1,200
Alternative

Press

The Courier Journal
525 W Broadway,
PO Box 740031
Louisville KY 40201-7431
502-582-4011
Daily newspaper

Louisville Eccentric Observer (LEO)
3900 Shelbyville Rd., Ste 14A
Louisville KY 40207
502-895-9770
Weekly alternative newspaper

Louisville Music News
PO Box 148
Pewee Valley KY 40056
502-239-9004 (fax)
Monthly music newspaper

River City Music News
6801 Dixie Hwy
Louisville KY 40258
812-284-3646

Radio

WFPL 89.3 fm
301 York St.
Louisville KY 40203-2257
502-574-1640
Jazz, Blues, Folk, Bluegrass

WLCV 570 am
University of Louisville
Rm W320F SAC Bldg
Louisville KY 40292
502-852-6966
All styles, mostly Alternative

Record Stores

Better Days Records
1591 Bardstown Rd.
Louisville KY 40205
502-456-2394
CD, CA, LP

Ear X-Tacy
1140 Bardstown Rd.
Louisville KY 40204
502-452-1799
CD, CA, LP

Music Stores

Doo Wop Music
1587 Bardstown Rd.
Louisville KY 40205
502-456-5250
Most instrument sales and
rentals

Guitar Emporium
1610 Bardstown Rd.
Louisville KY 40205
502-459-4153
Guitars; guitar and amp repairs

Mom's Musicians General Store
2920 frankfort Ave.
Louisville KY 40206
502-897-3304
800-467-MOMS
Most instruments; electronic
repairs

Music Warehouse
3204 Bardstown Rd.
Louisville KY 40205
502-456-4730
Most instrument sales, rentals
and repairs.

LOUISIANA
Baton Rouge
Venues

The Bayou
124 W. Chimes St
Baton Rouge LA 70802
504-346-1765
Capacity: 350
Alternative, rock

The Corner Bar
1108 Highland Rd.
Baton Rouge LA 70802
504-338-1005
Capacity: 250
Rock, Blues, R&B

Pappa Joes's
1580 Nicholson Dr.
Baton Rouge LA 70802
504-387-0091
Capacity: 600
Hard rock, metal, alternative

Phil Brady's
4848 Government St.
Baton Rouge LA 70806
504-927-3786
Capacity: 250
Blues.

Varsity Theatre
3357 Highland
Baton Rouge, LA 70894
504-383-7018
Capacity: 800
Alternative

Press

The Advocate
525 Lafayette St.
Baton Rouge, LA 70802-5410
504-383-1111
Daily

Radio

KLSU
Lousiana State University
39 Hodges Hall
Baton Rouge LA 70803
504-388-4620
Alternative

WBRH
2825 Government St.
Baton Rouge LA 70806
504-383-3243
Jazz, New Age, Alt.

Record Stores

Paradise Records
226 W. State St.
Baton Rouge LA 70802
504-344-2324

Music Stores

Be-Bop
2560 Government
Baton Rouge LA 70806
504-343-7433
Rentals, sales, repairs

Ziegler Music
7003 Florida Bl.
Baton Rouge LA 70806
504-923-0769
Rentals, sales, repairs

New Orleans
Venues

Cafe Brasil
2100 Chartres St.
New Orleans LA 70116
504-947-9386
Capacity: 300
Jazz, Latin, Reggae

Checkpoint Charlie's
504 Esplanade Ave.
New Orleans LA 70116
504-947-0979
Capacity: 275
Rock, R&B, Alternative

Howlin' Wolf
828 Peters St.
New Orleans LA 70130
504-529-2341
Capacity: 500
All styles, a good place for indie bands

Jimmy's
8200 Willow St.
New Orleans LA 70118
504-838-6981
Capacity: 900
All styles

Maple Leaf
8316 Oak St.
New Orleans LA 70118
504-866-9359
Capacity: 350
Cajun, Reggae, Rock
Mostly local bands

Margaritaville Cafe
1104 Decatur St.
New Orleans LA 70116
504-592-2565
Capacity: 600
Country, Latin, Zydeco, Cajun, Rock
Jimmy Buffet's bar, (at least he isn't living off of his laurels or anything)

Mermaid Lounge
1100 Constance St.
New Orleans LA 70130
504-524-4747
Capacity: 200
All styles.

Mid-City Bowling Lanes
4133 S Carrollton Ave.
New Orleans LA 70119
504-482-3133
Capacity: 400
R&B, Zydeco, Blues
"Rock and Bowl"

Muddy Waters
8301 Oak St.
New Orleans LA 70118
504-866-7174
Capacity: 550
Various styles, mostly blues and alternative

RC Bridge Lounge
1201 Magazine St.
New Orleans LA 70131
504-523-9190
Capacity: 200
Alternative
This is the punk rock club.
Careful with that axe Eugene.

Tipitina's
501 Napolean Ave.
New Orleans LA 70115
504-891-8477
Capacity: 1,000
All styles
Books mainly "established" artists, and I use that term loosely.

Warehouse Cafe
1179 Annunciation St.
New Orleans LA 70130
504-586-1282
Capacity: 200
Various styles

Press

Gambit
4141 Bienville
New Orleans LA 70119
504-486-5900
Weekly news magazine
Mainly Jazz and R&B

Offbeat
333 St. Charles St., Ste 614
New Orleans LA 70130
504-522-5533
Monthly music magazine

Times Picayune
3800 Howard Ave.
New Orleans LA 70140
504-826-3470
Daily newspaper

Radio

WCKW 92.3 fm
PO Box 5905
Metairie LA 70002
504-831-8811
Commercial Rock

WTUL 91.5 fm
Tulane University
New Orleans LA 70118
504-865-5887
All styles

WWOZ 90.7 fm
PO Box 51840
New Orleans LA 70151
504-568-1238
Jazz, Blues, Cajun, International

Record Stores

Brown Sugar Records
2334 Louisiana Ave.
New Orleans LA 70115
504-895-8087
CD, CA, LP

ADVICE FROM THE ROAD

TIPS ON EATING WELL ON TOUR

By Zuzu's Petals

1. Bring a cooler (buy your own food)

2. Stock up on vitamins and herbal cures

3. If you don't have a contract or rider, ask for meals anyway (when you book the show and again at the club)

4. If you do have a rider take the buyout $ whenever possible (unless you're playing at Maxwell's or Cicero's)

5. Don't dine at salad bars in Iowa (unless you love Miracle Whip)

6. Avoid Bob Evans, Stuckey's and Rax

7. Don't eat anything in England

VANS

The backbone of any band.

1. Always get a tune-up before each tour (Laurie's diligence in this matter enabled us to get an additional 100,000 miles on our last vehicle)

2. Get as many gas and credit cards as your bohemian credit rating will allow (these will come in handy when you don't get paid or need repairs)

3. Get a AAA Gold Card, among its special features is a free tow within 100 miles of your breakdown (this came in handy more than once, especially the time we rode 70 miles in a tow truck on Laurie's birthday)

4. If you do break down (and you will) call the club immediately. Ask someone you know to recommend an honest mechanic; otherwise put some grease on your face and pretend to understand car jargon.

5. Don't speed in Pennsylvania, it is a $96 fine for going 1 mile an hour over the speed limit.

The Minneapolis-based Zuzu's Petals have toured nationally and throughout Europe.

Odyssey Records & Tapes
Carrollton Shopping Center
3920 Dublin
New Orleans LA 70118
504-468-8018
CD, CA, LP

Record Ron's
1129 Decatur St.
New Orleans LA 70116
504-524-9444
CD, CA, LP

Underground Sounds
735 Octavia St.
New Orleans LA 70115
504-897-9030
LP, CD, CA, alternative.

Music Stores

Allied Music
4417 Bienville Ave.
New Orleans LA 70119
504-488-2674
Most instruments; electronic and guitar repairs; no rentals

Rock 'N' Roll
4805 Baudin St.
New Orleans LA 70119
504-486-7625
Most instruments; electronic, guitar, and PA repairs and rentals

Uptown Music
4514 Magazine St.
New Orleans LA 70115
504-891-6515
Most instrument sales and rentals; guitar and amp repairs

Werleins for Music
229 Decatur St.
New Orleans LA 70130
504-883-5080
Most instrument sales and rentals; guitar and electronic repairs

Food & Etc.

Go to the **French Quarter!!!** This is going to be the town you blow all of your money in, but enjoy doing it all the same. Find a restaurant where you can get crawdads, raw oysters, catfish, crawfish etouffee, gumbo, and red beans and rice. (**Seaport**, on Bourbon St. has a killer buffet - a little of everything) Try a shrimp po boy at one of the mom and pop type grocery stores in the quarter - they're half the price of those in the restaurants and twice as good. Also check out **Cafe Beignet**, across from Jackson Square, for some Cajun coffee with chicory. Another "don't miss" is an Original **Pat O'Brien's** Hurricane - get it from Pat O's side bar because the main bar is pretty cheesy. Also, if you have some time to kill between 8:00 and 10:30p.m., I highly suggest the MAGIC Vampire and Ghost Hunt. It's a walking tour through the darker parts of the Quarter. They arm you with a stake and some holy water, show you real haunted houses, and tell you some freaky stories about the city! (It costs about $13, but it's worth it) One last word of advice: **DO NOT EAT A LUCKY DOG!!!!!**

MAINE
Portland
Venues

Geno's
13 Brown St.
Portland ME 04101
207-772-7891
Capacity: 200
Alternative

Granny Killam's
55 Market St.
Portland ME 04112
207-761-2787
Capacity: 200
Rock, alternative, reggae.

Raoul's Roadside Attraction
865 Forest Ave.
Portland ME 04103
207-773-6886
Capacity: 225
Alternative, folk, R&B, etc.

State Theater
609 Congress St.
Portland ME 04101
207-773-5540
Capacity: 900
All styles.

T-Bird's
126 N. Boyd St.
Portland ME 04101
207-773-8040
Capacity: 525
Rock, alternative.

Zootz
31 4th Ave.
Portland ME 04101
207-773-8187
Capacity: 350
Rock, alt., reggae

Press

Cradle
P.O. Box 4811
Portland ME 04112
207-772-1711
Bi-weekly music mag.

Face Magazine
19 Commercial St.
Portland ME 04101
207-774-9703
Bi-weekly entertainment paper.

Portland Press Herald
390 Congress St.
Portland ME 04104
207-780-9000
Daily

Radio

WBOR 91.1
Moulton Union
Bowdoin College
Brunswick ME 04011
207-725-3210
College, all styles

WMPG
University of Southern Maine
96 Falmouth St.
Portland ME 04103
207-780-4974
College, all styles

Record Stores

Bad Habits
10 Exchange St.
Portland ME 04101
207-773-1310
CD, LP, CA

Enterprise Records
613-A Congress St.
Portland ME 04101
207-773-7672
LP, 7"

Music Stores

Crazy Ed's
200 Gorham Rd.
S. Portland ME 04106
207-774-7592

Daddy's Junky Music
1064 Brighton Ave.
Portland ME 04103
207-772-3293

Portland Percussion
5 Deering Ave.
Portland ME 04101
207-775-2230

MARYLAND
Baltimore
Venues

8 X 10
10 E Cross St.
Baltimore MD 21230
410-625-2001
Capacity: 300
All styles, mainly alternative
18 and up

The Barn
9527 Harford Rd.
Baltimore MD 21234
410-882-6182
Capacity: 200
Rock

Chambers
203 Davis St.
Baltimore MD 21202
Bernie, 410-539-3255
Variety - Reggae, Jazz, Alternative

Dead Freddy's
7209 Harford Rd.
Baltimore MD 21214
410-254-8373
Capacity: 170
Rock

Fat Lulu's
1818 Maryland Ave.
Baltimore MD 21201
410-685-4665
Capacity: 200
Rock, Underground, Soul, Jazz

Hammerjack's
1101 S Howard St.
Baltimore MD 21230
410-752-3302
Capacity: 1,900
Rock, Alternative

J. Strapp's
7653 Harford Rd.
Baltimore MD 21214
Capacity: 165
Rock

Karaoke Bar
113 W 2nd St.
Baltimore MD 21218
410-727-5455
Paul Hutzler

Max's on Broadway
735 Broadway
Baltimore MD 21231
410-675-6297
Capacity: 300
All styles

Memory Lane
1433 W. Hamburg St.
Baltimore MD 21230
410-837-5070
Capacity: 400
Rock, alternative.

The Paradox
1310 Russel St.
Baltimore MD 21230
410-837-9110
Capacity: 1,500
Alternative Techno, Industrial,
Dance, Rap

The Rendezvous
205 W 25th St.
Baltimore MD 21211
410-467-3860

Press

The Baltimore Sun
501 N Calvert St.
Baltimore MD 21278
410-332-6605
Daily newspaper

The City Paper
800 Charles St., Ste 350
Baltimore MD 21201
410-523-2300
Weekly alternative newspaper
Send info to Jim Maher

Dirty Linen
PO Box 66600
Baltimore MD 21239
410-583-7973
Folk music magazine

The Foster Child
7635 Marcy Ct
Glen Burnie MD 21060
410-766-5218
Quarterly alternative fanzine

Music Monthly
7510 Harford Rd., 2nd Fl
Baltimore MD 21234
410-494-0566
Monthly music magazine

Rox
1714 Alicenna St.
Baltimore MD 21231
410-880-6155
Monthly music magazine

Radio

According to our sources, there may as well be no college radio in Baltimore.

WHFS 99.1 fm
8201 Corporate Dr, Ste 550
Landover MD 20785
301-306-0991
Commercial Alternative

WRNR 103.1 fm
12 Main St., 3rd Fl
Annapolis MD 21401
410-626-0103
Commercial Rock, Alt.

WIYY 97.9 fm
3800 Hooper Ave.
Baltimore MD 21211
410-889-0098
Commercial Rock

WJHU 88.1 fm
Johns Hopkins University
2216 N Charles St.
Baltimore MD 21218
410-516-9548
Classical, Jazz, Acoustic

WTMD 89.7 fm
Towson State University
Media Center
Towson MD 21204
410-830-8937
New Age, Jazz

Record Stores

An Die Musik
1 Investment Pl., Annex Bldg
Towson MD 21204
CD, CA

Modern Music
241 W Read St.
Baltimore MD 21201
410-675-2172
CD, CA, LP

Musical Exchange
422 N Charles St.
Baltimore MD 21201
410-528-9815
CD, CA, LP

Normal's
429 E 31st St.
Baltimore MD 21218
410-243-6888
CD, CA, LP

Record Masters
711 W 40th St.
Baltimore MD 21211
410-366-1250
CD, CA

Reptilian
403 S Broadway
Baltimore MD 21231
410-327-6853
CD, CA, LP
This is the hip indie store for all those hipsters who were curious

Vinyl Discoveries
5615 Belair Rd.
Baltimore MD 21206
410-325-1020

Music Stores

Appalachian Bluegrass
643 Frederick Rd.
Baltimore MD 21228
410-744-1144
Acoustic instrument sales and repairs

Bill's Music
733 Frederick Rd.
Baltimore MD 21228
410-747-1900
Most instrument sales, repairs, and rentals

Coffey Music
15 E Main St.
Westminster MD 21157
410-848-5003
Most instrument sales and repairs; PA rentals

Gordon Miller Music
8804 Orchard Tree Ln
Baltimore MD 21286
410-825-2558
Most repairs; PA and keyboard rentals

The Guitar Exchange
17 Melrose Ave.
Catonsville MD 21228
410-747-0122
Guitars; guitar and amp repairs and rentals

Metro Broker, Ltd
4 N Eutaw St.
Baltimore MD 21201
410-752-1233
New and Vintage guitars; bass and amp sales and repairs

Ted's Musician's Shop
11 E Center St.
Baltimore MD 21202
410-685-4198
Most instruments; guitar repairs

Contact **Jef Brown** for instrument repairs in the area, 410-728-6270. He is supposedly "the best"

Food

A list of restaurants: **Paper Moon Cafe** (24 hours), **The Buttery, Louie's Bookstore, Daily Edition.**

Etc.

Go see: **Fort McHenry, Aquarium, Normal Books, Atomic Books.**

MASSACHUSETTS
Boston
Cambridge
Venues

Avalon
15 Lansdowne St.
Boston MA 02215
617-262-2424
Capacity: 1,300
Alternative, Rock, Dance

Ave. C
25 Boylston Pl.
Boston MA 02116
617-423-3832
Capacity: 700
Alternative

Axis
13 Lansdowne St.
Boston MA 02215
617-262-2437
Capacity: 1,000
Alternative, Rock

Bill's Bar / Venus De Milo
5 1/2 Lansdowne St.
Boston MA 02215
617-421-9595
Capacity: Bill's 200; Venus 900
Rock, Reggae, Acoustic

Causeway
65 Causeway St.
Boston MA 02211
617-523-9151
Capacity: 75
Alternative, indie.

Club 3
608 Somerville Ave.
Somerville MA 02143
617-623-6957
Capacity: 350

Harper's Ferry
158 Brighton Ave.
Allston MA 02134
617-254-9743/7380
Capacity: 340
Blues

House of Blues
96 Winthrop St.
Cambridge MA 02138
617-491-2583
Capacity: 250
Blues, Gospel

Johnny D's
17 Holland Ave.
Somerville MA 02144
617-776-7450
Capacity: 300
Various styles

Local 186
186 Harvard Ave.
Allston MA 02134
617-351-2660
Capacity: 300
Rock

Mama Kin
36 Lansdowne St.
Boston MA 02215
617-536-2100
Capacity: 350
Owned by Aerosmith, so you
know it's rock.

Man Ray
21 Brookline St.
Cambridge MA 02139
617-864-0406/0400
Capacity: 800
Dance, Alternative

Middle East Cafe
Middle East Underground
472 Massachusetts Ave.
Cambridge MA 02139
Cafe: 617-492-9181
Booking: 617-492-1886
Underground: 617-354-5434
Capacity: upstairs 150; down-
stairs 400
Alternative, Rock, Jazz, World
Beat. Downstairs occasionally
does all-ages shows. A great
place to play.

The Paradise
967 Commonwealth Ave.
Boston MA 02215
617-562-8800
Capacity: 650
All Styles

Passim
47 Palmer St.
Cambridge MA 02138
617-492-7679
Capacity: 150
Acoustic

The Rathskeller
528 Commonwealth Ave.
Boston MA 02215
617-536-2750
Capacity: basement 271; all
three floors 500
Rock

Regattabar
Charles Hotel
1 Bennett St.
Cambridge MA 02138
617-864-1200 / 876-7777
Jazz

Ryles
212 Hampshire St.
Inman Sq
Cambridge MA 02139
617-876-9330
Jazz

Scullers Grill & Lounge
Guest Quarters Hotel
400 Soldiers Field Rd.
Boston MA 02134
617-562-4111
Capacity: 150
Jazz, Soul, R&B, Blues

The Tam
1648 Beacon St.
Brookline MA 02146
617-277-0982
Capacity: 120
Rock, Blues, Acoustic

T.T. the Bear's Place
10 Brookline St.
Cambridge MA 02139
617-492-0082
Capacity: 350
Rock, Blues, Alternative
Management known to pull the
plug on loud bands.

Western Front
Cambridge MA 02139
617-492-7772
Capacity: 150
Reggae, World, Jazz

Zoots
251 Old Concord Rd.
Billerica MA 01821
508-667-6393
Capacity: 285
Blues, Rock

Press

The Boston Globe
PO Box 2378
Boston MA 02107-2378
617-929-2000
Daily newspaper

The Boston Herald
PO Box 2096
Boston MA 02106
617-426-3000
Daily newspaper

Boston Phoenix
126 Brookline Ave.
Boston MA 02215
617-536-5390
Weekly newspaper

Boston Rock
Box 371 New Town Branch
Newton MA 02258
617-244-6803
Monthly Magazine

Buzz Magazine Boston
Boston University Station
PO Box 319
Boston MA 02215

The Improper Bostonian
17 Station St., Ste 7A
Brookline MA 02146-7307
617-232-3507
Biweekly newspaper

New England Folk Almanac
PO Box 336
Cambridge MA 02141
617-661-4708
Bimonthly newsletter

New England Performer
11 Riverside Ave., Ste 4
Medford MA 02155
617-395-7055
Monthly music magazine

The Noise
74 Jamaica St.
Boston MA 02130
617-524-4735
Monthly fanzine

Pit Report
PO Box 120905
Boston MA 02112-0905
617-464-4262
Monthly fanzine

Popwatch
PO Box 440215
Somerville MA 02144
617-628-5333
Monthly fanzine

The Tab
1254 Chestnut St.
Newton MA 02164
617-969-0340
Weekly newspaper

Radio

WAAF 107.3 fm
200 Friberg Pkwy, Ste 4000
Westboro MA 01581
508-836-9223
Commercial Rock

WBCN 104.1 fm
1265 Boylston St.
Boston MA 02215
617-266-1111
Commercial Rock

WBRS 100.1 fm
Brandeis University
415 South St.
Waltham MA 02254
617-736-5277
All styles

WECB 640 am cc
Emerson College
100 Beacon St.
Boston MA 02116
617-578-8851

WERS 88.9 fm
Emerson College
128 Beacon St.
Boston MA 02116
617-578-8892
All styles

WFNX 101.7 fm
25 Exchange St.
Lynn MA 01901
617-595-6200
Commercial Alternative

WGBH 89.7 fm
125 Western Ave.
Boston MA 02134
617-492-2777
Jazz, Blues, Folk, World Beat

WHRB 95.3 fm
Harvard University
45 Quincy St.
Cambridge MA 02138
617-495-4818
Classical, Jazz, Alternative
A good college station for indie
bands

WJUL 91.5 fm
University of Lowell
One University Ave.
Lowell MA 01854
508-452-9073
All styles

WMBR 88.1 fm
MIT
3 Ames St.
Cambridge MA 02142
617-253-4000
All styles
This station comes recom-
mended for indie bands and
they do on-air interviews and
performances.

WMFO 91.5
Tufts University
Curtis Hall 3rd Fl
490 Boston Ave.
Medford MA 02153
617-625-0800
All styles

WMLN 91.5 fm
Curry College
1071 Blue Hill Ave.
Milton MA 02186
617-333-0311
All styles

WRBB 104.9 fm
Northeastern University
360 Huntington Ave.
Boston MA 02115
617-373-4338
All styles

WSFR clc
Suffolk University
41 Temple St.
Boston MA 02115
617-573-8324

WTBU
Boston University
640 Commonwealth Ave.
Boston MA 02215
617-353-6400

WUMB 91.9 fm
University of Massachusetts
Harbor Campus
Boston MA 02125
617-287-6900
Fax: 617-265-7173
Folk, Acoustic, Jazz, Blues

WMWM 91.7 fm
Salem State College
352 Lafayette St.
Salem MA 01970
508-745-9401
Fax: 508-740-7204
All styles, Mostly Alternative and
Rap. Another good station for
indie bands.

WZBC 90.3 fm
Boston College
107 McElroy Commons
Chestnut Hill MA 02167
617-552-3511
Alternative
A good station for indie bands

Record Stores

Disc Diggers
401 Highland Ave.
Somerville MA 02144
617-776-7560
CD, CA

HMV
1 Brattle Square
Cambridge MA 02138
617-868-9696
CD, CA, LP

In Your Ear
957 Commonwealth Ave.
Boston MA 02215
617-787-9755
CD, CA, LP
This is the highly recommended
store in the area, especially for
indie stuff

Kids Will Have Their Say
12 Elliot St. 2nd Floor
Cambridge MA 02138
617-270-2914

Looney Tunes
1106 Boylston St.
Boston MA 02215
617-247-2238
CD, CA, LP

Mystery Train
1208 Massachusetts Ave.
Cambridge MA 02138
617-497-4024
CD, CA, LP

Newbury Comics
38 Everett St.
Allston MA 02134
617-254-1666
CD, CA, LP
This is the main office for a
number of branch stores in the
Boston/Cambridge area

Nuggets
486 Commonwealth Ave.
Boston MA 02215
617-536-0679
CD, CA, LP

Planet Records
536 Commonwealth Ave.
Boston MA 02215
617-353-0693
CD, CA, LP

Second Coming
1105 Massachusetts Ave.
Cambridge MA 02138
617-576-6400
CD, CA, LP

Skippy White's
315 Centre St.
Jamaica Plain Plaza
Jamaica Plain MA 02130
617-524-4500
CD, CA, LP

Tower Records
360 Newbury St.
Boston MA 02115
617-247-5900
CD, CA

Music Stores

Cambridge Music
1906 Massachusetts Ave.
Cambridge MA 02140
617-491-5433
Used and vintage guitar and
amp sales; guitar repairs; no
rentals

Daddy's Junky Music
159 Massachusetts Ave.
Boston MA 02115
617-247-0909
Most instrument sales and
repairs; no rentals

Jack's Drum Shop
1096 Boylston St.
Boston MA 02215
617-266-4617
Drums, percussion, acoustic
guitars; drum and percussion
repairs; no rentals

Mack's Music Center
14 Wareham St.
Middleboro MA 02346
508-946-1107
Most instruments; guitar, amp,
keyboard, electronic repairs; no
rentals

Mr. Music
128 Harvard Ave.
Allston MA 02134
617-783-1609
Most instruments; amp repairs;
no rentals

Steve's Quality Instruments
18 Waters St.
Danvers MA 01923
508-777-3221
Most instrument sales and
rentals; guitar, keyboard and
elecronic repairs

Taft Sound
17 Taft St.
Uxbridge MA 01569
800-244-7491
PA rentals

Turn 2 Music
128-132 Prospect St.
Waltham MA 02154
617-899-0030
Most instruments; guitar and
amp repairs; PA rentals

E.U. Wurlitzer
922 Commonwealth Ave.
Boston MA 02215
617-738-7000
and
180 Massachusetts Ave.
Boston MA 02115
617-738-7001
Repairs
This place comes highly recommended by the locals.

Food

If you play at the **Middle East**,
eat there. That place rules,
whether you are vegetarian or
not.

Shelter

Days Inn on Soldiers Field Rd. in Boston. If you play at the Middle East, you get a discount here. You can go north of the city on Route 1 for about 10 or 15 minutes and there are cheap hotels/motels in Saugus and Peabody.

Etc.

Go to **Harvard Square** for cool shops, restaurants and people. This is a mellow area to hang out in while you wait for a sound check that will turn out to be a complete waste of time. Soundmen at clubs generally suck and only give you a soundcheck to humor you. Notice how they never mark anything while you check, and then change all the nobs when the other bands play. Go to **Fenway Park** and see the Red Sox play if it is baseball season, and quit pretending musicians never played Little League and hate all sports.

MICHIGAN
Detroit
Ann Arbor
Venues

Alvin's
5756 Cass Ave.
Detroit MI 48202
313-832-0589
Capacity: 300
Various styles

The Attic Bar
11667 Joseph Campau
Hamtramck MI 48212
313-365-4194
Capacity: 125
Blues

The Blind Pig
208 S First St.
Ann Arbor MI 48104
313-996-8555
Capacity: 425
All styles

The Falcon Club
3515 Caniff
Hamtramck MI 48212
313-368-6010
Capacity: 960
Alternative

The Heidelberg
215 N Main St.
Ann Arbor MI 48104
313-663-7758
Capacity: 250
Alternative, Jazz, Blues

The Impound
17320 Harper Ave.
Detroit MI 48224
313-884-9441
Capacity: 225
Alternative, Rock

Intersection
1520 Wealthy St.
Grand Rapids MI 49506
616-554-3102
Capacity: 400
Alternative

I-Rock Nightclub
16350 Harper Ave.
Detroit MI 48224
313-881-7625
Capacity: 600
Rock

Lili's 21
2930 Jacob St.
Hamtramck MI 48212
313-875-6555
Capacity: 150
Alternative

The Majestic Theater
4140 Woodward
Detroit MI
313-833-9700
Capacity: 900
All styles

The Reptile House
139 S. Division Ave.
Grand Rapids MI 49503
616-242-9955
Capacity: 300
Alternative, rock.

Rick's Cafe
611 Church St.
Ann Arbor MI 48104
313-996-2747
Capacity: 400
Blues, Rock, R&B, Jazz, Reggae

The Ritz
17580 Frazho
Roseville MI 48066
810-778-6404
Capacity: 1,800
Rock

St. Andrew's Hall
431 E Congress
Detroit MI 48226
313-961-8137
Capacity: 1,000
Alternative, Rock, Jazz, Blues

The Shelter
431 E Congress
Detroit MI 48226
313-963-7237
Capacity: 550
Alternative, Rock, Jazz, Blues
This is the place if you are a relatively new act.

Sully's
4758 Greenfield
Dearborn MI 48126
313-846-1920
Capacity: 175
R&B, Jazz, Blues

Press

Anti-Matter
47500 Winthrop
Utica MI 48317
313-254-0828
Monthly Paper

Detroit Monthly
1400 Woodbridge
Detroit MI 48207
313-446-0330
Monthly Lifestyle Magazine

Jam Rag
PO Box 20076
Ferndale MI 48220
810-542-8090
Biweekly Alternative News

Metro Times
743 Beaubien
Detroit MI 48226
313-961-4060
Weekly

The Michigan Daily
420 Maynard Ave.
Ann Arbor MI 48109
313-763-0379
Daily College Paper

Orbit
919 Main St. Ste 2001
Royal Oak MI 48067
810-541-3900
Monthly Entertainment

Slack
P.O. Box 230167
Grand Rapids MI 49523
616-454-9371
Monthly alternative music
magazine.

Weekender Entertainment
68364 S. Main St.
Richmond MI 48062
810-727-9297
Monthly entertainment magazine.

Radio

CIMX 88.7 fm
30100 Telegraph Rd., Ste 465
Birmingham MI 48025
313-961-9811
Alternative

WCBN 88.3 fm
530 SAB
University of Michigan
at Ann Arbor
Ann Arbor MI 48109
313-763-3501
World Beat to College Rock

WDET 101.9
6001 Cass Ave.
Detroit MI 48202
313-577-4146
Contemporary, Alternative

WEMU 89.1 fm
PO Box 350
Ypsilanti MI 48197
313-487-2229
Jazz, Blues

WHFR 89.3
Henry Ford Community College
5101 Evergreen Rd.
Dearborn MI 48128
313-845-9676
Alternative

WXOU 90.1
Oakland University
69 Oakland Center
Rochester MI 48309
313-370-4272
All styles.

Record Stores

Absolute Music
34910 Gratiot Ave.
Clinton Township MI 48035
810-791-2990
CD, CA

Car City Records
21918 Harper Ave.
St. Clair Shores MI 48080
810-775-4770
CD, CA

Desirable Discs II
13939 Michigan Ave.
Dearborn MI 48212
313-581-1767
CD, CA, LP

Off the Record
322 S. Main
Royal Oak MI 48067
810-398-4436
CD, CA

Play it Again
503 S. Main St.
Royal Oak MI 48067
810-542-7529
CD, LP, CA

Record Time
25110 Gratiot Ave.
Roseville MI 48066
810-775-1550
CD, LP, CA

Repeat the Beat
1116 N. Telegraph
Dearborn MI 48128
313-562-6318
CD, CA

Schoolkids
523 E. Liberty St.
Ann Arbor MI 48104
313-994-8031
CD, LP, CA

Wazoo Records
336 1/2 S. State St.
Ann Arbor MI 48104
313-761-8686
CD, CA

Music Stores

Al Nally's
312 S. Ashley St.
Ann Arbor MI 48104
313-665-7008
Repairs & rents everything; full
product line

Arnold & Williams Music
5701 Canton Center Rd.
Canton MI 48187
313-453-6586

Drum House
25525 Five Mile Rd.
Redford MI 48239
313-531-4982

Gordy's Music
23263 Woodward
Ferndale MI 48220
810-546-7447
Guitar sales and rentals; amps;
no rentals

Joe's Music Quarters
24525 Gratiot
East Pointe MI 48021
810-777-2333
Sales, rentals & repairs; full-line
of products

Limelight Music
3068 Walton Blvd.
Rochester Hills MI 48309
810-375-0220

Music Box
42383 Garfield
Clinton Township MI 48038
810-263-1994
Guitar & amp rentals and
repairs; full product line

Music Stand
3063 W. 12 Mile
Berkley MI 48076
810-543-2330

Food

Xoshimilco, on Baegly Ave., near
bridge to Canada, has great
mexican food, more than
reasonably priced. **Cosmic Cafe**,
87 W. Palmer, Downtown, 313-
832-0001, off Woodward near
College, good vegetarian food.
There are tons of vegetarian
places in Ann Arbor, as well as
the greasy spoons found in just
about every college town.

Shelter

Try the **Days Inn** Downtown or
Motel 6's in the suburbs.

Etc.

Sweetwater, a British pub,
Downtown. Next door to St.
Andrews, a dive, is **Steve's Place**
- everyone goes there. Under St.
Andrews, **The Shelter** - a cool
club depending on what night of
the week. Near this area is
Greektown, which is a cool area
of town to waste time in. There
are a lot of Greek restaurants,
but **Nikki's** is the cheapest and
the best. **Locobar** is next to
Nikki's and has good, cheap
Mexican food. In Hamtramck,
Shadowbox ,2971 Trowbridge,
313-873-CAFE, cool coffehouse,

hangout, spoken word, etc.
Royal Oaks Noir Leather -
Renowned bondage clothing
store, leather jackets, nipple
rings, etc. **Brazil Coffeehouse** on
S. Main. **Dave's Comics** in Royal
Oak and Ann Arbor.

Kalamazoo
Venues

Club Soda
340 E. Michigan Ave.
Kalamazoo MI 49007
616-342-8067

Press

Insight Magazine
PO Box 51592
Kalamazoo MI 49005-1592
616-345-8446
A very cool alternative monthly.

Radio

WIDR 89.1 fm
Western Michigan University
Faunce Student Services Bldg
Kalamazoo MI 49008
616-387-6301
All styles
They have a lot of specialty
shows and some on-air perfor-
mances

WJMD 650 am cc
Kalamazoo College
Kalamazoo MI 49006
616-337-7218
All styles

Record Stores

Flipside Records
309 N Burdick
Kalamazoo MI 49007
616-343-5865
CD, CA, LP

Boogie Records
773 W Michigan
Kalamazoo MI 49007
616-385-4288
CD, CA, LP

Music Express
5049 W Main
Kalamazoo MI 49006
616-342-1239
CD, CA

Music Stores

Dillon's Music World
5252 Portage Rd.
Kalamazoo MI 49002
616-344-0397
Some sales; all kinds of repairs

Food

The Flame in downtown
Kalamazoo has a $1.49 break-
fast special.

Shelter

Stay at somebody's house (our
most frequent response to this
question).

Etc.

Thieves Market on Westnedge,
Bell's Brewery downtown on
Kalamazoo Ave., **The Mermaid
Lounge** (if you like scumbags),
The Boy in the Plastic Bubble is
off Route 20.

MINNESOTA
Minneapolis
St. Paul
Venues

7th St. Entry
29 North 7th St.
Minneapolis MN 55403
612-338-8388
Capacity: 250
A famous punk rock club attached to the even more famous 1st Ave. This is a great place to play and, unlike CBGB's in New York, the people who run this place are totally cool and helpful. Ask them to tell you a good Replacements or Husker Du story and they'll talk all night.

The 400 Bar
400 Cedar Ave. S.
Minneapolis MN 55454
612-332-2903 club, 612-332-3844 booking
Capacity:475
Shows 7 nights a week, all styles, a good place for indie bands to play

Blues Saloon
601 N. Western Ave.
St. Paul MN 55103
612-228-9959
Capacity: 300
Basically blues, some rockabilly, hillbilly & cajun

Bunker's
761 Washington Ave. N.
Minneapolis MN 55401
612-338-8188 club, 612-332-3904 booking
Capacity: 299
Roots rock, blues, R&B, country; 7 nights a week

Cabooze
917 Cedar Ave.
Minneapolis MN 55404
612-338-6425
Capacity: 1,000
Various styles, they will book indie touring bands

The Dakota Bar & Grill
1021 E. Bandana Blvd.
St. Paul MN 55108
612-642-1442
Capacity: 150
Live jazz 7 nights a week

Fine Line Music Cafe
318 1st Ave. N.
Minneapolis MN 55401
612-338-8100
Capacity: 500
Jazz, folk, R&B, reggae & soul; classy showcase 7 nights a week indie bands can sometimes do shows here

First Ave.
701 1st Ave. N.
Minneapolis MN 55403
612-338-8388
Capacity: 1,300
This is a large club for large bands, but attached is the 7th Street Entry and they will sometimes book unknown bands.

Five Corner's
501 Cedar Ave. S.
Minneapolis MN 55454
612-338-6424
Capacity: 120
Mostly R&B, reggae, soul & blues

Glam Slam
110 N. 5th St.
Minneapolis MN 55403
612-338-3383
Capacity: 1,200
Prince's club; funk, jazz, hip-hop, rap

The Mirage
792 29th Ave. SE
Minneapolis MN 55414
612-729-2387
Capacity: 1,550
Mainly major club acts, smaller capacity stage for regional & local bands

Uptown
3018 Hennepin S.
Minneapolis MN 55408
612-823-4719
Capacity: 350
Progressive pop to grunge
This is one of the best clubs for indie touring bands to play.

What's Up Lounge
701 N. Riverfront Dr.
Mankato MN 56001
507-387-5034
Capacity: 225
Rock, alternative, etc.

Whiskey Junction
901 Cedar Ave.
Minneapolis MN 55404
612-338-9550
Capacity: 600
Rock, blues, R&B

The Whole
220 CMU
300 Washington Ave. SE
Minneapolis MN 55455
612-624-8638
Capacity: 440
Located in the University of Minnesota student union; all-ages; alternative

Press

Buzz
401 N. 3rd St., Ste 550
Minneapolis MN 55401
612-375-1015
Tabloid found in City Pages

Cake Magazine
3028 Ewing Ave. S. #201
Minneapolis MN 55416
612-781-9178
This is a great magazine to be reviewed in.

City Pages
401 N. 3rd St., Ste 550
Minneapolis MN 55401
612-375-1015
Free weekly news & art paper

Minnesota Daily
University of Minnesota at Minneapolis
10 Murphy Hall
206 Church St. SE
Minneapolis Mn 55455
612-627-4080
Daily Newspaper

Minneapolis Star/Tribune
425 Portland Ave. S.
Minneapolis MN 55488
612-673-4000
Major daily newspaper

Request
7630 Excelsior Blvd.
Minneapolis MN 55426
612-932-7418
Monthly music magazine

The Skyway News
33 S. 5th St.
Minneapolis MN 55402
612-375-9222; 612-375-9208 fax
Weekly arts paper

St. Paul Pioneer Press
345 Cedar St.
St. Paul MN 55101
612-228-5591
Major daily newspaper

Twin Cities Reader
Colonnade Bldg, Ste 800
5500 Wayzata Blvd.
Minneapolis MN 55416
612-591-2598
Free weekly news & entertainment

The Wrap-Up
PO Box 3901
Minneapolis MN 55403
612-472-1381
Monthly fanzine
This is a good paper for indie bands

Your Flesh
PO Box 583264
Minneapolis MN 55458
Quarterly music fanzine
If you think you're punk rock, send your stuff here. Finicky.

Radio

KBEM 88.5 fm
1555 James Ave. N.
Minneapolis MN 55411
612-627-2833
Non-commercial jazz

KFAI 90.3 fm
1808 Riverside Ave.
Minneapolis MN 55454
612-341-3144
Various styles

WMCN 91.7 fm
Macalester College
1600 Grand Ave.
St. Paul MN 55105
612-696-6082
Various styles

KMOJ 89.9
501 Brant Ave. N.
Minneapolis MN 55405
612-377-0594
Urban contemporary

KTCZ 97.1
100 N. 6th St., Butler Square
Minneapolis MN 55403
612-333-2997; 612-339-0000 fax
Adult album alternative

KUOM 'Radio K' 770 am
University of Minnesota
550 Rarig Center
330 27th Ave. SE
Minneapolis MN 55455
612-625-3500
Non-commercial alternative
Probably the only station that will play your band's record

Record Stores

Aardvark
8913 Penn Ave.
Bloomington MN 55431
612-885-9737

Electric Fetus
2010 4th Ave. S.
Minneapolis MN 55404
612-870-9300
CD, CA
recommended

Garage D'Or
2548 Nicollet Ave. S.
Minneapolis MN 55404
612-871-0563
CD, LP, CA
recommended

Let It Be
1001 Nicollet Mall
Minneapolis MN 55403
612-339-7439
CD, LP, CA
Recommended for indie stuff even though the store is dance-music oriented

Oar Folkjokeopus Records
2557 Lyndale Ave. S.
Minneapolis MN 55405
612-872-7400
CD, LP, CA
Another very good store

Roadrunner
4304 Nicollet Ave. S.
Minneapolis MN 55409
612-822-0613
CD, LP, CA
recommended

Music Stores

Aabe's
11 E. 58th St.
Minneapolis MN 55419
612-866-2620
Repairs, rents & sells a full-line of new/used products

Eclipse Concert Systems
153 E. Thompson Ave.
W. St. Paul MN 55118
612-451-8878
Minor instrument repairs; PA, lights, laser rentals; full-line of products, except drums & keyboards

General Music
1219 Arcade
St. Paul MN 55106
612-774-1908
Guitar repair; sound reinforcement rentals; full product line

The Good Guys
1111 Grand Ave.
St. Paul MN 55105
612-292-9165
All electronic, digital and analog repairs; no rentals

Groth Music Co
7800 Dupont Ave. S.
Bloomington MN 55420
612-884-4772
Band instrument repairs; band & string rentals; full product line

Hoffman Guitars
2219 E. Franklin Ave.
Minneapolis MN 55404
612-338-1079
Repairs string instruments; no rentals; full-line of guitars

Knut Koupee
2536 Hennepin Ave. S.
Minneapolis MN 55405
612-377-2000
Full-line of repairs, rentals & sales, recommended

Metro Sound & Lighting
1731 University Ave.
St. Paul MN 55104
612-647-9342
Sound, lighting, recording
equipment repairs; no rentals;
sound & lighting sales

The Music Connection
77 8th Ave.
Forest Lake MN 55025
612-464-5252
PA and band instrument repairs;
full product lines; no rentals

Music Go Round
1301 W Lake St.
Minneapolis MN 55408
612-822-7602
Most instruments; some guitar
repairs

Schmitt Music
88 S. 10th St.
Minneapolis MN 55403
612-339-4811
Full-line of rentals, repairs &
sales

Food

The **Uptown Bar** has good food
for the money, (for $6 you can
get a huge plate of food), and
the menu is very diverse.
Mudpie on Lindow and 26th is a
good vegetarian place.

Shelter

In the Uptown area, the **Fair
Oaks** is a cheap place on 3rd
Ave., near the College of Design.
The Uptown area is called the
Rock'N'Roll Ghetto, supposedly
many of the people who play in
local bands live is this part of
the city.

Etc

The **Mary Tyler Moore House** is
in Minneapolis, find someone
who knows where it is and go
check it out. You can't really go
inside, but you can drive by.
First Ave. is where *Purple Rain*
was filmed. The **Hennepin Ave.
Bridge** is worth driving over. As
you leave the city, at the end of
the bridge, look to the right and
you may catch a glimpse of

Nye's Polynaise, the coolest
piano bar in Minneapolis. There
is a woman playing piano who
knows all the old hits. Come
and sing a Sinatra classic, or go
downstairs and play a little
poker.

**(Mississippi intentionally
omitted.)**

MISSOURI
Columbia
Kansas City
Venues

The Bassment
816 E. Broadway
Columbia MO 65201
314-874-9211
Capacity: 250
All sorts of alternative.

Blayney's
415 Westport Rd.
Kansas City MO 64111
816-561-3747
Capacity: 250
Blues, classic rock & reggae

The Blue Note
17 N. 9th St.
Columbia MO 65201
314-874-1944
Capacity: 750
Great sound; regional & national
acts; various styles

Davey's Uptown Ramblers Club
3402 Main St.
Kansas City MO 64111
816-753-1909
Capacity: 200
Alternative, blues & rock

The Foundry
2805 Southwest Bl.
Kansas City MO 64108
816-931-5266
Capacity: 300
Alternative.

Grand Emporium
3832 Main St.
Kansas City MO 64111
816-531-7557
Capacity: 350
Main venue for live blues & jazz

Harling's Upstairs
3941 Main St.
Kansas City MO 64111
816-531-0303
Capacity: 274
Alternative Irish music

The Hurricane
4048 Broadway
Kansas City MO 64111
816-753-0884
Capacity: 350
Alternative rock/rock in a pub-
like atmosphere

The Lone Star
4117 Mill St.
Kansas City MO 64111
816-561-1881, 816-756-0288
booking
Capacity: 500
Premier rock/metal club

NightMoves
5110 NE Vivian
Kansas City MO 64119
816-452-8399; 816-452-8399
booking
Capacity: 200
Blues from Wed-Sat nights

Press

The New Times
1509 Westport Rd.
Kansas City MO 64111
816-753-7880; 816-561-9625
contact Melissa
Weekly newspaper

Pitch
3701 Summit
Kansas City MO 64111
816-561-6061
Weekly news & arts

Radio

KCOU 88.1 fm
101 F Pershing Hall
Columbia MO 65201
314-882-8262
Various styles

KKFI 90.1
PO Box 10255
Kansas City MO 64111
816-931-3122
Various styles

KWWC 90.5 fm
Stevens College
1405 Broadway
Columbia MO 65215
314-876-7272
Various styles

Record Stores

Avalon
3841 Main St.
Kansas City MO 64111
816-931-9060
CD, LP, CA, Video

Groove Farm
827 Westport Rd.
Kansas City MO 64111 basement
816-531-8800
CD, LP, CA, 7"

Love Records
4041 Broadway
Kansas City MO 64111
816-753-0078
CD, LP, CA, Video

The Music Exchange
207A Westport Rd.
Kansas City MO 64111
816-931-7560
CD, LP, CA, Video

Pennylane
4128 Broadway
Kansas City MO 64111
816-561-1580
CD, LP, CA, Video

Recycled Sounds
3941 Main St.
Kansas City MO 64111
816-531-4890
CD, LP, CA, Video

Spiney Norman
900 Westport
Kansas City MO 64111
816-931-9903
CD, LP, CA, Video

Music Stores

Big Dudes Music
3817 Broadway
Kansas City MO 64111
816-931-4638
Full-line of products and repairs;
drum, amp, keyboard, and small
PA rentals;

Guitar World
10600 B Metcalf Ave.
Overland Park KS 66212
913-341-0915
Guitar repairs; PA & guitar-
related rentals; guitar equipment

Quigley Music
7800 Troost
Kansas City MO 64131
816-361-2050
Guitar, amp, minor keys & drum
repairs; no rentals; full-line
products

St. Louis
Venues

The Bernard Pub
214 Morgan
St. Louis MO 63102
314-621-4020
All-ages
Punk, metal, thrash, and some
alternative

Cicero's
6510 Delmar
St. Louis MO 63130
314-862-0009, 314-862-5999
booking
Capacity: 200
All styles.
This is definitely a great place to
play, and the food upstairs is
amazing!

Club 367
9973 Lewis and Clark Blvd.
St. Louis MO 63136
314-868-3419
Capacity: 1,200
Hard rock, thrash & metal

Hi-Pointe
1001 McCausland
St. Louis MO 63117
314-781-4716
Capacity: 200
Alternative, rock, reggae
This is a good venue for up-and-
coming independent bands;
lesser-known unsigned bands
can get slots as openers.

Just Jazz
1019 Pine St.
St. Louis MO 63101
314-436-2355
Capacity: 150
Jazz

THINGS ARE GOING PRETTY WELL

By John Andrew Fredrick of the Black Watch

You've been on tour a week now and things are going pretty well. You've played three noon shows at colleges and five club gigs (two excellent, two not-so-hot, one appalling). You've sold a few dozen CDs and some 7"s. You've set up two interviews at college radio stations along the way and although the djs asked sweet, stupid questions you acquitted yourselves well and felt like bona fide artists discussing your work while bolting donuts and nursing soapy coffee.

You've only had to cough up for a hotel two of the nights on account of your being mindful of calling friends of friends and sometimes announcing half-kiddingly from the stage that you could use a place to crash that night (it usually works!). You only marginally despise your bandmates; they're not that boring and bothersome — a sentiment that, three weeks from now, will be amended to full-blown screaming contempt and frustration, yowling inner torment and lung-crushing depression that you ever thought for a second that you had anything in common with these unmitigated oafs.

Your back hurts from sleeping on unforgiving floors but, really, things are not that bad. Besides, tonight you have a gig in the neat-o college town you played two days ago. You're going back to play the University Pub. You've played there before — two months ago, in fact. The Joe College booker, Habib, went fucking crazy for you. "I fucking love you guys," he said. "I've gotta get you back in here! You're coming up on tour in a couple of months? Great! How about a Saturday night? Two sets and we'll guarantee $250, okay? Excellent! See you on the 14th!"

Late Saturday afternoon you're shambling out to the van to go to your soundcheck. You've been drinking in a new friend's sunsplashed backyard and everyone's all excited! Saturday night! The University Pub! There were easily 400 kids at the noon show on Thursday. There'll probably be a million-thousand there tonight! All right! Let's mobilize! Big gig! Hey!? What the fuck's the matter with the front right tire?!! Fuck! There's a screw in it the size of Idaho!! Oh no! We'd better get this fixed!

Two hours later there you are at the University Pub. Obviously you missed your soundcheck; it was an hour and a half ago. Fucking hell — there's some band up there on the stage! You go over to the girl at the bar who looks in charge. You smile insincerely, insecurely, 'cause you've got a more-than-semi queasy feeling. "Hi," you say.

"We're The Fill In the Blanks," you say. "Oh hi," she says, "I remember you guys." "Is Habib around?" you ask. "Habib?" she says. "No, he got fired or something about a month ago; I think he dropped out of school or something too. What are you guys doing up here?"

Oh-oh. You explain to the girl the whole story: Habib booked the band; the band is on tour; the van got a screw in the tire, etc. "Gosh," she says. "Do you have a contract from him or something like that? You don't? Oh. Well, Bob the owner took over the bookings and he mentioned something about you guys but he never heard from you, so I guess he just booked that band over there, The Frat Guys, for tonight. Bob's unfortunately not here right now and he's not at home 'cause I just tried to call him. Maybe you can talk to The Frat Guys and the two of you could work something out."

You approach The Frat Guys and force another smile. You remind yourself that The Frat Guys are musicians, and musicians are very, very likely to be all of the following: selfish, touchy, egocentric, unreasonable, vainglorious and indigent. You calmly explain the sitch to them and they start hemming and hawing. At last the drummer, an ogre-at-large, says, "Hey man, I didn't lug my kit down here so we could just do one set, man, and our whole frat is gonna be here, man, and you guys shouldn't have missed your soundcheck, man, and Bob said we could have the whole night and $150 so... Sorry dudes! No way!! It's our gig now."

Things are not going very well now. Things are not going very well at all. You can't forfeit a Saturday night! You can't forgo a gig for 250 bucks! This can't happen! It can't!

But it just did.

Love and mayhem,

the black watch

p.s. Get a contract for every single gig and call to confirm it.

The Black Watch is signed to the label Zero Hour, who insist that the band keep touring.

Kennedy's
612 N 2nd St.
St. Louis MO 63102
314-421-3655
Capacity: 350
This club does mostly local alternative bands, but if you are willing to play for little or no money, you may be able to play here on your first trip to St. Louis.

Mississippi Nights
914 N. 1st St.
St. Louis MO 63102
314-421-3853
Capacity: 1,000
This is the area's premier mid-sized venue for national, major-label touring bands. You may get a slot, but chances are not that great for unknown bands.

Oasis Coffee Shop
8130 Big Bend
St. Louis MO 63119
314-968-3038
This club features mostly acoustic music and spoken word in a small, intimate setting.

Off Broadway
3509 Lemp
St. Louis MO 63118
314-773-3363
Capacity: 300
Blues, rock, roots, folk and swing

The Other World
1624 Delmar
St. Louis MO 63103
314-436-2114
Capacity: 600
This is a new hot-spot in the area. It is a warehouse space divided between techno dance music and live alternative music. This place is definitely worth checking out.

Red Sea
6511 Delmar
St. Louis MO 63130
314-863-0099
Capacity: 300
Reggae, alternative, funk
This club is across the street from Cicero's, but features mostly local bands.

The Sheldon Concert Hall & Ballroom
3648 Washington Ave.
St. Louis MO 63108
314-533-9900
Capacity: 732 seated
This is a large venue that features anything from classical to jazz, blues and the avant garde.

Washington University
The Gargoyle
314-935-5917
Dawn Barger
Every Thursday night, shows only opened to students
All-ages with a bar

Press

The Riverfront Times
1221 Locust, #900
St. Louis MO 63103
314-231-6666
Weekly arts & entertainment newspaper

Sample
c/o KWUR Washington University
Box 1182
St. Louis MO 63130
314-935-5952
Quarterly; record reviews, features, interviews

Spotlight Magazine
PO Box 63423
St. Louis MO 63163
314-773-5454
Fax 314-773-3466
The premier monthly music newspaper of St. Louis since 1987. A mostly local focus, but will preview some shows and review indie products. Lead times are longer for monthlies, so get your materials mailed out ASAP.

St. Louis Post Dispatch
900 N. Tucker
St. Louis MO 63101
314-340-8000
Major daily newspaper

Radio

KCFV 89.5 fm
St. Louis Community College
3400 Pershall
St. Louis MO 63135
314-595-4478
Various styles

KDHX 88.1 fm
3504 Magnolia
St. Louis MO 63118
314-664-3955
Blues, bluegrass rock, ethnic
10 hours of rock per week

KWMU 90.7 fm
University of Missouri
8001 Natural Bridge
St. Louis MO 63121
314-553-5968
Classical, jazz

KWUR 90.3 fm
Washington University
PO Box 1182
St. Louis MO 63130
314-935-5952
Everything except top 40
The only good station in the city for independent music

Record Stores

Disc Connection
7253 Manchester
St. Louis MO 63143
314-644-1171
CD, LP, CA

Sound Revolution
7751 N. Lindberg
Hazelwood MO 63042
314-839-3520
CD, LP, CA

Streetside Records
(24 Locations)
2055 Walton Rd.
St. Louis MO 63114
314-426-2388 (main office)
CD, LP, CA, Video, 7"

Vintage Vinyl
6610 Delmar
St. Louis MO 63130
314-721-4096
CD, LP, CA, 7"
A highly recommended store.

West End Wax
389 N. Euclid
St. Louis MO 63108
314-367-0111
CD, CA, 7"
Also recommeded

Music Stores

Dales' Music
6235 N. Lindbergh Rd.
St. Louis MO 63042
314-895-3403
Full-line of repairs, rentals &
products

Drum Headquarters
7241 Manchester
St. Louis MO 63143
314-644-0235
No rentals; drum & percussion
sales and repairs

J. Gravity Strings
1546 S. Broadway
St. Louis MO 63104
314-241-0190
Guitar, bass & amp repairs &
sales; amp rentals

Silver Strings Music
8427 Olive
St. Louis MO 63132
314-997-1120
Guitar repairs; no rentals;
vintage & new guitar sales

Etc.

Go to **The Arch.**

MONTANA
Bozeman
Venues

Cat's Paw
721 N. 7th Ave.
Bozeman MT 59715
406-586-3542
Capacity: 300
Various styles

The Filling Station
2005 N. Rouse
Bozeman MT 59715
406-587-5009
Capacity: 250
All-ages with a bar
Varying styles
This is a great venue for indie
bands to play if the show is
promoted well.

The Gallatin Gateway Inn
PO Box 376
Gallatin Gateway MT 59730
406-763-4672
Capacity: 350
Folk, Bluegrass, Blues

Little John's
515 W Aspin
Bozeman MT 59715
406-587-1652
Capacity: 300
Country

Press

The Bozeman Daily Chronicle
PO Box 1188
Bozeman MT 59771
406-587-4491
Daily newspaper
Monday is a good day

The Exponent
Montana State University
Strand Union Bldg, Rm 305
Bozeman MT 59717
Twice weekly college newspaper

The Tributary
503 W Olive St.
Bozeman MT 59715
406-586-4322
Monthly alternative arts magazine

Radio

KGLT 91.9 fm
Montana State University
Strand Union bldg
Bozeman MT 59717
406-994-6483
Rock, Alternative
This station has an excellent
reputation for playing cool indie
records.

KMMS 95.1 fm
125 W Mendenhall
Bozeman MT 59715
406-586-2343
Commercial Rock, Alternative

Record Stores

Cactus Records
29 W Main St.
Bozeman MT 59715
406-587-0245
CD, CA

Music Stores

Music Villa
34 W Main St.
Bozeman MT 59715
406-587-4761
Most instrument sales and
rentals; guitar repairs

Food

Four B's on Main St., typical
diner food and they are open
late.

Shelter

Most of the small motels near
the downtown area are relatively
inexpensive.

Missoula
Venues

Buck's
1805 Regent St.
Missoula MT 59801
406-543-7436
Capacity: 300
Rock, Top 40 (no alternative)

Copper Commons / Ballroom
University of Montana
University Center 104
ASUM Programming
Missoula MT 59812
406-243-6661
Capacity: 500, 1,000
All styles, open to indie bands

Top Hat
134 W Front St.
Missoula MT 59802
406-728-9865
Capacity: 250
Blues, Bluegrass, R&B,
Rockabilly, Reggae
This is the favorite club of the touring indie bands. Maybe try to play here and do a college show.

Press

The Kaimin
University of Montana
School of Journalism, Rm 204
Missoula MT 59812
406-243-6541/4310
Daily newspaper

The Missoulian Daily
PO Box 8029
Missoula MT 59802
406-523-5200
Daily newspaper

The Independent
PO Box 8275
Missoula MT 59807
406-543-6609
A politically oriented weekly alternative paper that has a section for reviews of upcoming shows and new records. The best source for press in the Missoula area.

Radio

KUFM 89.1 fm
University of Montana
Missoula MT 59812
406-243-4931
Classical, Jazz, Blues, World Beat, Alternative
This is the station most likely to play any independent music.

KZOQ 100.1 fm
2701 N Reserve St.
Missoula MT 59807
406-728-5000
Commercial Rock, Alternative
Mostly syndicated radio shows.

Record Stores

Rockin' Rudy's
237 Blaine St.
Missoula MT 59801
406-542-0077
CD, CA, LP
This is pretty much the store in Missoula.

Music Stores

Electronic, Sound, & Percussion
819 S Higgins
Missoula MT 59801
406-728-1117
Most instrument sales and rentals; guitar repairs

Stringed Instrument Division
123 W Alder
Missoula MT 59802
406-549-1502
Most instrument sales and repairs; no rentals

Food
The **Thai Deli** is the recommended restaurant in the area.

Shelter
There are a number of cheap motels in the Downtown area and along the 93 highway.

Etc.
There is plenty to see around Missoula, here in Big Sky country. Missoula is 120 miles from **Flathead Lake**, one of the largest lakes west of the Great Lakes. If you want to see grizzly bears, there are plenty in the area as well. The downtown area is really the hub of this small town.

NEBRASKA
Lincoln
Venues

Duffy's Tavern
1412 O St.
Lincoln NE 68508
402-474-3543
Capacity: 220
Alternative, Rock
Wednesday and Sunday nights they do indie, alternative type bands. This is a very established club in the area.

Hurricane's
1118 'O' St.
Lincoln NE 68508
402-435-6989
A larger venue for big bands
Alcohol served but you don't have to be 21.

Knickerbockers
901 O St.
Lincoln NE 68508
402-476-6865
Capacity: 125
21 and up
Alternative bands Friday and Saturday Nights. Talk to Ernie, "a very good guy"

Shakes
14th and 'O' St.
PO Box 94695
Lincoln NE 68509
Dave Rabe
All-ages coffee shop, will probably do a show any time.

University of Nebraska at Lincoln
University Program Council
Nebraska Union, Rm 200
Lincoln NE 68588
402-472-8146
Capacity: 1,000
All styles

Zoo Bar
136 N 14th St.
Lincoln NE 68508
402-475-3094
Capacity: 150
Blues, R&B

Press

The Daily Nebraskan
University of Nebraska
1400 R St., Rm 34
Nebraska Union
Lincoln NE 68588
402-472-2588
Daily newspaper

The Lincoln Journal Star
926 P St.
Lincoln NE 68501
402-473-7244
Daily.

Radio

KRNU 90.3 fm
University of Nebraska
203 Avery Hall
Lincoln NE 68588-0131
402-472-3054
Attn: Andy
All styles
This is the station to be on.
They don't do on-air shows but
they may do an interview.

KZUM 89.3 fm
Sunrise Communications
941 O St., Ste 1025
Lincoln NE 68508
402-474-5086
Blues, Jazz, Folk, Reggae, Rock
Alternative late at night

Record Stores

Homer's Records
1637 P St.
Lincoln NE 68508
402-474-3230
CD, CA, LP
This is a decent store

Recycled Sounds
824 P St.
Lincoln NE 68508
402-476-8240
CD, CA, LP
A very cool place with a lot of
vinyl and the owner is into
promoting smaller bands.

Twister's
1339 O St.
Lincoln NE 68508
402-434-2500
CD, CA

Music Stores

Dietz Music
1208 O St.
Lincoln NE 68508
402-476-6644
Most repairs; guitar, keyboard,
and PA rentals, full product
lines. They have everything, and
as an added bonus, John from
Mercy Rule may be spotted
working here.

Food

Yia Yia's on 'O' Street has
incredible pizza by the slice,
different than any other pizza.
Dave doesn't know what it is
about it, but he knows it is
great. **Shakes** has good vegetarian food and really great soup -
different every day.

Shelter

"Don't bands usually just stay
with people in the audience?"

Etc.

'O' Street downtown is the
cultural hub of Lincoln NE. Go
there pretty much for everything
on this list. **The Haymarket** is
the original area of commerce
where you may take in a little
history. **Shakes** is the place
where "band type" people hang
out these days, they are welcome to just sit around and
smoke cigarettes. **The Ozone** is
a place to get hip alternative
clothes, shoes, hats, jewerly,
some music and of course a
body piercing.

Omaha
Venues

**McKenna's Blues, Booze and
Barbecue**
7425 Pacific St.
Omaha NE 68114
402393-7427
Capacity: 150
Blues

Omaha Ranch Bowl
1606 s 72nd St.
Omaha NE 68124
402-393-0900
Capacity: 600
Hard rock, metal, reggae, rap,
jazz & blues at this bowling
alley/club/bar

Sharky's Brewery
7777 Cass St.
Omaha NE 68114
402-390-0777
Capacity: 500
Reggae, world beat, jazz &
alternative

Press

The Fast Lane
PO Box 371 137
Omaha NE 68137
800-238-8078
Free biweekly entertainment
guide

The Gateway
University of Nebraska
at Omaha
Annex 26
Omaha NE 68182
402-554-2470
Twice weekly newspaper

Omaha World Herald
14th and Dodge
Omaha NE 68102
402-444-1000
Daily newspaper

The Reader
7777 Cass St.
Omaha NE 68114
402-341-7323

Sound, News and Art
PO Box 31104
Omaha NE 68132
402-346-7133
Monthly arts magazine

Radio

KEZO 92.3 "Z-92"
11128 John Galt Blvd.
Omaha NE 68137
402-592-5300
New and classic rock

KRRK 93.3 "93 K-Rock"
1606 S. 72nd St.
Omaha NE 68124
402-393-8780
Commercial Rock

Record Stores

The Antiquarium
1215 Harney St.
Omaha NE 68102
402-341-8077
CD, LP, CA

Dirt Cheap Records
1026 Jackson St.
Omaha NE 68102
402-341-9500
CD, LP, CA, Video

Drastic Plastic
1209 Howard St.
Omaha NE 68102
402-346-8843
CD, LP, CA

Homer's Records
1114 Howard St.
Omaha NE 68102
402-346-0264
CD, LP, CA, Video

Stagedoor Music
1415 Farnam St.
Omaha NE 68102
402-341-1502
CD, LP, CA

Tunes Music and Video
7926 S 84th St.
La Vista NE 68128
402-339-3577
CD, CA

Music Stores

D-Rocks
2505 S 120th St.
Omaha NE 68144
402-330-1310
Guitar repairs; no rentals; full product lines

Joe Voda's Drum City
602 S 72nd St.
Omaha NE 68114
402-397-1060
Drum sales, rentals, and repairs

Note Works Omaha
7357 Pacific St.
Omaha NE 68114
402-399-0109
Full-line of rentals, repairs & products

Paragon Music
4829 Dodge St.
Omaha NE 68132
402-558-6850
Full-line of products & repairs; guitar, keyboard, and PA rentals

NEVADA
Las Vegas
Venues

Boomers
3200 Sirius
Las Vegas NV 89102
702-593-2446
Capacity: 250
Hard rock, metal

Fremont Street
400 E. Fremont
Las Vegas NV 89101
702-474-7209
Capacity: 600
Alt., rock, blues, world.

Huntridge Theater
1208 E Charlston Bl.
Las Vegas NV 89104
702-477-7069
Capacity: 800
Alt., rap, jazz, rock

Money Plays
4755 W. Flamingo
Las Vegas NV 89103
702-368-1828
Capacity: 150
Alternative

Shifty's Cocktail Lounge
3805 W Sahara
Las Vegas NV 89108
702-871-4952
Capacity: 150
Rock, blues

Sports Pub
4440 S maryland Pkwy
Las Vegas NV 89121
702-796-8870
Capacity: 500
Rock and alternative.

Tom and Jerry's
4550 S Maryland Pkwy
Las Vegas NV 89109
702-736-8550
Capacity: 400
All styles

Press

The New Times
5300 W Sahara #100
Las Vegas NV 89102
702-871-6780
Weekly newspaper

The Review Journal
1111 Bonanza Rd
Las Vegas NV 89106
702-383-0211
Daily newspaper

Scope
8170 W Sahara #207
Las Vegas NV 89117
702-256-6388
Monthly music and entertainment newspaper

Radio

KEDG 103.5 fm
1455 E Tropicana #650
Las Vegas NV 89119
702-795-1035
Commercial alternative

KUNV 91.5 fm
4505 Maryland Pkwy
Las Vegas, NV 89541-8020
702-895-3877
College alternative, jazz, reggae, world beat et. al.

Record Stores

Benway Bop
4800 S Maryland Pkwy
Las Vegas NV 89119
702-597-9440
Indies and imports
CD, CA, LP, Video

Odyssey Records
1600 S Las Vegas Bl
Las Vegas NV 89119
702-384-4040
CD, CA, LP, Video

Music Stores

Mahoney's Pro Music
608 S Maryland Pkwy at Charlston
and
4972 S Maryland Pkwy at Tropicana
Las Vegas NV 89101
702-382-9147
Full-line sales, rentals, and repairs.

Etc.

Gambling, gambling, gambling. If you're looking for cheap blackjack, avoid the strip and head downtown, but the strip hotels are always worth a look for the sheer spectacle. Vegas is the town of the 75¢ 1/2 pound hotdog and a beer, and there's always **Sassy Sally's** dollar pizzas. Cheap food is not a problem, but cheap lodging can be, depending on what day of the week or time of the year you're here. Obviously, weekends and holidays are tough. Cheap strip hotels include the **Imperial Palace** and the **Hacienda**. Most of the downtown hotels are cheap, unless there's a convention in town. Definitely check out the new **Hard Rock Casino**, it's a hipster hangout and they have Sid Vicious slot machines; need we say more. If you see a roulette wheel, put 5 bucks on 28 black.

Reno
Venues

Casa Margarita
1065 S Virginia
Reno NV 89502
702-329-7263
Capacity: 150 and 200 (two rooms)
All styles. All ages shows.

Del Mar Station
701 S Virginia St
Reno NV 89501
702-322-7200
Capacity: 500
Rock, metal.

Discopolis
515 S Virginia
Reno NV 89501
702-333-5269
Capacity: 750
Hard rock, alternative

The Fallout Shelter
100 N Sierra
Reno NV 89501
702-333-2800
Capacity: 350
Alternative

Little Waldorf "The Wall"
1661 N VIrginia
Reno NV 89503
702-323-3682
Capacity: 500
Mainly alternative.

Rodeo Rock Cafe
1537 S Virginia
Reno NV 89502
702-323-1600
Capacity: 1000
Country and alternative

The Zephyr
1074 S Virginia
Reno NV 89502
702-322-8177
Capacity: 50
All styles, eclectic

Press

Reno Gazette-Journal
PO Box 22000
Reno NV 89520-2000
702-788-6420

Reno News & Review
900 W First St
Reno NV 89503
702-324-4440
Weekly news. Will review

Record Stores

Insurrection Sound & Image
1470 S Wells Ave
Reno NV 89502
702-329-5526
Imports and indies
CD, CA, LP, Video

Mirabelli's Music City
154 E Plumb Ln
Reno NV 89502
702-825-7210
CD, CA, LP, 45s

Recycled Records
4930 S Virginia
Reno NV 89502
702-826-4119
CD, CA, LP

Soundwave CDs
940 W Moana St. #105
Reno NV 89509
702-825-5044
CD

Music Stores

Bizarre Guitar
2677 Oddie Bl.
Reno NV 89512
702-331-1001
Guitar, amp and drum sales, repairs. Amp rentals.

Maytan Music Center
777 S Center
Reno NV 89501
702-323-5443
Full-line repairs, rentals, sales

Etc.

Lake Tahoe and surrounding mountains are the main attractions here. That fresh air will clean out your secondhand-smoke-filled lungs.

NEW HAMPSHIRE
Portsmouth
Dover
Venues

The Elvis Room
142 Congress St
Portsmouth NH 03081
603-436-9189
Capacity: 200
Rock, alternative, country and acoustic.

Meadow Brook Inn
Portsmouth Traffic Circle
Portsmouth NH 03081
603-436-2700
Capacity: 250
Rock

Mike Libby's
47 Main St
Durham NH 03824
603-868-5542
Capacity: 150
College

Portsmouth Brewery
56 Market St
Portsmouth NH 03802
603-431-1115
Capacity: 80
All styles

The Press Room
77 Daniel St
Portsmouth NH 03801
603-431-5186
Capacity: 200
Blues, jazz, folk, some rock

Press

IQ Demo Review
13 Roberts Rd Box 8
Brookfield NH 03872
603-522-6290
Quarterly news

Portsmouth Herald's Spotlight
111 Maplewood Ave
Portsmouth NH 03801
603-436-1800
Weekly arts and entertainment

Seacoast Times
Towle Office Park
1 Merrill Industrial Dr
Hampton NH 03842
603-926-5777
Weekly news

Radio

WUNH 91.3 fm
U of New Hampshire
Memorial Union Bldg
Durham NH 03824
603-862-2087
All styles

Record Stores

Lost Chord Records
491 Central Ave
Dover NH 03820
603-749-3859
CD, CA, LP, Video

Rock Bottom Records
86 Pleasant St
Portsmouth NH 03801
603-436-5618
CD, CA, LP, Video

Sessions Music
10 Congress St
Portsmouth NH 03801
603-431-8244
CD, CA

Music Stores

Ear Craft
14 4th St
Dover NH 03820
603-749-3138
Repairs, PA rentals, full sales

Gary's Guitars
69 Albany St
Portsmouth NH 03801
603-427-6133
PA, amps, repair and rentals, guitar sales

NEW JERSEY
Northeast Jersey & Hoboken
Venues

Cricket Club
415 16th Ave.
Irvington NJ 07111
201-374-1062
Capacity: 1,200
Alternative and heavy rock

Elysian Cafe
1001 Washington St.
Hoboken NJ 07030
201-659-9110, 201-659-9344 booking
Capacity: 75-100
R&B club

Del's
125 Washington St.
Hoboken NJ 07030
201-795-9606
Capacity: 360
Original alternative, pop & rock

Maxwell's
1039 Washington
Hoboken NJ 07030
201-656-9632
Capacity: 200
All types of music, always a good crowd. This is the club most likely to book an indie touring band in the Hoboken area.

Studio 1
88-90 Verona Ave.
Newark NJ 07104
201-482-1150
Capacity: 500+
Huge metal & heavy metal club, all ages allowed

Press

The Aquarian Weekly
PO Box 137
Montclair NJ 07042
201-783-4346
Weekly arts & entertainment

The Hudson Reporter
The Hudson Current
1321 Washington St.
Hoboken NJ 07030
201-798-7800
Weekly arts & entertainment newspaper

Jersey Beat
418 Gregory Ave.
Weehawken NJ 07087
201-864-9054
Quarterly fanzine
This is the hip fanzine in the area.

Jersey Journal
30 Journal Square
Jersey City NJ 07306
201-653-1000
Daily paper
Send info to Jim Testa

Lava
7 Oak Place
PO Box 137
Montclair NJ 07042
201-783-4346
Biweekly news. Will review

Radio

WFDU 89.1 fm
Fairleigh Dickenson University
1000 River Rd.
Teaneck NJ 07666
201-692-2806
Various styles

WFMU 91.1 fm
Upsala College
580 Springdale Ave.
E Orange NJ 07017
201-678-8264
All styles

WNTI 91.9 fm
Centenary College
400 Jefferson St.
Hackettstown NJ 07840
908-852-4545
College Alternative, hip-hop, more

WRPR 90.3 fm
Ramapo College
505 Ramapo Valley Rd.
Mahwah NJ 07430
201-825-1234
Top 40, alternative, rap, metal

Record Stores

Crazy Rhythms
561 Bloomfield Ave.
Montclair NJ 07042
201-744-5787
CD, LP, CA, 7"

Flipside Records
120 Wanaque Ave.
Pompton Lakes NJ 07442
201-835-8448
CD, LP, CA, 7"

Pier Platters Records
56 Newark St.
Hoboken NJ 07030
201-795-4785
CD, LP. 7"

Tower Records
809 Rte 17
Paramus NJ 07652
201-444-7277
CD, CA

Music Stores

Sam Ash Music
1831 Rt 27- Plainfield Ave.
Edison NJ 08817
908-572-5595
Full line of sales, rentals, and repairs

NJRC
6-8 Franklin Ave.
Ridgewood NJ 07450
201-612-9222

Stirling Audio Services
239 Main Ave.
Stirling NJ 07980
908-647-0327
Rents sound equipment, drums, staging, lighting & generators

Food

Go into New York City or eat at **Maxwell's**.

Shelter

There are no cheap hotels in the area, and beware of the scummy motels in Jersey City, across from Manhattan.

Trenton
Venues

Campus Club
5 Prospect Ave.
Princeton NJ 08540
609-924-5122
Capacity: 300
Alternative and industrial

City Gardens
1701 Calhoun St.
Trenton NJ 08638
609-392-8887, 215-862-0852
Randy for booking
Capacity: 950
Industrial, hard rock, alternative.

Press

Metal-Core Magazine
13 Carriage Ln
Marlton NJ 08053
609-596-1975
Quarterly fanzine

Radio

WPRB 103.3 fm
Princeton University
PO Box 342
Princeton NJ 08542
609-258-3655
Block - alternative, classical,
jazz, world beat, jazz, folk

WTSR 91.3 fm
Trenton State College
Kendall Hall 50-4700
Hillwood Lakes NJ 08625
609-771-2420
Block - alternative, metal, rap,
world beat, techno, classical

WRRC 107.7 fm
Rider College
2083 Lawrenceville Rd.
Lawrenceville NJ 08648
609-896-5211
Metal, urban, classic rock,
reggae, alternative

Record Stores

Princeton Record Exchange
20 S Tulane St.
Princeton NJ 08542
609-921-0881
CD

Music Stores

Russo Music Center
1989 Arena Dr
Trenton NJ 08610
609-888-0620
Sales and repairs; recording
equipment rentals

Zaph's
5811 S Crescent Bl Rt #130
Pennsauken NJ 08015
609-488-4333
Repairs, rentals, sales

NEW MEXICO
Albuquerque
Santa Fe
Venues

909 Club
3222 Central
Albuquerque NM 87106
505-266-9708
Capacity: 300
Punk, alternative

Beyond Ordinary
211 Gold Southwest
Albuquerque NM 87102
505-764-8858
Capacity: 300
Alternative

Cadillac Ranch
9800 Montgomery Blvd. NE
Albuquerque NM 87111
505-298-2113
Capacity: 600
Mostly country and western

Club Alegria
PO Box 22963
Santa Fe NM 87502
505-471-2324
Capacity: 300
All styles

The Dingo Bar
313 Gold SW
Albuquerque NM 87102
505-243-0663
Capacity: 250
Blues, jazz, alternative

The Fat Chance Bar & Grill
2216 Central SE
Albuquerque NM 87106
505-265-7531
Capacity: 150
Alternative, rock, blues, jazz

The Kachina Lodge
413 N Pueblo Rd.
Taos NM 87571
505-758-2275
Capacity: 350
Rock, R&B, country, and reggae;
it's a ski resort.

The Outpost Performance Space
112 Morningside SE
Albuquerque NM 87108
505-268-0044
Capacity: 100
Jazz, acoustic.

Time Out
618 Central SE
Albuquerque NM 87102
505-764-8887
Capacity: 300

Press

Albuquerque Journal
Albuquerque Tribune
7777 Jefferson NE
Albuquerque NM 87109
505-823-4444
Daily papers

The Health City Sun
P.O. Box 1517
Albuquerque NM 87103
505-242-3010
Weekly

The Lobo
University of New Mexico
Arts Desk - Daily Lobo
UNM Box 20
Albuquerque NM 87131
505-277-5656
Daily newspaper

Nucity
2118 Central Ave. SE #151
Albuquerque NM 871016
505-268-8111
Weekly news

The New Mexican
202 E. Marcy
Santa Fe NM 87501
505-983-3303
Weekly arts newspaper

Santa Fe Reporter
132 E Marcy
Santa Fe NM 87501
505-988-5541
Weekly newspaper

Radio

KRUX 91.5 fm
New Mexico State Universtiy
PO Box 30004, Dept CC
Las Cruces NM 88003
505-646-4640
College alternative

KUNM 89.9 fm
University of New Mexico
Onate Hall
Albuquerque NM 87131
505-277-4806/8018
Jazz, rock, folk, blues

Record Stores

Bow Wow Records
3103 Central Ave. NE
Albuquerque NM 87106
505-256-0928
CD, LP, CA

The Music Shop
3721 Cerrillos Rd.
Santa Fe NM 87501
505-471-2833
CD, CA, Video

Music Stores

The Candyman
851 St. Michael's Dr
Santa Fe NM 87501
505-988-8933
Sales and rentals

Encore Music
5314 Menaul NE
Albuquerque NM 87110
505-888-0722
Guitar & amp repairs, rentals,
sales

Grandma's Music & Sound
800 S-T Juan Tabo NE
Albuquerque NM 87123
505-292-0341
Sales, repairs

NEW YORK
Albany
Saratoga
Venues

Bogie's
297 Ontario
Albany NY 12208
518-482-4368
Capacity: 300
Alternative

Caffe Lena
47 Philadelphia St.
Saratoga NY 12866
518-583-0022
Capacity: 85
Mainly acoustic, folk, jazz, blues.

The Chance
6 Crannell St.
Poughkeepsie NY 12601
914-471-1966
Capacity: 650
All styles.

Mother Earth's
217 Western Ave.
Albany NY 12203
518-434-0944
Capacity: 60
Blues, folk, jazz, rock, alternative

Nepenthe Cafe
154 Madison Ave.
Albany NY 12202
518-436-0329
Capacity: 45
Acoustic rock & folk

Pauly's Hotel
337 Central Ave.
Albany NY 12206
518-426-0828
Capacity: 200
Blues, rock, reggae

QE2
12 Central Ave.
Albany NY 12210
518-434-2023, 434-2697
Charlene for booking
Capacity: 225
Industrial, alternative.

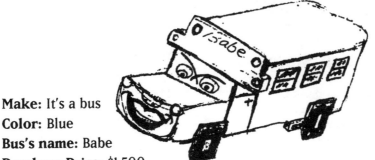

Make: It's a bus
Color: Blue
Bus's name: Babe
Purchase Price: $1,500
Mileage at Purchase: Don't know
Current Mileage: Dunno
The van runs on: Petroleum now.
The band runs on: Malt liquor, wheat grass
Miles per gallon: 10 to 15 but these things I'm not sure.
Number of people who tour in it: 6-7
Stereo: Radio Shack cassette player
Favorite thing to listen to: Zeppelin. Damon complaining.
Coolest thing about our van: It's actually a half school bus that's painted blue and it has a "Why Be Normal?" sticker on the back.
The coolest thing we did to our bus was: Put it up for sale.
The suckiest thing about our bus: That it broke down the first night of our six-week tour and we had to rent another one. And those square tires were really a pain.
Is there anybody's bus you'd trade it for? Velocity Girl's
Anything else? We fell in love with the blue bus. We had to have it. The guy we bought it from replaced the diesel engine with a regular one, although he forgot to rewire the electrical system accordingly. He said, "It's got a new engine, sure it'll make it across the country." The night we broke down, The Doors' song *The End* came on the radio..."The Blue Bus is calling us."

Saratoga Winners
PO Box 541
Cohoes NY 12047
518-783-1010
Capacity: 600
Metal, alternative, hardcore.

Press

Buzz
PO Box 3111
Albany NY 12203
518-489-0658
Monthly fanzine

Metroland
PO Box 6370
Albany NY 12206
518-272-0022
Weekly news & arts paper

Albany Time Union
News Plaza, Box 15000
Albany NY 12212
518-454-5694
Weekly arts & entertainment guide

Source
PO Box 66385
Albany NY 12206
518-453-3070
Biweekly entertainment newsmag

Radio

WCDB 90.9 fm
SUNY Albany Campus Center
1400 Washington Ave.
Albany NY 12222
518-442-5262
Alternative rock, contemporary soul, jazz

WRPI 91.5 fm
Rennsselaer Polytechnic Institute
1 WRPI Plaza
Troy NY 12180
518-276-6248
Alternative, rock, jazz, world beat

WSPN 91.1 fm
Skidmore College
Saratoga Springs NY 12866
518-584-7378
Blues, jazz, rock, alternative.

WVCR 88.3 fm
Siena College
515 Louden Rd.
Loudonville NY 12211
518783-2990
Mostly rock, heavy metal

Record Stores

Music Shack
65 Central Ave.
Albany NY 12206
518-436-4581
CD, LP, CA, Video

Music Shack
295 River St.
Troy NY 12180
518-273-1400
CD, CA

Coconut's
Stuyvesant Plaza
Albany NY 12203
518-438-3003
CD, CA

World's Records
132 Central Ave.
Albany NY 12206
518-462-5271
CD, CA

Rhino Records
900 Central Ave.
Albany NY 12206
518-438-0732
CD, CA, 7"
This store is usually open to in-store performances. Ask.

Music Stores

Adirondack Strings
1316 Central Ave.
Albany NY 12205
518-458-7717
Stringed instruments

Drome Sound Music Store
3486 State St.
Schenectady NY 12304
518-370-3701
Full-line of products

New Music
40 Russell Rd.
Albany NY 12206
518-459-8298
Sales, repairs, and rentals

Only Guitar Shop
1774 Rt 9
Clifton Park NY 12065
518-371-1232
Sales and rentals; guitar and electronic repairs

Ithaca Syracuse
Venues

ABC Cafe
308 Stuart Ave.
Ithaca NY 14850
607-277-4770
Capacity: 50
Acoustic, jazz, blues, more.

East LA
505 Westcott St.
Syracuse NY 13210
315-471-1148
Capacity: 181
Rock, country, alternative.

The Haunt
114 W Green St.
Ithaca NY 14850
607-277-2726
Capacity: 300
Rock, alternative

Lost Horizon
5863 Thompson Rd.
Syracuse NY 13214
315-446-1934
Capacity: 350
Rock, alternative

The Nines
311 College Ave.
Ithaca NY 14850
607-272-1888
Capacity: 200
Blues, rock

Oliver's
415 College Ave.
Ithaca NY 14850
607-273-9720
Capacity: 120
Blues, jazz, acoustic

Rongovian Embassy
One W Main St., Box 397
Trumansburg NY 14886
607-387-3334
Capacity: 200
All styles.

Stylene's
314 S Franklin St.
Syracuse NY 13202
315-472-2665
Capacity: 400
R&B, blues rock

Press

Ithaca Journal
123 W State St.
Ithaca NY 14850
607-274-9262
Daily newspaper

Ithaca Times
PO Box 27
Ithaca NY 14851
607-277-7000
Weekly newspaper

The Music Press
Box 154
Chenango Fork NY 13746
Monthly all-music newspaper

Radio

WICB 91.7 fm
Ithaca College
Park School of Communications
Ithaca NY 14850
607-274-1040
Rock, Jazz, urban, folk, blues

Record Stores

Knuckleheads
406 S Main St.
N Syracuse NY 13212
315-452-5592
CD, LP, CA

The Last Unicorn
1907 Genesse St.
Utica NY 13501
315-724-0007
CD, LP, CA

Oliver's
107 Marshall St.
Syracuse NY 13210
315-471-2275
CD, LP, CA

Bebop Records
409 College Ave.
Ithaca NY 14850
607-273-0737
CD, LP, CA

Sound's Fine
171 E. State St., Box 111
Ithaca NY 14850
607-277-4766
CD, CA

Music Stores

Hickey's
104 Adams St.
Ithaca NY 14850
607-272-8262
Full product lines

Ithaca Guitar World
215 No. Cayuga St.
Ithaca NY 14850
607-272-2602
Repairs, sales, rentals

Buffalo
Rochester
Venues

Club Utica
527 W Utica St.
Buffalo NY 14213
716-886-8621
Capacity: 120
Country rock, bluegrass

Continental Lounge
212 Franklin St.
Buffalo NY 14202
716-842-1292
Capacity: 400
Alternative

Horizontal Boogie Bar
204 N Water St.
Rochester NY 14604
716-325-5600
Capacity: 1,000
Wide variety.

Impaxx
652 S Ogden St.
Buffalo NY 14206
716-824-0752
Capacity:750-1,200
Rock, blues, pop, alternative

Lafayette Tap Room
391 Washington St.
Buffalo NY 14203
716-855-8800, 716-847-6511
Capacity: 300
Mostly blues, some cajun

Marquee at the Tralf
100 Theater Pl.
Buffalo NY 14202
716-852-0522
Capacity: 800
All styles, mostly jazz.

Milestone's
50 East Ave.
Rochester NY 14604
716-325-6490
Capacity: 350
All styles

Mohawk Place
47 E Mohawk St
Buffalo NY 14203
716-838-2146
Capacity: 175
Alternative, pop

Nietzsche's
248 Allen St.
Buffalo NY 14201
716-886-8539
Capacity: 400
Blues, world beat, folk, rock

Topic Cafe
224 Allen St.
Buffalo NY 14222
716-883-4760
Capacity: 100
Mainly acoustic music

Press

Art Voice
124 Elmwood Ave.
Buffalo NY 14201
716-881-6604
Jamie Moses
Bi-monthly music & arts newspaper. A good place to send
your information for a listing
and possible interview.

The Avenue Player
400 W. Utica
Buffalo NY 14222
716-885-RODS
Chris Celeste
Interviews and listings. All
styles, except metal and country.

Buffalo News
PO Box 100
1 News Plaza
Buffalo NY 14240
716-849-4484
Daily newspaper

Free Time
850 University Ave.
Rochester NY 14607
716-473-2266
Biweekly arts & entertainment
mag

Metro Weekend
25 Boxwood Lane
Buffalo NY 14227
716-668-5223 x389
Weekly newspaper

Night Life
1620 Niagara Falls Blvd. #216
Tonawanda NY 14150
716-834-3348
Weekly dining & entertainment
newspaper

Radio

WBER 90.5 FM
2596 Baird Rd.
Penfield NY 14526
716-381-4353
Alternative

WBNY 91.3 fm
State Univ. College of Buffalo
1300 Elmwood Ave.
Buffalo NY 14222
716-878-3080
Alternative rock - pop
This station is formatted to play
indie records.

Record Stores

Doris Records
286 E Ferry St.
Buffalo NY 14208
716-883-2410
CD, CA, 12"

Home of the Hits
1105 Elmwood Ave.
Buffalo NY 14222
716-883-0330
CD, LP, CA
Despite the name, this is the
store to find your indie records.

New World Record
512 Elmwood Ave.
Buffalo NY 14222
716-882-4004/0225
CD, LP, CA, Video
It is also recommended that you check out this store.

Record Archive
1394 Mt Hope Ave.
Rochester NY 14620
716-473-3820
CD, LP, CA

Record Theater
3500 Main St.
Buffalo NY 14208
716-837-2090

Music Stores

Airport Music
448 Cayuga Rd.
Cheektowago NY 14225
716-634-5649
Full line of products

Buffalo Drum Outlet
934 Walden Ave.
Buffalo NY 14211
716-897-0950
Drum repairs & sales; no rentals

Elmwood Music
1630 Elmwood Ave.
Buffalo NY 14207
716-874-6775
No rentals; guitar & amp repairs; guitar & combo sales

House of Guitars
645 Titus Ave.
Rochester NY 14617
716-544-3500
Full line

Top Shelf Music
1232 Hertel Ave.
Buffalo NY 14216
716-876-6544
Guitar sales & repairs; no rentals

Unistage
330 Genesee St.
Buffalo NY 14204
716-853-6500
Full line

Food

Elmwood Ave. is kind of the area in Buffalo where the "younger folks tend to live and hang out." **Preservation Hall**, on Elmwood Ave., is a good vegetarian type restaurant. Unfortunately, it is not real cheap. **The Town Restaurant** on the corner of Allen and Elmwood Ave. has good greasy Greek food. There are a lot of good Greek restaurants in the area.

Shelter

Out in the burbs you may be able to find cheap lodging; consult the Buffalo section of your Triple A guide to the Northeast (you do have a Triple A guide to the Northeast under the passenger's seat don't you?).

Etc.

Niagra Falls is 14 minutes north of Buffalo. Our source says, in reality, it is just a big dump for chemical waste surrounded by lame old tourist hotels, but the Falls themselves are nice to see. **Darien Lake** is a big "modern" amusement park near Buffalo with big, neat roller coasters. **Canada** is across the bridge, you can go take a look at an actual foreign country!

New York City
Venues

The Bank
225 E Houston
New York NY 10002
212-505-5033
Capacity: 650
Wide variety, mostly alternative.

The Bitter End
147 Bleecker St.
New York NY 10012
212-673-7030
Capacity: 220
Acoustic, alternative.

The Bottom Line
15 W 4th St.
New York NY 10012
212-228-6300
Capacity: 400
Rock, country, R&B, blues, jazz and folk.

Brownie's
169 Ave. A
New York NY 10009
212-420-8392
Capacity: 250
Alternative.

CBGB
315 Bowery St.
New York NY 10003
212-982-4052
Capacity: 285
Legendary punk rock venue

CB's 313 (CB's Gallery)
313 Bowery
New York NY 10003
212-677-0455
Capacity: 250
Country, blues, jazz, etc.

Coney Island High
15 St. Marks Pl
New York NY 10003
212-674-7959
Capacity: 300
Punk

Continental Club
17 Irving Place
New York NY 10003
212-533-0453
Capacity: 480
Mainly alternative and hard rock, but also blues, R&B, and country.

Downtime
251 W 30th St.
New York NY 10001
212-695-3373
Capacity: 350
Most styles.

Gonzalez Y Gonzalez
625 Broadway
New York NY 10012
212-473-8787
212-532-7592 Marc for bookings
Capacity: 300
Latin, funk, and jazz; also a Tex-Mex dinner place.

Indigo Blues
221 W 46th St.
New York NY 10036
212-221-0033
Capacity: 150
Jazz, blues, world music.

Kenny's Castaways
157 Bleecker St.
New York NY 10012
212-473-9870
Capacity: 250
Variety, including folk, blues and alternative.

Knitting Factory
47 E Houston St.
New York NY 10012
212-219-3006
Capacity: 250
Alternative rock, jazz fusion and avant-garde.

Lauterbach's
335 Prospect Ave.
Brooklyn NY 11215
718-788-9140
Capacity: 140
Rock, hard rock and country.

Limelight
47 W 20th St.
New York NY 10011
212-807-7850
Capacity: 2,000
Alternative, rock.

The Lion's Den
214 Sullivan St.
New York NY 10012
212-477-2782 (after 6pm)
Capacity: 400
Alternative, rock.

Ludlow Street Cafe
165 Ludlow St.
New York NY 10002
212-353-0536
Capacity: 100
All styles.

Manny's Car Wash Blues
1558 3rd Ave.
New York NY 10128
212-369-2583
Capacity: 150
Blues, rock.

Mercury Lounge
225 E. Houston
New York, NY 10009
212-260-4700
Local and touring bands, mostly alternative, folk, jazz. One room for talking, another for rocking.

Nightingale Bar
213 2nd Ave
New York, NY 10002
Capacity: 150
Punk, pop, alternative

Remedy
179 Varrick St.
New York NY 10014
212-463-0509
Capacity: 600 on both floors
Rock.

Rodeo Bar
375 3rd Ave.
New York NY 10016
212-683-6500
212-532-7592 Marc for bookings
Country, rock.

S.O.B.'s
204 Varrick St.
New York NY 10014
212-243-4940
Capacity: 500
World music.

The Spiral
244 E Houston St.
New York NY 10002
212-353-1740
Capacity: 200
All styles.

Tramps
51 W 21st St.
New York NY 10010
212-727-7788
Capacity: 900
Blues, R&B, zydeco, country, more.

Under Acme
9 Great Jones St
New York NY 10012
212-420-1934
Sharon 212-260-1145
Alternative.

Wetlands
161 Hudson St.
New York NY 10013
212-966-4225
Capacity: 500
Alternative, rock, hip-hop, funk.

Press

Big Takeover
249 Eldridge St. #14
New York NY 10002
212-533-6057
Twice yearly music fanzine

Cover
PO Box 1215
Cooper Station
New York NY 10276
212-673-1152
Mag published 9 times a year

Fast Folk Magazine
PO Box 938
Village Station
New York NY 10014
212-274-1636
Folk music mag plus CD
10 issues a year

Good Times
PO Box 33
Westbury NY 11590
516-334-9650
Biweekly newspaper

Musician's Exchange
PO Box 304
Manhasset NY 11030
212-614-0300
516-883-8898
Monthly music mag

New York Newsday
780 Third Ave.
New York NY 10016
212-339-7540
Daily. Music Editor Ira Robbins and staff writer Dave Sprague are very supportive of young, new bands.

New York Post
210 50th St.
New York NY 10002
212-815-8000

New York Press
295 Lafayette St.
The Puck Bldg 9th Fl
New York NY 10012
212-941-1130
Weekly alternative arts and
entertainment newspaper

New York Times
229 W. 43rd St.
New York NY 10036
Daily paper
212-556-1234

Propaganda Magazine
PO Box 26
New Hyde Park NY 11040
516-248-8143 fax
Quarterly Gothic/metal mag

Sound Views
96 Henry St., Ste 5W
Brooklyn NY 11201
718-797-5350
Bimonthly magazine

Under the Volcano
PO Box 236
Nesconset NY 11767
516-265-8227
Bimonthly fanzine

Village Voice
36 Cooper Sq
New York NY 10003
212-475-3300
Weekly news, arts and entertainment newspaper

Radio

WBAI 99.5 fm
505 8th Ave.
New York NY 10018
212-279-0707
Punk rock, reggae, salsa, opera,
and jazz AOR blocks

WBMB 590 am
Baruch College
155 E 24th St.
New York NY 10010
212-447-3019
All styles, college format

WFMU 91.1 fm
Upsala College radio station in
East Orange, NJ, but it reaches
NYC and features some of the
best progressive programming in
the area. Check the Northeast NJ
listing.

WFUV 90.7 fm
Fordham University
Bronx NY 10458
718-817-4550
Acoustic-based alternative music

WKCR 89.9 fm
Columbia University
208 Ferris Booth Hall
New York NY 10027
212-854-5223
Jazz, classical, avant garde,
country & soul

WNYU 89.1 fm
New York University
721 Broadway 11th Fl
New York NY 10003
212-998-1658
Alternative, reggae, club music

Record Stores

Bleecker Bob's Records
118 W 3rd St.
New York NY 10012
212-475-9677
CD, LP, CA, 7"

Finyl Vinyl
89 Second Ave.
New York NY 10003
212-533-8007
Exclusively vinyl

Kim's Underground
144 Bleecker St
New York NY 10014
Recommended.

Midnight Records
P.O. Box 390
Old Chelsea Stn NY 10113
212-675-2768
CD, LP

Rebel Rebel Records
319 Bleecker St.
New York NY 10014
212-989-0770
CD, LP, 7"

Record Runner
5 Jones St.
New York NY 10014
212-255-4280
CD, LP, Video

Rocks in Your Head
157 Prince St.
New York NY 10012
212-475-6729

Subterranean
5 Cornelia St.
New York NY 10014
212-463-8900
CD, LP, CA, Video

Venus Records
8th & St. Mark's Pl.
New York NY 10003
212-598-4459
CD, LP

Music Stores

Aguilar Electronics
1600 Broadway, Ste 1004
New York NY 10019
212-757-2823
Analog and digital repairs; no
rentals; amp/amp related sales

Alex Music
165 W 48th St.
New York NY 10036
212-819-0070
Repairs woodwinds, brass, and
guitars; no rentals; full-line of
products

Andre Audio-Tronics
375 W 48th St.
New York NY 10036
212-765-4345
Amps, electronics, keys, speaker
re-coning repairs; no rentals

The Guitar Lab Repair Center
165 W 48th St.
New York NY 10036
212-704-2042
In-house repair and rush jobs;
no rentals

**International Woodwind and
Brass**
174 W 48th St.
New York NY 10036
212-575-1508
Repairs, rents, and sells brass &
woodwinds

Mandolin Brothers
629 Forest Ave.
Staten Island NY 10310
718-981-3226

Manny's Music
156 W 48th St.
New York NY 10036
212-819-0576
Full-line of product sales; no
rentals or repairs

Matt Umanov Guitars
273 Bleecker St.
New York NY 10014
212-675-2157
Guitar sales & repairs; no
rentals.

Mojo Guitars
102 St. Marks
New York NY 10009
212-260-7751
Guitar repairs; guitar & amp
sales.

Play It Productions
106 W 32nd St., 3rd Fl
New York NY 10001
212-695-6530

Rougue Music
251 W 30th St., 10th Floor
New York NY 10001
212-629-5073
Full-line of repairs, rentals, and
sales

Rudy's Music
169 W 48th St.
New York NY 10036
212-391-1699
Sales and repairs; acoustic
guitar rentals

Sadowsky Guitars Ltd.
1600 Broadway Rm 1000B
New York NY 10019
212-586-3960
Guitar repair and custom
building; no rentals; guitar &
bass product lines

Sam Ash
160 W 48th St.
New York NY 10036
212-719-2625
Sales and rentals

Toy Specialists
333 W 52nd St., 7th Floor
New York NY 10019
212-333-2206
Rentals, audio equipment sales

Guest Commentary

Because New York is so big,
we've decided to add this
information straight from the
horse's mouth, so to speak.
Here it is as told by our corre-
spondent in the "Big Apple,"
Keith Lyle.

Venues & Promoters

I really like **Brownies** on Ave. A
these days. They seem to put
together the swell package
shows of cool, up-and-coming
bands that, with all this 25th
anniversary business, CB's was
generously credited with in the
major press outlets.

In Jersey, I'd have to say that
perhaps the coolest booking guy
is Randy Ellis out at venerable
City Gardens in Trenton. (609)
695-2483 or (215) 862-0852.
Though Randy seems to sometimes overplay his Rodney
Dangerfield status, he has a
good ear for cool music and is
usually prepared to give new
bands a chance. All ages shows
at all times. Before being signed
to Warners, he booked Green
Day to their biggest show ever.
It was a total sell-out because
the hardcore kids in the area
dutifully read their zines and
listened to Princeton U. radio
(WPRB) punk shows. Any
Epitaph, Lookout (related) act
will draw like crazy here and sell
a ton of merch. Just ask
Pennywise.

Don't listen to people who
suggest that booking a show at
the **Fast Lane** or **Stone Pony** in
Asbury Park precludes a booking
at City Gardens. Those venues
draw a totally different audience
from a totally different part of
the state. If it comes down to
either Trenton or Asbury, I'd go
to Trenton. Plus, Asbury is a
fucking miserable place, even
compared to Trenton, and will
do much to bring down the
morale of the bands.

If you're dealing with speed or
death metal, you might want to
look into **Obsessions** in
Randoph (Northern Central

Jersey - 201-895-3243). It's a bit
divey and usually caters to a
depressing meat market/Jersey
singles crowd but the occasional
metal shows they book do fairly
well. Most of the kids who go
there for shows never go to NYC
and seldom leave the confines
of Morris County except to hit
the shore in the summer.
They're desperate for some local
mosh action. If you're looking to
spend the night in the area,
there are a bunch of motels on
nearby Route 10 and, for fun,
there's a mini-golf course about
5 minutes down the road.

Record Stores

You know about **Pier Platters** in
Hoboken. The only suggestions I
can add to this list would be
Crazy Rhythms in Montclair and
even better is **Flipside Records**
in Pompton Lakes.

Radio

I've been listening to **WSOU**
from Seton Hall in South Orange
NJ for a while now but they're
not the cool station they were
even two years ago. They don't
play much of the indie rock/
metal mix they once did. Now
it's mostly the cheesier side of
metal with a lot of classic metal
and AC/DC reverence.

Hotels

I just read somewhere that there
are actually a number of reasonably priced Bed & Breakfast
spots in Manhattan. They might
be worth looking into. I know
there's a travel book dedicated
to American B&B's that would
have more info and phone
numbers. This might be worth
investigating for smaller bands
with not too much gear.

Sightseeing & Fun

The Great American Backrub -
958 Third Ave. near 57th St. Pay
$7.95 for an almost 9 minute
massage -by the way, you keep
your shirt on. House rules. A
sure bet stress reducer for pre-
gig jitters.

Village Chess Shop Ltd. - 230 Thompson St. - open 7 days 'til midnight. Bring a friend or go in search of some hot competition. The chess pieces fly at all hours, whether you're into speed or skill. Geek paradise.

Dave! - Unless he's on vacation, the Letterman show tapes every afternoon from the Ed Sullivan Theater on 53rd St. and Broadway. You can chance getting stand-by tickets by showing up early (call for exact time) and being very patient. You'll have a better chance of scoring **Conan O'Brien** tickets at the spur of the moment if you don't deal well with rejection.

Restaurants

(near the Academy)
Howard Johnson's - 1551 Broadway at 46th. The New Yorker recently said this spot offers "food for nostalgia buffs." I guess that's because this is the last fully operating Ho Jos restaurant in Manhattan. It's a throwback in a Times Square increasingly haunted by the '90s image obsessed Disney monster and enormous CK billboards featuring the haunting stares of Kate Moss and Marky Mark. Japanese tourists pose in front of these billboards to impress the folks at home. Yes, people watching is incredible from the Ho Jo windows. The interior offers an eyeful as well. Every Friday, Penn Gilette hosts his movie night outings (all welcome) with a pre-flick snack at the rear of the restaurant. Arrive around 11:15 pm or so.

(near Wetlands)
The Moondance Diner - 6th Ave. at Grand St. They do the honest diner faves but also have a selection of tastier deserts. The counter staff play some killer mix tapes.

(East Village)
Brunetta's - 190 First Ave., between 10th and 11th. Small but bright and cozy. Big pasta plates for not too much. Once inside, you totally forget you're on the grittier end of First Ave.

Odessa - 117 Ave. A between 7th and 8th. Greg Ginn asked Henry Rollins to join Black Flag at this famous spot across from Tompkins Park. Traditional dinner fare but with an Eastern European flair for meaty delights, which I stay well away from. They've just gone 24 hours and will fill you up cheap. Watch out for the Belgian Waffles because sometimes they don't cook them long enough. Also, roaches have been spotted at all levels so go elsewhere if you are squeamish. And on crowded weekend mornings they'll give you the bums rush.

Leshko's Coffee Shop - 111 Ave. A at 7th. Rival to Odessa. Take your pick. Here, you can also get tons of Pirogi Kielbasy, stuffed cabbage, blintzes and borscht for not too much. They call it home cooking.

Old Devil Moon - 511 East 12th St., between A & B. Home cooking and a wait staff that will sit down and chat when they're not too busy. Small but solid menu with a variety of vegetarian items. True country breakfast on Saturday and Sunday mornings.

Cooper Square - 87 2nd Ave., at the corner of 5th St. Open 24 hours offering more reliable food on sometimes confusing surroundings. Also, there's the chance you'll catch a taping of NYPD Blue. The station exterior is just east of here on 5th. The restaurant has been spotted during the show in arty Bochco-esque quick edits.

9: A Coffee House at 110 St. Marks. Part of the new coffee intensive trend towards "neat" places to eat. Great sprout-type sandwiches and a complete menu of caffeinated and decaffeinated coffee varieties. Cool but not too cool wait staff. Too drafty on sub-freezing days.

NORTH CAROLINA
Charlotte
Venues

Aardvark's
5600 Old Concord Rd.
Charlotte, NC 28256
704-596-1342
Capacity: 200
All styles.

The Double Door
218 E Independence Bl.
Charlotte, NC 28204
704-376-1446
Capacity: 150
Mainly blues, zydeco.

The Tremont Music Hall
400 W Tremont Ave.
Charlotte, NC 28203
Capacity: 500
All styles.

Press

Break Magazine
PO Box 32188
Charlotte, NC 28232
704-358-5910
Weekly arts and entertainment. Reviews CDs and demos.

Charlotte Observer
PO Box 30308
Charlotte, NC 28232-0308
704-358-5000
Daily newspaper

Creative Loafing
1620 S Bl.
Charlotte, NC 28203
704-375-2121
Weekly alternative. Reviews demos.

Indie File
1711 Central Ave.
Charlotte, NC
Monthly music paper

Record Stores

Milestone Records
1711 Central Ave.
Charlotte, NC 28205
704-377-2350
CD, CA, LP

The Record Exchange
210 S Sharon Amity Rd.
Charlotte, NC 28211
704-364-9400
CD, CA, LP

Repo Records
2516 Central Ave.
Charlotte, NC 28205
704-334-7376
CD, CA, LP

Music Stores

Action Music
6903 E Harris Bl.
Charlotte, NC 28215
Full-line repairs and products;
PA and equipment rentals

Fordham Music
251 Watauga Village Dr.
Boone, NC 28607
704-264-9361
Repairs wind instruments; PA
rentals; Full-line products

Musician's Workshop
319 Merriman Ave.
Asheville, NC 28801
704-252-1249
All electric repairs; PA rentals;
Full-line products

Reliable Music
650 E Stonewall St
Charlotte, NC 28202
704-375-8662
Full line sales and repairs

Greensboro Winston-Salem

Venues

Blind Tiger
2115 Walker Ave.
Greenboro, NC 27403
910-272-9888
Capacity:150
R&B, rock.

Kilroy's
708 W Market St
Greensboro, NC 27403
910-274-2166
Capacity: 500
Alternative, rock, reggae..

Somewhere Else
5713 W Friendly Ave
Greensboro, NC 27410
910-292-5494
Capacity 300
All styles

The Turtle
807 S Aycock St
Greensboro, NC 27403
910-272-0801
Capacity: 400
All styles

Ziggy's Tavern
433 Baity St
Winston-Salem, NC 27105
910-748-1064
Capacity: 900 (larger tented area
and smaller indoor area with
pool table)
Most styles

Press

Crunchy Music Stuff
908 Spring Garden St.
Greesboro, NC 28403
910-230-0201
Monthly fanzine. Alternative and
punk. Reviews shows and
submitted material.

ESP Magazine
5601 Roanneway #111
Greensboro, NC 27409
910-294-4377
Weekly magazine

Triad Style
PO Box 20007
Greensboro, NC 27420
910-373-7374
Weekly entertainment

Winston-Salem Journal
418 N Marshall St
Winston-Salem, NC 27102
910-727-7284
Send tour and band info. for
possible reviews.

Radio

WQFS 90.9 fm
Guilford College
PO Box 17714
Greensboro, NC
910-316-2352
College alternative, jazz metal.
Indie show Mon 8-9pm.

WUAG 103.1 fm
U. of No Carolina
N Tate St.
Greensboro, NC 27413
910-334-5688
Mixed alternative, jazz, rap,
heavy metal

Record Stores

Crunchy Music
908 Spring Garden St.
Greensboro, NC 27403
910-230-0201
CD, CA, LP

Mighty Quinn Music
3722 Reynolda Rd
Winston-Salem, NC 27106
910-922-2919
CD, CA, LP, Video
Also a store in Raleigh

Record Exchange
2403-5 Battleground ave
Greensboro, NC 274408
910-288-2300
CD, CA, LP

Spins
2144 Lawndale Dr.
Greensboro, NC 27408
910-274-8530
CD, CA, LP, 7"

Music Stores

Carey Sound
216 N Church St
Greensboro, NC 27401
910-379-1943
Sales, repairs, rentals.

Music Barn
920 S Chapman St
Greensboro, NC 27403
910-272-2118
Large drum selection. Sales and
repairs.

Music Loft
501 Baity St
Winston-Salem, NC 27103
910-721-1991
Reliable full-line repairs and products. PA and some amp rentals.

Chapel Hill Durham Raleigh

Venues

The Brewery
3009 Hillsborough St.
Raleigh NC 27607
919-834-7018
Capacity: 350
This is one of two clubs in the Raleigh area that will have indie touring bands play. The crowd is mainly students from the nearby university.

The Cat's Cradle
300 E. Main St.
Carrboro NC 27510
919-967-9053
Capacity: 900
Frank Heath
18 and up
More well-known national acts, some regional. The biggest venue, nationally known.

The Duke Coffeehouse
PO Box 90689
Durham NC 27706
Contact Jeremy Seckler
919-684-2957
Fax: 919-684-3260
Capacity: 200
Shows sponsored by WXDU
This is an all-ages venue that does a lot of up-and-coming indie acts coming through the area. Bands take the door and this is pretty much the only place in Durham to play. The Coffeehouse is the place to get a good toe-hold before going on to play a larger club.

The Lizard and Snake
110 N Columbia St
Chapel Hill, NC 27514
Capacity: 75
Acoustic, rock.

Local 506
506 W Franklin
Chapel Hill NC 27516
919-942-5506
Capacity: 150
18 and up
Alternative, other styles.

Mad Monk
127 S College Rd.
Wilmington NC 28403
910-395-0281
Capacity: 1,000
Rock, alternative.

Seldom Blues Cafe
Tryon Rd. & Kildare Farm Rd.
Cary NC 27511
919-851-2583
Capacity: 400
Blues

Skylight Exchange
405 1/2 W Rosemary St.
Chapel Hill NC 27516
919-933-5550
Capacity: 150
Blues, folk, reggae and jazz.

Snookers
2109-E Avent Ferry Rd.
Raleigh NC 27606
919-828-0052
Capacity: 300
Rock, alternative, metal.

Southwest
2 S. West St.
Raleigh NC 27603
919-832-8855
Capacity: 100
Mostly alternative, indie bands.

Press

The Daily Tarhill
PO Box 3257
Chapel Hill NC 27515
919-962-0245
Daily Newspaper

The Duke University Chronicle
Flowers Blvd., 3rd Flr
Durham NC 27706
919-684-2663
Daily newspaper

The Independent
PO Box 2690
Durham NC 27715
919-286-1972
Weekly alternative newspaper

Live Wire
PO Box 5097
Cary, NC 27511
Monthly fanzine

News and Observer
PO Box 191
215 S MacDowell St.
Raleigh NC 27602
919-829-4500
Daily newspaper

The Spectator Magazine
PO Box 12887
Raleigh NC 27605
919-828-7393
Weekly arts & entertainment magazine

Radio

WKNC 88.1 fm
North Carolina State University
Box 8607, North Carolina State University Mail Center
Raleigh NC 27695
919-515-2401
Heavy alternative, rap/urban, metal, jazz, blues

WXDU 88.7 fm
Duke University, PO Box 4706
Duke Station
Durham NC 27706
919-684-2957
Fax: 919-684-3260
All styles

WXYC 89.3 fm
UNC at Chapel Hill
Box 51, Carolina Union
Chapel Hill NC 27599
919-962-7768
Mixed - alternative rock, pop, jazz, urban

Record Stores

All three of these stores are highly recommended places to check out.

Poindexters
718 9th St.
Durham NC 27705
919-286-1852
CD, LP, CA

The Record Exchange
2109-144 Avent Ferry Rd.
Raleigh NC 27606
919-831-2300
CD, LP, CA, Video
Also a store in Chapel Hill

Schoolkids
144 E Franklin St.
Chapel Hill NC 27514
919-929-7766
CD, CA

Schoolkids
2316-104 Hillsborough St.
Raleigh NC 27606
919-821-7766
CD CA

Music Stores

Associated Sound Products
605 Creekside Dr
Raleigh NC 27609
919-829-1143
No repairs; PA & sound equipment rentals and sales.

Harry's Guitar Shop
616 Glenwood Ave.
Raleigh NC 27603
919-828-4888
Guitar & amp repairs and sales; no rentals

The Music Connection
900 W Hodges St.
Raleigh NC 27608
919-755-1776
Sales, rentals, some repairs.

The Music Loft
2101 New Hope Church Rd.
Raleigh NC 27604
919-872-0331
No repairs; PA's & sound rentals; full-line sales.

Food

Honey's, **Shorey's**, and **Burgers** are all good eats. Nothing is really open 24 hours in this area. **International Delights** on 9th in Chapel Hill has a decent vegetarian menu. **Pepper's Pizza** in Chapel Hill has good cheap food. **The Pyewacket** in Chapel Hill on Franklin caters to the vegetarian diet, and you can't beat the name.

Shelter

Cheap Hotels - you can't miss 'em. On Interstates 40 and 80, you may find the general chains such as **Motel 6**, etc, that have decent prices

Etc.

9th Street in Durham, **Hillsborough** in Raleigh and **Franklin Street** in Chapel Hill are the main drags in each town, normally pretty cool areas to hang out. **Thrift World**, **Grandma's Pantry**, and the **Salvation Army** are good thrift stores. **UNC Duke** Campus is a very beautiful school. The Chapel Hill community totally revolves around the activities of the university. **Moorehead Planetarium** in Chapel Hill is cool if you are into the stars, looking at them that is. **The Durham Bulls** play in the summer, for $3 you can watch a minor league baseball game. Raleigh is the state capital, and they have the **North Carolina Museum of Arts**, along with all the other typical state capital sights. There are many avenues for the arts in the Triangle area because of all the student activity. The **North Carolina Museum of Life and Sciences** is very cool. **Duke Gardens**, between Durham and Chapel Hill, is a very beautiful park, and someone once told me that when travelling the world, city parks are almost always the highlights of any given community, both aesthetically and historically.

NORTH DAKOTA
Fargo
Venues

Cactus Jack's
3402 Interstate Bl.
Fargo, ND 58103
701-232-8110
Capacity: 300
Bowling alley, bar and casino.
Rock, metal.

Kirby's
315 Main Ave.
Moorhead, MN 56560
218-233-2617
Capacity: 500
Rock, alternative.

Ralph's
23 Forest St. S
Moorhead, MN 56560
218-333-3351
Capacity: 200
Alternative, punk, blues.

Windbreak Lounge
3150 39th St. SW
Fargo, ND 58103
701-282-5507
Capacity: 280
Mostly country.

Press

The Forum
PO Box 2020
Fargo, ND 58107
701-235-7311
Daily newspaper

The Spectrum
No. Dakota State University
356 Memorial Union
Fargo, ND 58105
701-231-7414
Bi-weekly newspaper

Radio

KDSU
No. Dakota State U.
PO Box 5347
Fargo, ND 58105
701-231-8322
Jazz

Record Stores

Disc & Tape
4101 13th Ave S
Fargo, ND 58103
701-282-5624
CD, CA, LP, 7"

Mother's Records
542 6th Ave N
Fargo, ND 58102
701-241-9601
CD, CA, LP, 7"

Music Stores

Beehive Music
213 N P Ave.
Fargo, ND 58102
701-232-3667
PA, guitar, drum repairs, sales.

Schmitt Music
West Acres Mall
Fargo, ND 58103
701-281-1828
Sales, repairs, rentals.

OHIO
Cincinnati
Venues

The Blue Wisp
19 Garfield Place
Cincinnati OH 45202
513-721-9801
Capacity: 145
Jazz

Bogart's
2621 Vine St.
Cincinnati OH 45219
513-872-8801
513-221-7625 bookings
Capacity: 1,300
All styles.

The Greenwich Tavern
2442 Gilbert Ave. at McMillian
Cincinnati OH 45206
513-221-6764
Capacity: 300
Jazz and blues.

Ripley's
2507 W. Clifton
Cincinnati OH 45219
513-861-6506
Capacity: 400
All styles.

Sudsy Malone's
2626 Vine St.
Cincinnati OH 45219
513-751-2300
Capacity: 250
18 and up
A laundromat which features a full bar and stage along with laundry-cleaning facilities. Bands can hang out here all day, do their laundry and drink beer or soda pop at discount prices. This is pretty much the only place that will book indie touring bands.

Press

Cincinnati City Beat
23 East 7th St. #617
Cincinnati OH 43229
513-665-4700
Entertainment weekly

Cincinnati Enquirer
312 Elm St.
Cincinnati OH 45202
513-721-2700
Daily

Cincinnati Post
125 E. Court St.
Cincinnati OH 45202
513-721-2700
Daily

Entertainer Magazine
803 Scott St.
Covington KY 41011
606-581-6585
Bimonthly entertainment magazine

Everybody's News
1310 Pendelton
Cincinnati OH 45210
513-381-2606
Biweekly arts newspaper

Radio

WAIF 88.3 fm
PO Box 6126
Cincinnati OH 45206
513-961-8900
Jazz, blues, college alternative

WOXY 97.7 fm
5120 College Corner Pike
Oxford, OH 45056
513-523-4114
Rock, alternative.

WVXU 91.7 fm
Xavier University
3800 Victory Parkway
Cincinnati OH 45207
513-731-9898
All styles featured
Send your stuff to Night Waves, a late night show that features indie and alternative music.

Record Stores

Everybody's Records
6106 Montgomery Rd.
Cincinnati OH 45213
513-531-4500
CD, LP, CA

Mole's Records
2615 Vine St.
Cincinnati OH 45219
513-861-6291
CD, CA, LP

Wizard Records
2629 Vine St.
Cincinnati OH 45219
513-961-6196
CD, CA, Video

Music Stores

Buddy Roger's Music
1939 West Galbraith Rd.
Cincinnati OH 45239
513-931-6780
Sales, repairs, rentals.

Jimmy D's Music
2627 Vine St.
Cincinnati OH 45219
513-861-2583
Guitar and electronic repairs, sales. Across the street from Sudsy Malone's.

Food

Perkin's is a 24-hour restaurant chain near Sudsy's. **Camp Washington Chili** on Colerain, chili is a big deal in Cincinati. Have it on spaghetti or however you like. They do it more ways than you could imagine. **Skyline Chili** is another good chili place. **Daniel's** is open late, a very good Mexican Restaurant on Vine, near Sudsy's. **Mayura's**, a whole world restaurant, **Floyd's**, a very good Greek Restaurant, and **Vindu Hindu** are all on Calhoun. Vindu Hindu is a great Indian Place that is cheap and highly recommended. **BW3's**, a wings place on Vine. **In the Woods** on Calhoun is a good restaurant for breakfast. **Fergusons Country Restaurant** on Kellog Ave., connected with an antique mall and thrift store, is a cool little Ma and Pa type place in an interesting area. **White Castle** on Central Parkway is cheap and a must experience for anyone who has yet to go there, they have great coffee, everything else is questionable.

Shelter

Somebody's floor. All the hotels are $40 and up.

Etc.

The best thrifting is in Cincinati, supposedly the most for your dollar. The **Norwood Thrift**, off the Norwood lateral or Route 536. There is no sightseeing worth mentioning according to our sources except (there is always an exception to the rule, right?) one can see the **Cincinati Symphony** for $6 with any old student I.D., call 513-345-4490. There are also a lot of cheap movies, the **Reel Movies** downtown is one theater with good prices, for others check a local paper. There is a whole menagerie of $1.50 theaters.

Cleveland
Venues

The Agora / The Agora Ballroom
5000 Euclid Ave.
Cleveland OH 44103
216-881-6700
216-881-6700
Capacity:1600/400(ballroom)
All styles.

The Barking Spider
11310 Juniper
University Circle
Cleveland OH 44106
216-421-9294
Capacity: 60
Acoustic, folk.

Cedar's
23 N. Hazel
Youngstown OH 44503
216-743-6560
Capacity: 300
Jazz, reggae, rock, blues, alternative, folk.

The Daily Double
370 Orleans
Akron OH 44311
216-535-1855
Capacity: 250
Reggae, jazz, pop.

The Euclid Tavern
11629 Euclid Ave.
Cleveland OH 44106
216-229-7788
Capacity: 250
Alternative
This is the main venue in town for indie touring bands.

The Grog Shop
1765 Coventry
Cleveland Heights OH 44118
216-321-5588
Capacity: 200
Rock, alternative.

Odeon Concert Club
1295 Old River Rd.
Cleveland OH 44113
216-574-2525
Capacity: 950
Mostly rock, but it varies.

Peabody's Downunder
1059 Old River Rd.
Cleveland Flats OH 44113
216-241-2451
Capacity: 600
Jazz, blues, rock, folk and reggae.

Phantasy Nightclub /Symposium
11794 Detroit Ave.
Lakewood OH 44107
216-228-6300
Capacity: 1200 theatre/350 nightclub
Alternative, Rock and Metal

Splash
1575 Merwin Ave.
Cleveland OH 44115
216-589-9797, 721-4623 booking
Capacity: 150
Reggae

The Symposium
11794 Detroit Ave.
Cleveland OH 44107
216-521-9696
Capacity: 125
Rock, blues, rockabilly, alternative, and some folk.

Trilogy
2325 Elm St.
Cleveland OH 44113
216-241-1444
Capacity: 1,500
Wide variety.

Wilbert's
1360 W 6th St.
Cleveland OH 44113
Katherine Isenhart
216-771-2583
Blues

Press

Cleveland Plain Dealer
1801 Superior Ave.
Cleveland OH 44114
216-999-5000
Weekly entertainment magazine

The Free Times
11610 Euclid Ave. Ste 100A
Cleveland OH 44106
216-229-1600
Alternative weekly with advertising and listings for touring indie bands.

Scene Magazine
1375 Euclid Ave. #312
Cleveland OH 44115
216-241-7550
Weekly arts/entertainment
A great place for indie bands to send information for listings, etc.

US Rocker
6370 York Rd. #281
Cleveland, OH 44130
216-264-1274
Monthly regional

Radio

WBWC 88.3 fm
Baldwin-Wallace College
Berea OH 44017
216-826-2145
Alternative college format, similar to a commercial alternative format

WCPN 90.3 fm
3100 Chester Ave.
Cleveland OH 44114
216-432-3700
Jazz

WCSB 89.3 fm
Cleveland State University
#956 Rhodes Tower
Cleveland OH 44115
216-687-3721
Blues, world, rock, metal, jazz
Will play indie records

WENZ 107.9 fm "The End"
1510 Euclid Ave.
Cleveland OH 44115
216-861-0100
Commercial alternative, varied programming

WOBC 91.5 fm
Oberlin College
Wilder Hall
Oberlin OH 44074
216-775-8107
Fax 216-775-8107
Alternative
This station will play indie records, and are rather supportive of indie touring bands.

WRUW 91.1 fm
Case Western Reserve
11220 Bellflower Rd.
Cleveland OH 44106
216-368-2207
College alternative
This station is very likely to play indie records.

WUJC 88.7 fm
John Carroll University
20700 N. Park Blvd.
University Heights OH 44118
216-397-4437
College alternative
WUJC does play some indie records, but not as much focus as 91.1 FM.

Record Stores

Chris' Warped Records
13383 Madison Ave.
Lakewood OH 44107
216-521-4981
CD, LP, CA, Video

Record Revolution
1828 Coventry
Cleveland Heights OH 44118
216-321-7661
CD, LP, CA, Video

Wax Stacks
2254 Lee Rd.
Cleveland Heights OH 44118
216-321-7935
CD, CA
These people will take indie "product," and this is a highly recommended store.

Music Stores

Central Music
10508 Lorain Ave.
Cleveland OH 44111
216-671-0093
Guitar & amp repairs; PA rentals; combo product line.

Lentine's Music
2210 Brook Park Rd.
Cleveland OH 44134
216-741-1400
Full-line of rentals and sales.

Midway Music Inc.
4503 Brookpark Rd.
Parma OH 44134
216-661-3298
Amp & guitar repairs; various rentals; full line of sales.

Sodja's Music
5148 Wilson Mills Rd.
Richmond Heights OH 44143
216-461-2995
Full-line of rentals & sales; electronic & guitar repairs.

Food

Minanh on Detroit at W. 55th is a good, cheap Vietnamese restaurant. **Arabica** on Coventry is the hepcat coffee shop, they call it "Arafreaka." **Shaker Diner** Coffee Shop in Shaker Square is open 24 hrs. If you're still in the mood for greasy diner food, this place is good. **Big Egg** on 5107 Detroit is "a really weird place" open 24 hours, but not in the best of neighborhoods.

Shelter

Holiday Inn Lakeside may have cheap rooms, but once again, when you're in a big city try to find people to stay with.

FIG DISH AT NMS. ADVICE FROM THE ROAD

We figured we had already learned our lesson at the NYU seminar in April. It was our first conference and we were pretty sure we would just cruise into town, play in front of a wildly enthusiastic crowd saturated with high-powered A&R types that would fold massive record contracts into paper airplanes and fling them at the stage. What happened is we got slotted at seven o'clock at night and played in front of about eleven people. We got really depressed.

When we got offered to play at the New Music Seminar, we thought we were pretty clever by changing our approach; we treated the whole thing like a vacation with the actual show being more of a distraction than the focal point of our trip. This way we wouldn't be devastated when the thing totally sucked. The trip got off to a bad start. We got a very expensive ticket in Indiana even though we had a radar detector (don't speed, it's rarely worth it). At five in the morning we rolled into some town in Ohio that had like fifteen motels that were all completely occupied. There was one on the edge of town that had a room. As we walked to our room we could hear people yelling at each other in the other rooms we passed. You could hear strange slapping noises. We got to our room and there was cigarette burns all over the beds and the floors. There was snot literally (and liberally) smeared on the walls. The drive had been so brutal, however, that we didn't care. We would just sleep in our clothes on top of our gear. Rick went over to lock the door and found that the thumb lock was broken. No big deal, we would just lock the latch. When we tugged on it to test it the whole fucking door frame came off in our hands. I brought the whole thing down to the front desk and demanded our money back. They accused *us* of breaking it. We fought for a while but they gave in and refunded our cash. We got back on the road and limped into Youngstown at dawn where we ran into our friends in the band Triple Fast Action at a Motel 6.

The next day we took off with Triple Fast Action, which was a good thing because we had a nasty blow-out. It was so bad that we had to take pictures of the tire because no one would believe it. It looked like we had been hit by a sniper. Our jack didn't work too well so we borrowed TFA's (always travel with friends when possible). If it had been a front tire we probably would all be dead.

We barely made it into New York in time for soundcheck. During soundcheck I blew my amplifier so I borrowed Ronnie's from TFA (always play with friends when possible). After the soundcheck we went down to a bar on the corner and got drunk, really not caring much about how we played for the eleven people that would be there. We walked in the club about fifteen minutes before we were to go on and the place was packed. Six different A&R people introduced themselves to me before I even got to the stage. I asked one of them why all these people were there and he told me it was because we had gotten three different write ups in industry papers that week calling us a "buzz" band and we didn't know about it. We got up on stage and the sound was bad because it was a Blues club and had a tiny P.A. that didn't suit our style at all which ultimately didn't matter because we were too drunk to do anything but totally suck anyway which we succeeded in doing.

After the show, we tried to go to another club to see some other friends of ours and got pulled over by the cops and hassled for an hour for absolutely no reason. We got inside the club in time to hear the last chord of their set. Later that night we forgot to take our drummer's hardware out of the van. It was stolen of course.

Besides practically flushing our careers down the toilet at our show, the trip ended up costing us about two thousand dollars which made us depressed. We are looking forward to CMJ Convention next month. Fuck.

Fig Dish is based in Chicago. They still play at seminars, and were recently signed to Atlas/A&M Records. The New Music Seminar has since gone out of business.

Etc.

Cleveland has a brand new baseball stadium, **Jacob's Field**, and there is also a new basketball sports arena next door. **Terminal Tower** is a1920s building that was once the fourth largest building in the world. If you go up to the top you can take a look at the whole Cleveland area, quite awe-inspiring. The **Rock and Roll Hall of Fame** is in Cleveland. No comment. There is a really good zoo. The **Cleveland Museum of Art** is the last free museum that you may find in the area. Along with the art museum, you may want to check out the **Natural History Museum** which is also in the University Plaza area.

OKLAHOMA
Oklahoma City
Venues

Liberty Drug
786 Asp
Norman OK 73069
405-321-1776
Capacity: 130
Blues, roots rock

VZD
4200 N. Western
Oklahoma City OK 73118
405-524-4200
Capacity: 150
All styles except metal.

Press

Daily Oklahoman
PO Box 25125
Oklahoma City, OK 73125
405-475-3311
Daily newspaper

The Oklahoma Daily
860 Van Vlett Oval
Norman, OK 73019
405-325-2521
College daily

The Oklahoma Gazette
PO Box 54649
Oklahoma City OK 73154
405-528-6000
Weekly arts & entertainment newspaper

Radio

KROU 105.7 fm
University of Oklahoma
780 Van Fleet Oval
Norman OK 73019
405-325-3388
Public radio; classical & jazz.

KSPI 93.7 fm
215 W 9th St
Stillwater, OK 74074
405-372-7800
Alternative after 6pm.

Record Stores

Rainbow Records
2401 N Classen Blvd.
Oklahoma City OK 73106
405-524-4682
CD, CA

Shadow Play Records
737 Asp St.
Norman OK 73069
405-364-1670
LP, CA, 7"

Music Stores

Davie Music
520 E. Memorial
Oklahoma City OK 73114
405-752-5221
Guitar repairs; PA rentals; guitar, PA, and amp sales.

Tina's Guitars
758 Asp
Norman OK 73069
405-364-7796
Guitar & bass repairs; PA rentals; guitar (new and vintage) & sound equipment sales.

Tulsa
Venues

Cain's Ballroom
423 N Main St.
Tulsa OK 74103
918-584-2306/9
Capacity: 1,200
All-ages
Big rock venue.

Eclipse
1336 E 6th
Tulsa, OK 74129
918-582-5212
Capacity: 250
Mainly alternative

Ikon
606 S Elgin
Tulsa OK 74120
918-583-4566
918-585-5969 Davit (booking)
Capacity: 450
All-ages
Alternative, industrial.

Joey's
6825 So Peoria St.
Tulsa OK 74136
918-481-8787
Capacity: 175
Blues

Tulsa City Limits
2117 So Garnett St.
Tulsa OK 74129
918-438-3263
918-456-5168 Chuck (bookings)
Capacity: 1,360
Country, oldies, rock

Xenophon
20 E Brady
Tulsa, OK 74103
918-599-0992
Capacity: 250
Alternative

Press

The Collegian
University of Tulsa
600 S College Ave.
Tulsa, OK 74104
918-631-3818
College weekly

Substance
PO Box 701416
Tulsa OK 74170
918-743-1060 David
Sophisticated fanzine

Tulsa World
PO Box 1770
Tulsa OK 74102
918-581-8364/8388
Daily newspaper

Urban Tulsa
PO Box 50499
Tulsa OK 74150
918-592-5550
Monthly newspaper

Radio

KMYZ 104.5
5810 E Skelly Dr #801
Tulsa, OK 74135
918-665-3131
Alternative, rock

KRSC 91.3
Rogers State College
Claremore, OK 74017
918-343-7913
College, varied styles

KSPI 93.7 fm
Oklahoma State University
PO Box 2288
Stillwater OK 74076
405-372-7800
Alternative, varied styles

Record Stores

Mohawk Music
6157 E 51 Pl.
Tulsa OK 74135
918-664-2951
CD, CA, 7"

Starship Records & Tapes
2813 E 11 St.
Tulsa OK 74104
918-583-0638
CD, LP, CA, 7"

Music Stores

Drum Central Superstore
5155A S Peona St.
Tulsa OK 74105
918-742-0111
Drum repairs; no rentals; drum
sets, accessories, & guitar sales

Drum World
7106 S Mingo
Tulsa OK 74133
918-459-0444
Drum rentals, repairs and sales

Fierey Bros Music
4818 E 11th St. (11th & Yale)
Tulsa OK 74112
918-838-9895, 800-875-9895
Full-line of almost everything

Guitar House
6924 E Admiral Pl.
Tulsa OK 74115
918-835-6959
Violin rentals; string instrument
sales; fretted instruments and
fiddles repaired in-house

Music Sound World
2715 S Memorial
Tulsa OK 74129
918-664-2555
Guitar repairs; amps, PA's, and
keyboard rentals; full product
line except drums

The Music Store
9122 E 31st St.
Tulsa OK 74145
918-664-7333
Band instrument repairs, rentals,
and sales

Food

Cheap Restaurants: **Hideaway II
Pizza, Impressions, New York
Bagel Shop.** Vegetarian: **Big Al's
Subs & Health Foods,** Akin's
Natural Foods Market. 24-hour:
**Taco Cabana, Village Inn,
Denny's.**

Shelter

Howard Johnson Hotel Downtown, 1-800-446-4656, **Darby
Lane Inn,** 918-584-4461

Etc.

Thrift Stores: **Goodwill,** 2800
Southwest Blvd., **Quality Thrift
Store, Salvation Army, Clothes
Encounters of the Second Kind.**
Sightseeing: **Oral Roberts
University** (The Praying Hands),
**Expo Square, Mohawk Park,
River Parks.**

OREGON
Eugene
Venues

John Henry's
136 E 11th St.
Eugene OR 97401
Capacity: 300
503-342-3358
Bruce Hartnell
21 and up
This is pretty much the place to play in Eugene if you are an indie touring band.

Icky's Teahouse
503-345-3019
304 Blair Blvd
Eugene OR 97402

Press

See Portland; Eugene gets Paperback Jukebox, the Rocket, and Snipehunt.

Radio

KWVA
University of Oregon
EMU Ste 4
Eugene OR 97403
503-346-4091
Fax 503-346-2573
Alternative, varied styles
This station will do interviews, and sometimes they do shows on the university campus or in Lyle Hall, which is the Community Center for the Performing Arts. The shows are all-ages, but not very frequent, focusing on more established bands.

Record Stores

Green Noise Records
468 Willamette
Eugene OR 97401
503-683-1584
Ryder
CD, CA, LP
This is a good record store.

House of Records
258 E 13th St.
Eugene OR 97401
503-342-7975
CD, CA, LP
This is also a good record store.

Mckenzie River Music
525 E 13th St.
Eugene OR 97401
503-343-9482

Buy and Sell Center
171 W 8th St.
Eugene OR 97401
503-344-9273

Food

Sandino's at 854 E. 13th, is open until 4:00am on weekends. **13th Street** is the main street that goes right through town and up to the campus. If you play at John Henry's you get 20% off at Sandino's and it is a cool place to hang out.

Shelter

The Timbers Lodge located downtown is "strange but cheap." The address is 1015 Pearl, call them at 503-343-3345.

Etc.

While staying in Eugene you could check out one of the many cool parks, or visit the **The Holt Center**, which is supposedly the most acoustically sound music center in the U.S. They hold the annual Bach Festival.

Portland
Venues

1201 Cafe and Lounge
1201 SW 12th Ave.
Portland OR 97205
503-225-1201
Capacity: 40
All Acoustic music

Belmont's
3357 SE Belmont St.
Portland OR 97214
503-232-1998
503-234-3714 Steve (bookings)
Capacity: 250
All-ages
This is a hard show to get, they do a lot of blues, reggae and hippy-type rock'n'roll. They will have an occasional alternative show and it is worth a call, but don't expect much.

Berbati's Pan
231 SW Ankeny St
Portland, OR 97204
503-248-4579
Capacity: 350
Wide variety of styles.

Bojangles
2229 SE Hawthorne
Portland OR 97215
503-233-1201
Capacity: 150
This club books touring acts and will do just about any kind of music, but they don't do a lot of rock. They do more mellow, college alternative music.

The Brasserie Montmartre
626 SW Park Ave.
Portland OR 97205
503-224-5552
Capacity: 100
This is the Cool Jazz place. Usually instrumental, you can catch a little Be-bop or New Orleans style jazz. The bar is open and serving food until 4:00am, but drinks stop at 2:30am, like every other bar in Portland.

Drum
14601 SE Division St.
Portland OR 97236
503-760-1400
Capacity: 500
Country

East Ave. Tavern
727 E Burnside St.
Portland OR 97214
503-236-6900
503-236-6132 Lisa (bookings)
Capacity: 75
Acoustic, folk, alternative, blues. This is a great place for solo performers, but it is not in a great area of town.

Key Largo
31 NW First Ave.
Portland OR 97209
503-223-9919
Capacity: 250
Kind of a yuppy R&B hangout, occasionally a Robert Johnson or someone like that will play here, but for the most part it is kind of a local scene, probably out of your little budget.

La Luna
215 SE 9th
Portland OR 97214
503-235-9696
Monqui Presents Books most big shows
Capacity: 1,023
This is the premier club as far as well known touring bands are concerned. La Luna is in an old, renovated brick building with a very modern interior. This is definitely the place to play in town, if you can get in you are happy. They feature shows by anyone from the Smashing Pumpkins to smaller acts. It is quite doubtful that your band would headline, but you could get an opening slot. If there is no show going on downstairs, ask about the balcony. It is a smaller venue, with a capacity of 2-300, located upstairs in the same building.

Madrona Hill Winery
2412 N Mississippi Ave.
Portland OR 97227
503-284-5153
Capacity: 400
All-ages with beer and wine
This club is in a big old warehouse, in a scary section of town. There are big casks of wine inside the warehouse, hence the name. This a pretty hip place in the Northern Portland area. They only do shows on Friday and Saturday nights but with the closing of X-Ray, this may become a more popular place to play.

Mark's Hawthorne Pub
3518 SE Hawthorne Blvd.
Portland OR 97215
503-233-1178
Capacity: 70
This club features low volume electric and acoustic shows.

Melody Ballroom
615 SE Alder
Portland OR 97214
503-232-2759
503-232-2759 Kathleen (bookings)
Capacity: 805
This venue does bigger shows every once in a while, but is not really a place for touring bands to play.

The Mount Tabor Pub
4811 SE Hawthorne
Portland OR 97215
503-238-1646
Capacity: 250
This place has a lot of potential, but people just don't seem to go there, yet. This could all change, however, as the number of clubs for rock and punk diminish and better bands begin to play there. Across the street from the Mount Tabor Pub is the highlight of the area, the infamous Space Room Lounge, located inside the Brite Spot Restaurant. This is a must see for any fan of cheap beer and 60s space decor.

Produce Row
204 SE Oak St.
Portland OR 97214
503-232-8355
Capacity: 50 on the patio
This venue features mainly acoustic but some electric bands. They have no PA, which is not convenient for touring bands, but they will give bands dinner and good free beer all night.

Roseland
8 NW Sixth Ave.
Portland OR 97209
503-224-7511
503-221-0288 Julie/Rick (bookings)
This is a big place that only opens to do particular shows such as a Lenny Kravitz or a big name country act. The shows happen every couple of months and they do an occasional eight band local bill, but this is not really a place you would be interested in playing.

Satyricon
125 NW Sixth Ave.
Portland OR 97209
503-243-2380
Ben
Capacity: 250
Located in the recently renovated old town, this club has again become a great place to play. They have expanded and opened a cafe next door where you can get cheap grub, and The **Sisters of the Road Cafe** is located on the other side of the bar. The Sisters Cafe has a $2 meal, done according to the theme for the day of the week, it could be Mexican food night or turkey and stuffing night, always the same price. Monday nights are easy nights to be booked, and they are good nights to play. It is new band night at the old Satyricon and there is really nothing else going on in the city that night, so its usually prety crowded, more so than a Tuesday or Wednesday.

White Eagle Cafe & Saloon
836 N. Russell
Portland OR 97227
503-282-6810
Capacity: 110
Blues and classic rock.

Press

Art Rag
Box 4966
Portland OR 97208
503-299-9798
Every 6-8 weeks arts newspaper
Not that frequent, but a decent paper.

The Oregonian
Daily
Marty Hugley
This is the major newspaper in Portland. Marty will review a lot of different stuff and in the Weekender section, which comes with the paper on Wednesdays or Thursdays there is a whole section for reviews and listings for shows.

Paperback Jukebox
1914 NW 24 Pl.
Portland OR 97210
503-243-6674
Arts newspaper
A big rock rag in Portland, they do reviews, interviews, live reviews, and listings.

PDXS
2305 NW Kearney
Portland OR 97210
503-224-7316
Biweekly arts & politics newspaper. This is the best rock rag in Portland for reviews, interviews and listings etc.

The Rocket
(see Seattle press)
The Rocket has a Portland edition that you can find anywhere in the city and they have a pretty thorough coverage of the local music happenings.

Snipe Hunt
PO Box 42416
Portland OR 97242
503-236-3138
Alternative quarterly newspaper Covers the northwest territory from San Francisco to Vancouver, and they are very thorough. They do endless reviews, more than 100 of all formats. The writers are said to be pretty good and not overly biased.

Two Louies
2745 NE 34th
Portland OR 97212
503-284-5931
Monthly music publication
This paper has decent distribution, and they do live reviews and listings. Send them a press release, but not a CD.

Willamette Week
822 SW 10th Ave.
Portland OR 97205
503-243-2122
Tim Casbeer
Weekly entertainment newspaper. This a very large paper, with a big circulation. They will list shows, review some albums, and review some shows. Send a bio and all that kind of stuff.

Radio

KBOO 90.7 fm
20 SE Eighth Ave.
Portland OR 97214
503-231-8032
Non-commercial rock, blues a good station, advertising for shows and possible opportunities for interviews.

KKEY 1150 am
PO Box 5757
Portland OR 97228
503-222-1150
Jazz, fusion, folk, blues

KLCC 104.1 fm
Lewis & Clark College
PO Box 122
Portland OR 97202
503-768-7133
College alternative, jazz
A good station, send them stuff. They sometimes will promote shows on campus in a cafe, but you need to bring a PA.

KRRC 107.5 fm
Reed College
3203 SE Woodstock Blvd.
Portland OR 97702
503-771-2180
College format
There is also a possibility of playing here. A typical college station with low wattage, but with a wide variety of music.

Record Stores

Crocodile Records
828 SW Park
Portland OR 97205
503-222-4773
CD, LP, CA, Video

Django Records
1111 SW Stark St.
Portland OR 97205
503-227-4381
CD, LP, CA, Video
recommeded

Locals Only
61 SW 2nd
Portland OR 97204
503-227-5000
CD, LP, CA, Video
Like the name says, they only carry music from Portland.

Music Millenium
3158 E Burnside
Portland OR 97214
503-231-8943
CD, LP, CA, Video
recommeded

The Ozone Records
1036 W Burnside St.
Portland OR 97209
503-226-0249
CD, LP, CD, Video
The best store for alternative music.

Second Ave. Records
418 SW Second Ave.
Portland OR 97204
503-222-3783
CD, LP, CA, Video

Tower Records
1307 NE 102 Ave.
Portland OR 97220
503-253-1314
CD, CA

Music Stores

12th Fret Guitar Shop
2402 SE Belmont
Portland OR 97214
503-231-1912
Guitar repairs; no rentals; guitars on consignment.

Apple Music
225 SW First Ave.
Portland OR 97204
503-226-0036
Electronics and guitar repairs; full-line of rentals and sales

Artichoke Music
3526 SE Hawthorne
Portland OR 97214
503-232-8845
Acoustic string repairs; no rentals; acoustic, string & percussion sales

Horseshoe Music
9220 SW Barbur Blvd., Ste 110
Portland OR 97219
503-245-8442
Drum repairs; no rentals; guitar & drum sales

Portland Music
125 NW Fifth Ave.
Portland OR 97209
503-226-3719
No repairs; full-line of rentals and sales

Portland Music 3rd Ave.
520 SW 3rd Ave.
Portland OR 97204
503-228-8437
Band instrument repairs & rentals; specialty acoustic instruments product line

Showcase Music and Sound, Inc.
3401 SE Hawthorne
Portland OR 97214
503-231-7027
Full-line of repairs & sales; concert equipment rentals

Food

Montage is open until 4:00am and there are always a lot of young folks hanging out. They come for the quality cheap cuisine. Order the Spicy Mac Pasta or the Cajun Potatoes. For a mere $2 you can get one of these delicious entrees along with an order of bread, and for an additional 75¢ have yourself a 16-ounce Ranier Beer. **Oasis Cafe** on Hawthorne has the best pizza in town, its cheap and sold by the slice. **The Hawthorne St. Cafe** on Hawthorne, excellent food and ask for Cabe, the man with blue hair and a bunch of tattoos. **The Baghdad Theatre**, is a combination brewery, pizza restaurant and movie theater. You can drink one of their fabulous beers, have a slice of pizza and sit down in their $1 movie and enjoy a fine film, all without stepping out into the rain.

Shelter

There is a youth hostel on Hawthorne. There are also plenty of cheap motels in Northeastern Portland, if you can't find someone with whom to stay.

Etc.

The parks and forest areas are a really great feature in the area. If you have time, take advantage of The Great Outdoors, go to one of the rivers, 84 east 40 min. from downtown and you are in the **Columbia River Gorge** where the windsurfing is the best in the country. **Saturday Market** under the Burnside bridge. Portland has an excellent rapid transit system, cheap and you can ride for free in the downtown area.

PENNSYLVANIA
Harrisburg
Venues

The Brewery
233 E Beaver Ave
State College, PA 16801
814-237-2892
Capacity: 270

Cafe 210
210 W College Ave.
State College PA 16801
814-237-3449
Capacity: 360
Rock, R&B, Alternative.

The Chameleon
223 N Water St.
Lancaster PA 17604
717-299-9684
Capacity: 600
Mostly alternative

Club Zee's/Gulliftys
1104 Carlisle Rd.
Camp Hill PA 17011
717-737-3469
Capacity: 350
Wide variety.

Crowbar
936 E College Ave
State College, PA 16801
814-237-0426
Capacity: 700
All styles

Metropolis
400 S Cameron St.
Harrisburg PA 17101
717-232-7000
717-232-7135 John (bookings)
Capacity: 1,000
One large and one smaller room.
Rock and alternative.

Midtown Tavern
1101 N 2nd St.
Harrisburg PA 17102
717-236-5783
Capacity: 250

The Vault
236 N 2nd St.
Harrisburg PA 17101
717-234-4930
Capacity: 650
Alternative

Press

Barfly Monthly
PO Box 5192
Lancaster PA 17606
717-293-9772
Monthly music & nightlife guide

The Patriot News
PO Box 2265
Harrisburg PA 17105
717-255-8159
Daily newspaper

Radio

WFNM
Franklin & Marshall University
Box 90
Lancaster PA 17604
717-291-4098
All styles

WPSU
Penn State University
202 James Bldg
University Park PA 16802
814-865-9191
All styles

Record Stores

3D Compact Discs
2081 Springwood Rd.
York, PA 17405
717-845-5285
In-store performances

Encore Books and Music
Hampten Center
Mechanicsburg PA 17055
717-761-2665
CD, CA

It's Only Rock & Roll
855 Market St.
Lemoyne PA 17043
717-737-6399
CD, LP, CA

Music Stores

BCR Music
902 Market St.
Lemoyne PA 17043
717-730-9775
Repairs; PA's & custom cabinet
rentals; full-line of PA products

THE DOUGHBOYS

Make: 1989 Ford Econoline 250
Color: White and Rusty
Purchase Price: Lease $450/month, finally paid off total about $23,000
Does it have a name? Nelly Bell
Mileage at Purchase: 20,000
Current Mileage: 160,000
Miles per gallon: 15
Number of people who tour in it: 7-8
The van runs on: Gas, oil, $1,000 and a visit to the dealer every fuckin' month!
The band runs on: P.O.s, sleep, sleep, sleep, smoke, coffee, sleep
Type of sound system: None. Why bother? Just another headache
Favorite thing to listen to: The new ALL record, then silence as everyone listens to their own shit on their walkmans.
Coolest thing about our van: No seats, just sleeping stacks. Big dents in rear from various trailer accidents. 2 gas tanks so when one runs out, flip a switch and on you go for another 2 to 3 hours! Oh joy!
The coolest thing we did to our van was: Break down after the trailer exploded on the highway during a snowstorm, only to have Venus Delight Miss Nude Universe rescue us with her huge van and trailer full of birds and snakes. She took us and our van to a hotel. We left what was left of the trailer at the side of the road and recovered most of our equipment from the highway and the ditch.
The suckiest thing about our van: Parking tickets, repair bills, huge dents, people wanting rides home after a show, strange whistling sound from rear of van (must be the holes made by the trailer when it fishtailed from side to side, slamming into the van's sides).
Is there anybody's van you'd trade it for? Yes. Any European mini-bus. They are so much better than any van in North America. They're designed for comfort and bigger than a van, but not a bus.
Other: Trailers suck. We've had three accidents with a trailer.

Dale's Drum Shop
4440 Fritchey St.
Harrisburg PA 17109
717-652-2466
Drums & hardware repair;
rentals; full-line of drum and
accessory sales

Market Street Music
13 E Main St.
Mechanicsburg PA 17055
717-691-9552
Repairs, rentals, sales

**Wray's Music House & Pro
Sound Center**
326 Market St.
Lemoyne PA 17043
717-761-8222
Repairs, rentals, sales

Philadelphia
Venues

The Barbary
955 Frankford Ave.
Philadelphia PA 19125
215-552-8971
Capacity: 150
Blues, rock, alternative.

The Barn
2000 Brown Ave.
Bensalem PA 19020
215-639-5590
Capacity: 1,400 (700 each floor)
Dance-rock, alternative.

Boot 'N' Saddle
1131 S Broad St.
Philadelphia PA 19147
215-336-1742
Capacity: 210
Country

Blue Water
735 S Columbus Blvd.
Philadelphia PA 19147
215-923-2500
Reggae, R&B, light rock
This outdoor club is located on
the Delaware River.

Doc Watson's
216 S 11th St.
Philadelphia PA 19107
215-922-3427
Capacity: 125
Acoustic, rock, alternative, blues.

Grape St Pub
105 Grape St
Philadelphia PA 19127
215-483-4890
Capacity: 165
Alternative

JC Dobbs
304 South St.
Philadelphia PA 19147
215-925-4053
215-925-6679 Kathy (bookings)
Capacity: 220
Rock, alternative. (Our sources
say they'll book just about
everything)

JJ's Grotto
27 S 21st St.
Philadelphia PA 19103
215-988-9255
Capacity: 85
Jazz, blues, all-ages, liquor
license, full menu.

Khyber Pass
56 South 2nd St.
Philadelphia PA 19106
215-440-9683
215-440-0932 David (bookings)
Alternative

Maggie's
624 N Front St.
Philadelphia PA 19123
215-592-1645
Mostly country, blues and rock.
Small club with a cool atmosphere.

The Middle East
126 Chestnut St
Philadelphia PA 19106
215-922-1003
Capacity: 450
Rock, metal, jazz

North Star Bar
27th & Poplar St.
Philadelphia PA 19130
215-235-7826
Blues, folk, alternative. This is
one of Philly's older clubs; it
has a cool eclectic vibe and will
also book acoustic acts and
poetry readings.

Ortlieb's Jazz Haus
847 N 3rd St.
Philadelphia PA 19123
215-922-1035
Capacity: 110
Jazz

Revival
22 S 3rd St.
Philadelphia PA 19106
215-627-4825
Capacity: 1,000
Mostly alternative, techno and
industrial.

Silk City
435 Spring Garden St.
Philadelphia PA 19123
215-592-8838
Capacity: 200
Rock, alternative, world.

TLA
334 South St.
Philadelphia PA 19147
215-922-1011
215-569-9400 Adam (bookings)
Capacity: 400 reserved, 700
general
All styles.

Tin Angel
20 S 2nd St.
Philadelphia PA 19106
215-928-0978
215-574-2900 Larry (bookings)
Capacity: 100
Acoustic

Trocadero
10th & Arch St.
Philadelphia PA 19147
215-923-7625
215-440-9685 Jo (bookings)
Capacity: 1,275
All styles.

Zanzibar Blue
301 S 11th St.
Philadelphia PA 19107
215-829-0300
Capacity: 60
Jazz

Press

The City Paper
Chancellor Building Mezzanine
206 S 13th St.
Philadelphia PA 19107
215-732-5542
Weekly newspaper

Daily News
400 N Broad St.
Philadelphia PA 19130
215-854-5960
Daily newspaper (except Sun.)

Gear
PO Box 747
Lansdowne PA 19050
610-284-7130
Monthly magazine

Inquirer
400 N Broad St.
Philadelphia PA 19130
215-854-4965
Daily & Sun newspaper

Magnet
1020 N Delaware Ave.
Philadelphia PA 19125
215-389-1559
Monthly magazine

Mapps
623 Spring St.
Bethlehem PA 18018
610-838-2295
Monthly magazine

Open Mike Monitor
3411 Tilden St.
Philadelphia PA 19129
215-848-5381
Monthly newsletter

Rockpile Magazine
PO Box 258
Jenkintown PA 19046
215-885-7625
Monthly magazine

Stain
702 N 5th St.
Philadelphia PA 19123
Steve Anderson
Fanzine

Street Buzz! Magazine
2533 W Willard St., Ste 203
Philadelphia PA 19129
215-602-2441
Bi-monthly

Underground Press
PO Box 11803
Philadelphia PA 19128
215-482-0890
Monthly magazine

The Welcomat
1701 Walnut
Philadelphia PA 19103
215-563-7400
Weekly newspaper

Radio

WKDU 91.7 fm
Drexel University
3210 Chestnut St.
Philadelphia PA 19104
215-895-2580/5920/5917
Free-form college programming

WMMR 93.3 fm
Independence Mall East
Philadelphia PA 19106
215-238-8000
Commercial and alternative

WRTI 90.1 fm
Temple Public Radio
Temple University
100 Annenburg Hall
Philadelphia PA 19122
215-204-8405
Blues, salsa, reggae, jazz

WXPN 88.5 fm
University of Pennsylvania
3905 Spruce St.
Philadelphia PA 19104
215-898-6677
Rock, blues, world, alternative

Record Stores

3rd Street Jazz and Rock
20 N 3rd St.
Philadelphia PA 19106
215-627-3366
CD, LP, CA, Video

Digital Underground
526 S 5th St.
Philadelphia PA 19147
215-925-5324
CD

Discovery Discs
3417 Spruce St.
Philadelphia PA 19104
215-573-5714
CD

Noise Pollution
619 S 4th St.
Philadelphia PA 19147
215-627-7246
CD, CA, LP

Philadelphia Record Exchange
608 S 5th St.
Philadelphia PA 19147
215-925-7892
CD, CA, LP

Plastic Fantastic
26 W Lancaster Ave.
Ardmore PA 19003
610-896-7625
CD, LP, CA

Record Cellar
6832 Bustleton Ave.
Philadelphia PA 19149
215-624-1650
CD, LP, CA, Video

Sounds of Market
16 S 11th
Philadelphia PA 19107
215-925-3150
CD, CA

Sound City USA
5709 Broad St.
Philadelphia PA 19141
215-424-0888
CD

Spruce Street Records
4004 Spruce St.
Philadelphia PA 19104
215-382-4554
CD, CA

Tower Records
610 South St.
Philadelphia PA 19147
215-574-9888
CD, CA

Music Stores

8th Street Music
1023 Arch St.
Philadelphia PA 19107
215-923-5040
Sales, rentals, repairs.

A-Z Music II
343 W Bridge St.
Morrisville PA 19067
215-295-1116
Sales, repairs, rentals

Bluebond Guitars
617 S 4th St.
Philadelphia PA 19147
215-829-1690
Guitar repairs and sales

Jerry's Guitar Shop
7704 Caster Ave.
Philadelphia PA 19152
215-742-6650
Guitar & amp repairs and sales

Music Museum
405 S Broad St.
Pitman NJ 08071
609-589-4318
Full-line of repairs and sales; PA and sound rentals

Robert Zatzman Music
8024 Germantown Ave.
Philadelphia PA 19118
215-247-5010
Rentals, repairs and sales

Zapf's Music Inc.
5429 N 5th St.
Philadelphia PA 19120
215-924-8736
Sales, repairs; band instrument rentals.

Food

Essene Natural Foods is a good vegetarian restaurant. Cheap restaurants: **Oregon Diner, Makam's Kitchen, Stolli's, Last Drop Coffeehouse.**

Etc.

Thrift Stores: **Something Blue** on 10th and Pine, **Time Zone** on South St.

Sightseeing:
Reading Terminal Market, Italian Market, Boot 'N Saddle (Italian Cowboy Club).

Pittsburgh
Venues

Bloomfield Bridge Tavern
4412 Liberty Ave
Pittsburgh, PA 15224
412-682-8611
Capacity: 100
Indie, hardcore and Polish eats

The Decade
223 Atwood St.
Pittsburgh PA 15213
412-682-1211/1258
Capacity: 350
Rock, R&B, some alternative

The Electric Banana
3887 Bigelow Blvd.
Pittsburgh PA 15213
412-884-4412
Capacity: 175
Alternative, reggae. Feisty management.

Graffiti
4615 Baum Blvd.
Pittsburgh PA 15213
412-682-4210
412-373-7693 Paul (bookings)
All styles.

Rosebud/Metropol
1600-1650 Smallman St.
Pittsburgh PA 15222
412-261-2221
Capacity: 400/1,200
Jazz, blues, world beat, spoken word.

Press

In Pittsburgh
PO Box 4286
Pittsburgh PA 15203
412-488-1212
Weekly newspaper

The Pittsburgh City Paper
1 Library Pl., Ste G-2
Duquesne PA 15110
412-560-2489
Weekly alternative newspaper

Pittsburgh Post Gazette
34 Boulevard of the Allies
Pittsburgh PA 15222
412-263-1100
Daily

Radio

WPTS 98.5 fm
University of Pittsburgh
411 William Pitt Union
Pittsburgh PA 15213
412-648-7990
Pop, commercial alternative, rock

WRCT 88.3 fm
Carnegie Mellon University
5020 Forbes Ave.
Pittsburgh PA 15213
412-621-9728
Jazz, rock, blues, rap, college alternative

WYEP 91.3 fm
PO Box 66, Woodland Rd.
Pittsburgh PA 15232
412-381-9900
Jazz, blues, pop alternative

Record Stores

Eide's
1111 Penn Ave.
Pittsburgh PA 15222
412-261-0900
CD, LP, CA, Video

Paul's CDs
4526 Liberty Ave.
Pittsburgh PA 15224
412-621-3256
CD

Record-Rama Sound Archives
4981 McKnight Rd.
Pittsburgh PA 15237
412-367-7330
CD

Music Stores

Pianos & Stuff
468 Freeport Rd.
Pittsburgh PA 15238
412-828-1003
Keyboard, guitar, and PA repairs & rentals

Pittsburgh Guitars
1409 E Carson St.
Pittsburgh PA 15203
412-431-0700
Used and new guitar and amp sales and repairs.

Food

Eat and Park - a chain restaurant and all of them are open 24 hours. **Ritter's Diner** on Baum Blvd. is close to some of the clubs. **Scotty's** on Penn Ave. is another good all night diner.

Etc.

Oakland is where the cultural hub of Pittsburgh currently resides. The universities and clubs are there, and so are a few museums. On the South Side, across the river, there are also a few cool clubs and restaurants.

RHODE ISLAND
Providence
Venues

AS220
11 Empire St.
Providence RI 02903
401-831-9327
Capacity: 125
This is an art complex that is home to a gallery, a space for theater and live music, and a group of artists who have homes and studios in the building. Avant garde rock or art rock bands may be able to play here, but the typical performer here is usually way off the beaten indie path.

CAV
14 Imperial Place
Providence RI 02903
401-751-9164
Capacity: 80 seated
Folk and world music is the mainstay at this upscale cafe. They like to book straight ahead folk musicians, but will have anything from Irish pipers to traditional Chinese folk. The scene here is rather eclectic, but will do some punk type bands. They are not, however, as willing to book national acts.

Chan's
267 Main St.
Woonsocket RI 02895
401-765-1900
Capacity: 125
This is a more sophisticated, classy jazz and blues bar.

Club Babyhead
73 Richmond St.
Providence RI 02903
401-421-1698, 751-4122
Capacity: 525
This is the most obvious place for indie bands to play. They feature punk, metal, rock and alternative. They also occasionally do all-ages shows.

Last Call Saloon
15 Elbow St.
Providence RI 02903
401-421-7170
Capacity: 375
All-ages on Sundays
This club does book indie rock, but likes to focus on traditional blues. This is a cool club.

The Living Room, Inc
23 Rathbone St.
Providence RI 02908
401-521-5200
Capacity:
This is the club in town where bands like the Talking Heads and Ramones used to play back in the early days of punk and new wave, before the big "alternative" takeover. They had been closed for four years, but have recently reopened (January of '94). It is an 18 and up venue and they definitely book indie bands.

Lupo's Heartbreak Hotel
239 Westminster St.
Providence RI 02893
401-831-4071, 272-5876
401-828-4889 Jack (bookings)
This club was also closed for a while, two years or so, but they have reopened and this is also a good place for indie bands to try to get a show. You can't beat the name.

The Met Cafe
130 Union St.
Providence RI 02893
401-861-2142
This place is next door to Lupo's, and is a cool club. They book anything from blues to gospel, from rock to folk. Indie bands are welcome here and they do some punk shows one or two nights per week.

Ocean Mist
895-A Matunuck Beach Rd.
Matunuck RI 02879
401-782-4799
Capacity: 550
This bar features mostly local bands, but is a good party place right on the beach.

The Strand
61 Washington St.
Providence RI 02903
401-272-8900
Capacity: 1,500+
It is possible to get opening slots here, this week they were featuring Edgar Winter and Bad Company.

Press

The Nice Paper
157 Clifford St.
Providence RI 02903
401-521-6211
Weekly entertainment paper
This publication came about when a number of people broke away from the other local arts paper because of employee relations problems, hence the name. This paper will definitely cover hip indie bands, doing listings and interviews.

The Providence Journal
75 Fountain St.
Providence RI 02902
401-277-7000
Daily

The Providence Phoenix
131 Washington St.
Providence RI 02903
401-273-6397
Weekly entertainment newspaper. A lot of the information in this paper comes from the Boston Phoenix, but this is also a good source for listings, etc.

Radio

WBRU 95.5 fm
Brown University
88 Benevolent St.
Providence RI 02906
401-272-9550
Blues, hip-hop, jazz, world.

WDOM 91.3 fm
Providence College
Providence RI 02918
401-865-2460
Urban contemporary, jazz, rock, heavy metal, alternative
A good station for indie music at this Catholic college. There is "rebellion" in the air here.

WRIU 90.3 fm
University of Rhode Island
326 Memorial Union
Kingston RI 02881
401-789-8390
Alternative, underground, jazz, metal, folk
This is the station to check out in the area for interviews and on-air performances.

WSMU 91.1 fm
University of Massachusetts - Dartmouth
285 Old Westport Rd.
North Dartmouth MA 02747
508-999-8149
Local, alternative, metal, reggae, urban
This station, although not in Providence, does cover the area. They play a lot of a good old-fashioned indie rock!

Record Stores

Fast Forward
5 Steeples St.
Providence RI 02903
401-272-8866
CD, LP, CA, Video
This store comes highly recommended

Goldy Compact Discs & Tapes
272 Thayer St.
Providence RI 02906
401-273-5666
CD, CA, Video

In Your Ear
297 Thayer St.
Providence RI 02906
401-861-1515
CD, LP, CA, Video
The best record store in the city.

Phoenix Discount Records
102 Waterman St.
Providence RI 02906
401-331-2620
LP,CD
This store carries mostly new and used jazz products.

'Round Again
278 Wickenden St.
Providence RI 02903
401-351-6292
Mostly used vinyl and used CDs and cassettes. (Try to sell back all those bad records that band members have been giving you, while they talk about how they should play with your band, in your town).

Tom's Trax
281 Thayer St.
Providence RI 02906
401-274-0820
CD, LP, CA, Video
Yes, another highly recommended store.

Rhode Island Records
759 N Main St.
Providence RI 02904
401-331-4533
Rap, R&B

Music Stores

Al Trombetti Music Center
2067 W Shore Rd.
Warwick RI 02889
401-739-0182
Amp & guitar repairs and rentals; band product sales

Al Drew's Music Center
526 Front St.
Woonsocket RI 02895
401-769-3552
Builds custom drum sets; they will do repairs, especially on drums. They "stock millions of parts."

Axelrod
2051 Weybosset Dr.
Providence RI 02903
401-421-4833

Hyde Music
706 Washington St.
Coventry RI 02816
401-823-1929
You can also pick up a fog machine here.

Luca Music
1530 Mineral Spring Ave.
North Providence RI 02904
401-353-3800
Repairs, rentals, sales. Recommended

Providence Music
67 Warren Ave.
East Providence RI 02914
401-722-5837
Repairs, rentals, sales

Rhode Island Music
70 Broad St.
Pawtucket RI 02860
401-725-7829
Recording service, rentals, repairs, sales

Ross Music
12543 Mineral Springs Ave.
North Providence RI 02904
401-726-8060

Twin City Music
489 1/2 Plainfield St.
Providence RI 02909
401-943-2622
Repairs, sales

Food

Thayer St. is the best place to go for late night eats. There are ten or so places of ethnic variety, and may of them are open late. **Wickenden St.** is another hub in Providence with a number of restaurants, there may be a couple of vegetarian places here. **Wes' Rib House** is open until 4am. It is located in the Olneyville section of Providence, and the wood fire burns all night, quite cozy.

Shelter

Downtown is not recommended, but there are a few hotel/motels on Route 95, 10 minutes south of Providence in Warwick.

Etc.

Take a drive to **Newport,** Rhode Island to see the beaches and mansions. This is a very cool place to hang out. It is an old seaport town, and is the place most people go when in the Providence area. Great seafood (try the clam cakes).

SOUTH CAROLINA
Charleston
Venues

Cumberland's
26 Cumberland St.
Charleston SC 29401
803-577-9469
Capacity: 300
Rock, Blues

The Music Farm
32 Ann St.
Charleston SC 29403
803-722-8904
Capacity: 850
All styles.

Sand Dollar
7 Center St.
Folly Beach SC 29439
803-588-9498
Capacity: 200
Mainly blues

The Windjammer
1000 Ocean Blvd.
Isle of Palms SC 29401
803-886-8596
Capacity: 750
Rock and reggae.

Press

Charleston's Free Time
PO Box 5144
N Charleston SC 29406
803-767-0123
Bi-weekly entertainment paper

The Up With Harold
334 E Bay St #164
Charleston SC 29401
803-577-5304
Bi-weekly newspaper

Radio

WAVF 96.1 fm
1964 Ashley River Rd
Charleston SC 29407
803-852-9003
Rock. Supports new artists, live on-air performances

Record Stores

Monkey Music
320 King St
Charleston SC 29401
803-723-7200
CD, CA

Music Stores

Fox Music
7643 Rivers Ave #H
Charleston SC 29418
803-572-7744
Repairs, rentals, sales
975 Savannah Hwy. location too

Precision Guitar Works
423 Coleman Bl
Mt Pleasant SC 29464
803-884-8597
Repairs, sales

Columbia
Venues

Alley Cats
362 Jacobs Rd.
Columbia SC 29210
803-731-0555
800-950-2263 Ed (bookings)
Rock

Annie's
1354 Rosewood Dr.
Columbia SC 29201
803-779-4933
Capacity: 400
All styles

Rockafella's
2112 Devine St.
Columbia SC 29205
803-252-7625
803-798-1733 Art (bookings)
Capacity: 300
Rock

Press

Columbia Star Reporter
716 Santee Ave.
Columbia SC 29205
803-771-0219
Weekly

Free Times
455 St. Andrews Rd.
Bldg D
Columbia SC 29210
803-798-5100
Biweekly arts & entertainment newspaper

GameCock
University of South Carolina
PO Box 85131
Columbia SC 29208
803-777-7726
Weekly newspaper

The Point
18 Bluff Rd.
Columbia SC 29201
803-254-1803
Monthly newspaper

The State
1401 Shop Rd.
Columbia SC 29201
803-771-6161
Daily

Radio

WUSC 90.5 fm
University of South Carolina
Drawer B
Columbia SC 29208
803-777-7172
Alternative

Record Stores

Manifest Discs & Tapes
(5 locations)
1563 Broad River Rd.
Columbia, SC 29210
803-798-2606
CD, CA, Video

Papa Jazz Records
2014 Green St.
Columbia SC 29205
803-256-0095
CD, LP, CA

Sounds Familiar
4420 Rosewood Extension
Columbia SC 29209
803-776-7208
CD, LP, CA

Vans OF THE STARS!

SISTER DOUBLE HAPPINESS

Make: 1993 Ford Econoline
Color: Spooge White
Van's Name: Mr. Shit
Purchase Price: Rental
Mileage at Purchase: 3,000
Current Mileage: 34,379
Miles per gallon: 18
Number of people who tour in it: 3 plus Danny's cat
The van runs on: Unleaded
The band runs on: Coffee and sugar
Stereo: Ford Delco radio and Miles' boom box
Favorite thing to listen to: Tube Bar tape with Red Flaming Lips, Nirvana, Jon Spencer Blues Explosion, Babes in Toyland, classical shit.
Coolest thing about our van: How bad it smells. Cracked windshield. The amount of floor space covered with garbage. Mogo bags hanging from mirror.
The coolest thing we did to our van was: The extra seat and security wall. Punch holes in roof. Put up pictures of the babe in Genitorturers.
The suckiest thing about our van: No tape deck. No CD player. No bar. No car phone.
Is there anybody's van you'd trade it for? Bomb's van.
Anything else? Other than the deer horns mounted on the front, no.

TENNESSEE
Knoxville
Venues

Bijou Theater
803 S Gay St
Knoxville TN 37902
615-522-0832
Capacity: 750
All styles

Gryphon's
2003 Highland Ave
Knoxville TN 37916
615-524-6996
Capacity: 80
All styles

Flamingo's
1836 Cumberland Ave.
Knoxville TN
615-546-0404
Capacity: 500
Mainly alternative.

The Library
1910 Cumberland Ave.
Knoxville TN
615-546-0066
Capacity: 250
Alternative

Manhattan's
101 S Central St
Knoxville TN 37902
615-525-4463
Capacity: 180
Rock, jazz, country

The Mercury Theatre
28 Market St.
Knoxville TN
615-637-8634
Capacity: 175
Alternative, blues, country

Press

The Daily Beacon
U of Tennessee, Knoxville
#5 Communications Bldg
Knoxville TN 37996-0314
615-974-5195
College news, will review demos.

Knoxville News-Sentinel
PO Box 59038
Knoxville TN 37950-9038
615-521-1824
Daily newspaper

Metropulse
505 Market St. #300
Knoxville TN 37902
615-522-5399
Weekly entertainment. Will review

Radio

WUTK
University of Tennessee
P103 Andy Holt Tower
Knoxville TN 37996
615-974-6897
Alternative, rock

Record Stores

Underdog Records
1705 Cumberland Ave.
Knoxville TN
615-673-8282

Music Stores

Joe Morrell Music
2306 W State St
Bristol TN 37620
615-764-2171
Sales, repairs, rentals

Rob Payne's Music Center
8078 Kingston Pike
Knoxville, TN 37919
615-531-1988
Repairs, sales

Etc.

There are lots of little thrift stores and pawn shops scattered around Knoxville; for serious searching try **Amvets** on Holston Dr. **Cumberland Ave.** near the University of Tennessee is a good hangout area with fast food and just some decent turf to walk around. **Pluto Sports** (1723 Cumberland) is the place for skateboarders. For good joe, try the **Java** coffeehouse in Knoxville Old City.

Memphis
Venues

616 Club
600 Marshall St.
Memphis TN 38103
901-526-6552
Capacity: 800
College rock, alternative

Antenna Club
1588 Madison Ave.
Memphis TN 38104
901-276-4052
Capacity: 350-400
Mostly alternative, but sometimes ethnic and world music.

Barrister's
147 Jefferson Plaza #103
Memphis TN 38103
901-523-9421
Capacity: 200
All styles

B.B. King's Blues Club
143 Beale St.
Memphis TN 38103
901-524-5464
Capacity: 400
Blues and R&B

Huey's
1927 Madison Ave.
Memphis TN 38104
901-726-4372
Capacity: 100
Jazz and R&B

Newby's
539 S Highland
Memphis TN 38111
901-452-8408
Capacity: 500
All styles

New Daisy Theatre
330 Beale St.
Memphis TN 38103
901-525-8981
Capacity: 800
All styles

Oasis
567 S Highland
Memphis TN 38111
901-327-1080
Capacity: 300
Alternative and indie

Rum Boogie Cafe
182 Beale St.
Memphis TN 38103
901-528-0150
Capacity: 250
Blues and R&B

Shooter's
4293 Fayette Rd.
Memphis TN 38128
901-388-4135
Capacity: 600
Country and Southern rock

The Stage Stop
2951 Cela Ln
Memphis TN 38128
901-382-1576
Capacity: 300
Rock

Press

Memphis Commercial Appeal
495 Union Ave.
Memphis TN 38103
Daily

The Memphis Flyer
460 Tennessee St.
Memphis TN 38101
901-521-9000
Weekly news & entertainment

Shake Rattle & Roll
1725 B Madison Ave., Ste3
Memphis TN 38104
901-276-1770
Monthly music & entertainment

Radio

WEVL 89.2
PO Box 40952
Memphis TN 38174
901-528-0560
All styles

Record Stores

Audiomania
1698 Madison Ave.
Memphis TN 38104
901-278-1166
CD, LP, CA, Video

Boss Ugly Bob's Records
726 E McLemore Ave.
Memphis TN 38106
901-774-6400

Cat's Compact Discs
3249 Austin Peay Hwy
Memphis TN 38128
901-385-2287
CD, LP, CA, Video

Cheap Skates
1576 Getwell Rd.
Memphis TN 38111
901-744-1312
CD, LP, CA, Video

Pop Lar Tunes
308 Poplar Ave.
Memphis TN 38103
901-525-6348
CD, LP, CA, Video

Shangri-La
1916 Madison Ave.
Memphis TN 38104
901-274-1916
CD, LP, 7"
Cool store and record label.

Music Stores

Colie Stoltz Music Co
2766 Broad Ave.
Memphis TN 38112
901-323-2263
Sales, repairs & rentals.

Consignment Music
3952 Park Ave.
Memphis TN 38111
901-458-2094
Repairs, sales

Pro Audio
2012 Madison Ave.
Memphis TN 38104
901-278-6000
Sales, repairs, rentals

Strings 'n' Things
1492 Union Ave.
Memphis TN 38104
901-278-0500
Repairs, sales

Yarbrough's Music
741 N White Station
Memphis TN 38122
901-761-0414
Repairs, rentals, and sales

Etc.
Graceland.

Nashville
Venues

12th & Porter Playroom
114 12th Ave. N
Nashville TN 37203
615-254-7236
Capacity: 200
All styles

328 Performance Hall
328 4th Ave. S
Nashville TN 37201
615-259-3288
615-256-6151 Steve (bookings)
Capacity: 1,200
Rock, country, jazz

The Ace of Clubs
114 2nd Ave. S
Nashville TN 37201
615-254-2237
615-244-5862 Bob (bookings)
Capacity: 300
Rock, roots and R&B

The Bluebird Cafe
4104 Hillsboro Rd.
Nashville TN 37215
615-383-1461
Capacity: 150
Country, acoustic, rock, jazz

Club Mere Bulles
152 Second Ave. North
Nashville TN 37201
615-256-CLUB
Capacity: 350
Mostly Blues

Douglas Corner Cafe
2106 Eighth Ave. S
Nashville TN 37204
615-298-1688
Capacity: 200
Country, pop, and blues.

Mainstreet
527 Main St.
Murfreesboro TN 37129
615-890-7820
Capacity: 500
All styles.

The Station Inn
402 12th Ave. S
Nashville TN 37203
615-255-3307
Capacity: 125
Bluegrass, acoustic folk

The Sutler
2608 Franklin Rd.
Nashville TN 37204
615-297-9195
Capacity: 110
Mainly blues

Press

The Metropolitan Times
939 Jefferson
Nashville TN 37208
615-254-5176
Weekly black community
newspaper

Nashville Banner
1100 Broadway
Nashville TN 37203
Daily

The Nashville Scene
209 10th Ave., Ste 222
Nashville TN 37203
615-244-7989
Weekly alternative entertainment
newspaper

The Tennessean
1100 Broadway
Nashville TN 37203
615-259-8000
Daily newspaper

Radio

WFSK 88.1 fm
Fisk University
1000 17th Ave. N
Nashville TN 37208
615-329-8754
College format

WMOT 89.5 fm
Middle Tennessee State
University, PO Box 3
Murfreesboro TN 37132
615-898-2800
Jazz

WRLT 100.1 fm
131 2nd Ave. N
Nashville TN 37201
615-242-5600
Commercial alternative

WRVU 91.1 fm
Vanderbilt University
PO Box 9100, Station B
Nashville TN 37235
615-322-3691
All styles

Record Stores

The Great Escape
1925 Broadway
Nashville TN 37203
615-327-0646
CD, LP, CA

Lucy's Record Shop
1707 Church St.
Nashville TN 37203
615-321-0882
CD, LP, CA, 7"

The Sound Shop
1000 Two Mile Pkwy
Goodlettsville TN 37072
615-859-0850
CD, LP, CA, Video

Music Stores

The Classic Ax
1024 16th Ave. S, Ste 203
Nashville TN 37212
615-254-8058
Acoustic repairs, sales.

Corner Music
2705 12th Ave. S
Nashville TN 37204
615-297-9559
Sales, repairs, rentals

Gruhn Guitars
400 Broadway
Nashville TN 37203
615-256-2033
Renown vintage guitar store. No
repairs or rentals.

Rock Block Guitars
2113 Elliston Pl.
Nashville TN 37203
615-321-0317
Sales, repairs, rentals

TEXAS
Austin
Venues

311
311 E 6th
Austin TX 78701
512-477-1630
Capacity: 250
Rock, blues

Antone's Blues Club
2915 Guadalupe St.
Austin TX 78705
512-474-5314
Capacity: 400
"Home of the Blues," R&B, rock

The Austin Outhouse
3510 Guadaloupe
Austin TX 78705
512-451-2266
Capacity: 50-75
Folk, acoustic, rock, alternative

Back Room
2015 E Riverside Dr
Austin TX 78741
512-441-4677
512-441-5838 Mark (bookings)
Capacity: 1,000
Hard rock, alternative

Broken Spoke
3201 S Lamar
Austin TX 78704
512-442-6189
Capacity: 661
Country

Cactus Cafe
Texas Union (on UT campus)
24th & Guadalupe
Austin TX 78713
512-471-8228
Capacity: 160
Acoustic

Chances
900 Red River
Austin TX 78701
512-451-7740
Capacity: 500
Alternative, acoustic and rock

Chicago House
607 Trinity
Austin TX 78701
512-473-2542
Capacity: 300
Acoustic folk

Continental Club
1315 S Congress Ave.
Austin TX 78704
512-441-2444
Capacity: 200
Rock, roots and country rock

Electric Lounge
302 Bowie St.
Austin TX 78703
512-476-3873
Capacity: 200
Alternative
A highly recommended place to
play for touring indie bands.

The Elephant Room
315 Congress
Austin TX 78701
512-473-2279
512-477-7777
Capacity: 125
Jazz

Emo's
603 Red River
Austin TX 78701
512-477-EMOS
Capacity: 200 inside/out
A great Alternative venue. Good
management, sound, and there's
rarely a cover.

Headliners East
406 E 6th St.
Austin TX 78701
512-478-3844
512-454-1135
Capacity: 200 down, 150
upstairs
Country, R&B, and blues.

Hole in the Wall
2538 Guadaloupe
Austin TX 78705
512-472-5599
Capacity: 191
All styles

Joe's Generic Bar
315 E Sixth St.
Austin TX 78701
512-480-0171
Capacity: 200
Blues

Liberty Lunch
405 W Second St.
Austin TX 78701
512-477-0461
512-476-7165 (bookings)
Fax: 512-476-1804
Capacity: 1,000+
All styles

The Lumberyard
16511 Bratton Ln
Austin TX 78728
512-255-4073
Capacity:, 1,000
Country

Maggie Mae's
512 Trinity
Austin TX 78701
512-478-8562
512-453-7256 Charlie (bookings)
Pop, country, folk, R & B

Pearl V's Oyster Bar
9033 Research Blvd.
Austin TX 78758
512-339-7444
Capacity: 250-300
R&B, blues, rock, jazz

Saxon Pub
1320 S Lamar
Austin TX 78704
512-448-2552
Capacity: 200
Country, acoustic, bluegrass,
soul

Scholz Garden
1607 San Jacinto
Austin TX 78701
512-477-4171
Capacity: 500 outside in beer
garden, 400 inside
Folk, rock, and country

Steamboat
403 E 6th St.
Austin TX 78701
512-478-2913
512-440-1949 Danny (bookings)
Capacity: 600
All styles

Top of the Marc
618 W 6th St.
Austin TX 78701
512-472-9849
512-472-8402 Doug (bookings)
Capacity: 250
Classic rock, jazz, blues, R&B

Waterloo Icehouse
600 N Lamar
Austin TX 78703
512-451-5245
Capacity: 140
Acoustic, country and rockabilly

La Zona Rosa
612 W 4th St.
(corner of 4th & Rio Grande)
Austin TX 78701
512-482-0662
Capacity: 250 inside, 1,300
outside
Folk, zydeco

Press

Austin American Statesman
305 S Congress
Austin TX 78704
512-445-3610
Daily newspaper

Austin Chronicle
PO Box 49066
Austin TX 78765
512-454-5766
Weekly newspaper

The Daily Texan
University of Texas
PO Box D
Austin TX 78713
512-471-4591
Daily newspaper

Music City Texas
1002 S First St.
Austin TX 78704
512-444-0693
Monthly magazine

Pop Culture Press
PO Box 43022
Austin TX 78745
512-445-3208
Quarterly music newspaper

Texas Beat
PO Box 4429
Austin TX 78765
512-441-2422
Monthly entertainment & music
mag

Radio

KAZI 88.7 fm
8906 Wall St., Ste 202
Austin TX 78754
512-836-9544
R&B, reggae, gospel, blues, jazz

KGSR 107.1 fm
505 Barton Springs Rd.,
Ste 700
Austin TX 78704
512-472-1071
Commercial adult alternative

KOOP 91.7 fm
505 San Jacinto
Austin TX 78701
512-472-1369
Mixed alternative format.
Frequency shared with KVRX.

KUT 90.5 fm
University of Texas
The Center for
Telecommunication Services
Austin TX 78712
512-471-6395
Mixed alternative

KVRX 91.7 fm
University of Texas, Austin
PO Box D
Austin TX 78713-7209
512-471-5106, 471-1576
All styles
Will do interviews and on-air
performances for indie touring
bands.

Record Stores

Antone's Record Store
2928 Guadalupe
Austin TX 78705
512-322-0660
CD, LP, CA

Inner Sanctum Records
504 W 24th
Austin TX 78705
512-472-9459
LP, CA

Musicmania
3909-D N H-35 #1
Austin TX 78722
512-451-3361
CD, LP, CA, Video

Sound Exchange
2100 A Guadalupe
Austin TX 78705
512-476-8742
CD, LP, CA, Video
Recommended.

Tower Records
2402 Guadalupe
Austin TX 78705
512-478-5711
CD, LP, CA, Video

Waterloo
600 A Lamar
Austin TX 78703
512-474-2500
CD, LP, CA, Video
Recommended.

Music Stores

Guitar Resurrection
3004 Guadalupe
Austin TX 78705
512-478-0095
Repairs, sales.

Mark Erlewine Guitars
4402 Burnet Rd
Austin TX 78705
512-472-4859
Sales and repairs.

Musical Exchange
123 E North Loop Blvd.
Austin TX 78751
512-451-8512
Repairs, sales.

Musicmakers Austin
517B S Lamar
Austin TX 78704
512-444-6686
Sales, repairs, rentals

South Austin Music
1402 S Lamar
Austin TX 78704
512-448-4992
Repairs, sales.

Strait Music
805 W. 5th St.
Austin TX 78703
512-476-6927

Food

El Azteca is a good Mexican restaurant located at 2600 E. 7th St., 512-477-4701. **Magnolia Cafe** is at 1920 S. Congress, 512-445-0000, it's a late night hangout, with great breakfast and plenty of vegetarian cuisine. **Hut's Hamburgers** (they have vegetarian burgers as well) is at 807 W. 6th St., 472-0693.

Shelter

Motel 6 at 2707 S. Hwy 35, 512-444-5882. **Live Oak Inn** at 2900 S. Congress, 512-441-0252. **Stars Inn** at 3105 N. Hwy 35, Exit 236 A, 32nd St., 1-800-725-ROOM.

Etc.

Lucy in Disguise has vintage clothing at 1506 S. Congress, 444-2002. **Room Service** has vintage clothes and furniture (we're sure you have space for a nice antique chair in the back of that huge van you're in) at 107 E. North Loop, 451-1057. Three good brew pubs are **Waterloo**, **Bitter End** and **Armadillo**.

Dallas Fort Worth
Venues

Bar of Soap
3615 Parry Ave.
Dallas TX 75226
214-823-6617
Capacity: 150
A laundromat and bar where you must be 21+ to play and do your laundry.

Blue Cat Blues Club
2617 Commerce St.
Dallas TX 75226
214-744-2293
Capacity: 250
Chicago-style blues bar.

Club Clearview
2803 Main St.
Dallas TX 75226
214-939-0222
Capacity: 550
Alternative, industrial

Club Dada
2720 Elm St.
Dallas TX 75226
214-744-3232
Capacity: 450 outside, 250 in
Alternative

Dallas City Limits
10530 Spangler Rd.
Dallas TX 75220
214-869-3582
Capacity: 1,200
Metal, hard rock

Deep Ellum Live
2727 Canton at Croweus
Dallas TX 75226
214-748-6222
Capacity: 1,000
Alternative

Galaxy Club
2820 Main
Dallas TX 75226
214-742-2582
Capacity: 500
Rock, alternative

J+J Blues Bar
937 Woodward
Fort Worth TX 76107
817-870-2337
817-346-2612 Dave (bookings)
R&B, rock

Orbit Room
2809 Commerce
Dallas TX 75226
214-748-5399
Capacity: 600
Alternative

The Pig & Whistle Pub
5731 Locke Ave.
Ft Worth TX 76107
817-731-4938
817-551-1143 Jo (bookings)
Capacity: 200+
Acoustic, rock, folk, Celtic

The Stone Pony
5627 Dyer St.
Dallas TX 75206
214-890-0944
214-363-2263 Doug (bookings)
Alternative

Rodeo Exchange
221 W Exchange
Fort Worth TX 76106
817-626-0181
Capacity: 450
Country, rock

Royal Rack
1906 Greenville
Dallas TX 75206
214-824-9733
Capacity: 200
Reggae

The Top Rail
2110 W Northwest Hwy
Dallas TX 75220
214-556-0797
Capacity: 550
Country, some pop and top 40

Trees
2709 Elm St.
Dallas TX 75226
214-748-5014
214-368-2263 Doug (bookings)
Capacity: 650
All styles

White Elephant Saloon
106 E Exchange Ave.
Ft Worth TX 76106
817-624-1887
817-624-8241 Joe (bookings)
Country

Press

Buddy Magazine
11258 Goodnight Ln Ste 102
Dallas TX 75229
214-484-9010
Monthly music magazine

Dallas Morning News
PO Box 655237
Dallas TX 75265
214-977-8222
Daily newspaper

The Dallas Observer
2130 Commerce St.
Dallas TX 75201
214-757-9000
Weekly arts & entertainment
paper

Jam Magazine
P.O. Box 2186
Mesquite TX 75185
214-329-2241
Monthly music magazine

Li'l Rhino Gazette
PO Box 14139
Arlington TX 76094
817-261-9813
Quarterly music magazine

U-Turn
8662 Glen Hollow
Fort Worth TX 76179
817-236-0044
Josh Robertson
Monthly music magazine
This publication features record
reviews, live reviews, and
interviews. This is a very good
source in the Dallas/Fort Worth
area, and we definitely recommend sending your material.

Radio

KDGE 94.5 fm "The Edge"
1320 Greenway Dr, #700
Irving TX 75038
214-770-7777
Alternative rock, pop

KERA 90.1 fm
3000 Harry Hines Blvd.
Dallas TX 75201
214-871-1390
Adult acoustic, alternative

KNON 89.3 fm
PO Box 710909
Dallas TX 75371
214-824-6893
Most styles

KNTU 88.1 fm
University of North Texas
PO Box 13585
Denton TX 76203
817-565-3459
Jazz, blues, all Texas music

WTCU 88.7 fm
PO Box 30793
Fortworth TX 76129
817-921-7631
Fax: 817-921-7634
They have specialty shows

Record Stores

Bill's Records
8118 Spring Valley Rd.
Dallas TX 75240
214-234-1496
CD, LP, CA, Video

Direct Hit Records
3609 Parry Ave.
Dallas TX 75226
214-826-8222/826-5222
CD, LP, CA, 7", Video

Fourteen Records
2913 Greenville Ave.
Dallas TX 75206
214-821-1470
CD, LP, CA, Video

Last Beat Records
2639 A Elm St.
Dallas TX 75226
214-748-5600
CD, LP, CA, Video

Offbeat Records
1100 W Arkansas Ste 810
Arlington TX 76013
817-795-5591
CD, CA, LP, 7"

Pagan Rhythms
5409 Greenville Ave.
Dallas TX 75206
214-739-6331
CD, LP, CA

RPM
1900 Oates Dr Ste 200
Mesquite TX 75150
214-681-8441
CD, CA, LP

VVV
3906 Cedar Springs
Dallas TX 75219
214-522-3470
CD, CA, LP, 7"

Food

Cheap: **Black Eyed Pea** and
Waffle House can be found in
various locations around the
city. Vegetarian: **Cosmic Cup** on
Oaklawn Ave. in Dallas, 214-
521-6127. 24-hour: South
Pancake House on University
Ave. in Fort Worth, 817-336-
0311; **Taco Cabana** can be found
in various locations around the
greater Dallas/Fort Worth area.

Shelter

Days Inn on Mockingbird at
Lovefield Airport in Dallas.

Etc.

The Grassy Knoll (site of JFK's
untimely death). Downtown Fort
Worth is pleasant; nearby
stockyards add that old-west
charm.

Houston
Venues

The Abyss
5913 Washington
Houston TX
713-863-7173

Emo's
2700 Albany Ste 101
Houston TX 77006
Capacity: 200 inside, a lot
outside
713-523-8503
18 and up
Alternative

Fitzgerald's
2706 White Oak Dr
Houston TX 77007
713-862-3838
Capacity: 600
Alternative, rock

Hurricane Alley
13331 Kuykendahl St. Ste 200
Houston TX 77090
713-875-3330
Capacity: 800
Alternative, metal, various styles

Mary Jane's
4216 Washington
Houston TX 77007
713-869-5263
Capacity: 150
Mostly alternative

McGonigel's Muckyduck
2425 Norfolk
Houston TX 77098
713-528-5999
Capacity: 170
Blues, folk, bluegrass, rock

Urban Art Bar
2801 Brozos
Houston TX 77006
713-526-8588
Capacity: 350
Mostly Alternative. This club is
in the process of changing its
name and location, call for info.

Rudyard's Pub
2010 Waugh Dr
Houston TX 77006
713-521-0521
Capacity: 150
Jazz & rock

Press

The Daily Cougar
U of Houston
Rm #151 Communications
Houston TX 77204-4071
713-743-5302
Daily, Fall and Spring, biweekly,
Summer semester

Houston Chronicle
801 Texas Ave.
Houston TX 77002
713-220-7171
Daily newspaper

The Houston Press
2000 W Loop S, Ste 1900
Houston TX 77027
713-624-1400
Weekly news & entertainment

Music News Magazine
1506 Pearl
League City TX 77573
713-480-6397
Monthly music magazine

Public News
1540 W Alabama
Houston TX 77006
713-520-1520
Alternative newsweekly

Radio

KPFT 90.1 fm
419 Lovett Blvd.
Houston TX 77006
713-526-4000
Various styles

KTRU 91.7 fm
Rice University
PO Box 1892
Houston TX 77251
713-527-4098
All styles

KTSU 90.9 fm
Texas Southern University
3100 Cleburne
Houston TX 77004
713-527-7591
Jazz, R&B, rap, reggae, gospel,
oldies

Record Stores

Cactus Music & Video
2930 S Shepherd
Houston TX 77098
713-526-9272
CD, LP, CA, 7"

Sound Exchange
1718 Westheimer
Houston TX 77098
713-666-5555
CD, LP, CA, Video
Recommended

Sound Plus
1403 Westheimer Rd.
Houston TX 77006
713-520-7323
CD, CA

Sound Revolution
850 FM 1960 W, Ste 1
Houston TX 77090
713-444-5454
CD, LP, CA, Video

Vinyl Edge Records
13171 Veterans Memorial Dr
Houston TX 77014
713-537-2575
CD, LP, CA, Video

Music Stores

Evans Music City
6240 Westheimer
Houston TX 77057
713-781-2100
Repairs, rentals, sales

H & H Music
11522 Old Katy Rd.
Houston TX 77043
713-531-9222
Repairs, rentals, and sales

L.D. Systems
483 W 38th St.
Houston TX 77018
713-695-9400
Repairs, rentals, sales

Lone Star Guitar
1212 College
S Houston TX 77587
713-946-8120
Repairs, rentals, sales

Parker Music
9941 N Freeway
Houston TX 77037
713-820-0021
Repairs and sales

Rockin Robin Guitars & Music
3619 S Shepherd
Houston TX 77098
713-529-5442
Repairs, rentals

Food

Montrose, West of Downtown, **Brazil Empire Cafe, Moveable Feast** on Alabama.

Shelter

Motels on Main St. near the Astrodome and Medical Center.

Etc.

Don't go to the **Galleria** or **NASA**. NASA is boring and filled with obnoxious kids and tourists, and the Galleria is too expensive for you anyway. **Astro World** is a cool amusement park. **Galveston Beach** is about 45 minutes away and a nice beach spot. It is too hot in the summer in Houston to do anything. "The best thing to do is stay inside until dark, and then go outside and get drunk." -Bliss Blood.

San Antonio
Venues

Billy Blues
330 E Grayson
San Antonio TX 78215
210-225-7409
Capacity: 200
All styles

Rocky's
13307-A San Pedro Ave
San Antonio TX 78216
210-402-0760
Capacity: 750
Hard rock, metal, alternative

Taco Land
103 W Grayson
San Antonio TX 78212
Capacity: 100
Alternative

Press

San Antonio Current
8750 Tesoro #1
San Antonio TX 78217
210-828-7660
Weekly arts and entertainment

San Antonio Express-News
PO Box 2171
San Antonio TX 78297-2171
210-225-7411
Daily newspaper

Radio

KSYM 90.1 fm
1300 San Pedro Ave
San Antonio TX 78212-4299
210-733-2787
All styles

Record Stores

Eclipse Records
6557 San Pedro
San Antonio TX 78216
210-344-0093
Specialties include alternative, house, industrial, pop.

Hogwild Records & Tapes
1824 N Main St
San Antonio TX 78212
210-733-5354
Alternative and underground

Music Stores

Alamo Music Center
425 N Main Ave
San Antonio TX 78205
210-224-1010
Full-line Repairs, Rentals, Products.

UTAH
Salt Lake City
Park City
Ogden
Venues

The Bar & Grill
60 E 800 S
Salt Lake City UT 84111
801-533-0341/0340
Capacity: 250
Alternative, college crowd

The Black Pearl
350 Main St.
Park City UT 84060
801-649-3140
Capacity: 350
Blues, rock

Charley's Club
2827 So State
Salt Lake City UT 84115
801-483-9167
Capacity: 250
Country, rock

Cinema Bar
45 W Broadway
Salt Lake City UT 84101
801-359-1200
Capacity: 250
Alternative

Cisero's
306 Main St.
Park City UT 84060
801-649-6800
Capacity: 125
Rock, blues

The Dead Goat Saloon
165 SW Temple
Salt Lake City UT 84101
801-328-4628
Capacity: 175
Blues, reggae, rock

The Gray Moose Pub
2327 Grant
Ogden UT 84401
801-399-0553
Capacity: 225
Blues, reggae, Top 40

The Green Parrot
155 W 200 S
Salt Lake City UT 84101
801-363-3201
Capacity: 350
All styles

The Holy Cow
241 S 500 E
Salt Lake City, UT 84102
801-359-5905
Capacity: 250
Alternative

Rafters
485 W 4800 So
Murray UT 84123
801-262-4149
Capacity: 400
Heavy metal/hard rock

The Westerner
3360 S Redwood Rd.
W Valley City UT 84120
801-972-5447
Capacity: 1,200
Country

Zephyr Club
301 SW Temple
Salt Lake City UT 84101
801-355-5646
Capacity: 350
All styles

Press

Blastin'
868 1/2 E. 1300 South
Salt Lake City UT 84105
801-467-4742
Monthly music publication

Catalyst Magazine
140 S McClelland
Salt Lake City UT 84102
801-363-1505
Monthly alternative newspaper

Daily Universe
Brigham Young University
538 ELWC
Provo UT 84602
801-378-2957
Daily newspaper

The Event Newspaper
1800 SW Temple, Ste 205
Salt Lake City UT 84115
801-359-4117
Twice a month arts newspaper

The Private Eye
68 W 400 S
Salt Lake City UT 84101
801-575-7003
Weekly alternative newspaper

Slug Magazine
2120 S 700th E #H200
Salt Lake City UT 84106
801-487-9221
Monthly alternative music zine.
Will review.

Radio

KRCL 90.9 fm
208 W 800 So
Salt Lake City UT 84101
801-363-1818
College alternative, metal, blues,
world, folk

KUER 90.1 fm
University of Utah
103 Kingsbury Hall
Salt Lake City UT 84112
801-581-6625
Jazz, classical, gospel

KXRK 96.1 fm
165 SW Temple, Ste 202
Salt Lake City UT 84101
801-364-9601
Commercial alternative

Record Stores

Audio Works
149 E 2nd S
Salt Lake City UT 84111
801-364-9999
CD

Gray Whale CD
248 S 1300 E
Salt Lake City UT 84102
801-583-3333
CD, CA, Video

The Heavy Metal Shop
1074 E 2100 S
Salt Lake City UT 84106
801-467-7071
CD, LP, CA, Video

Raspberry Records
4862 Highland Dr
Salt Lake City UT 84117
801-278-4629
CD, CA

Raunch Records
1121 Wilmington Ave.
Salt Lake City UT 84106
801-484-3778
CD, LP, CA, Video

Smokey's Records
1515 S 15th E
Salt Lake City UT 84105
801-486-8709
CD, CA, Video

Music Stores

The Music Factory
4850 S Redwood Rd.
Salt Lake City UT 84123
801-965-8811
Sales, repairs, rentals

Progressive Music
342 E 300 S
Salt Lake City UT 84111
801-364-4353
Sales, repairs, rentals

Wagstaff Music Co
206 E 6400 S
Murray UT 84107
801-261-4555
Repairs, sales

Woolf Music
434 E. S Temple, Ste 2
Salt Lake City UT 84111
801-359-1327
Instrument repairs, custom
guitar sales

VERMONT
Burlington
Venues

Club Metronome
188 Main St.
Burlington VT 05401
802-865-4563
Capacity: 300
Alternative, reggae

Club Toast
165 Church St
BUrlington VT 05401
802-660-2088
Capacity: 500
Alternative, punk

Press

Burlington Free Press
191 College St
Burlington VT 05401
802-863-3441
Daily newspaper

The Vermont Cynic
U of Vermont
Billings Student Center
Burlington VT 05405-0040
802-656-4413
Weekly college newspaper

Vox
PO Box 940
Shelburne, VT 05482
802-985-2400
Weekly news and arts. Will
review.

Radio

WEQX 102.7 fm
PO Box 1027
Manchester VT 05254
802-362-4800
Alternative

WRUV 90.1 fm
U of Vermont
Billings Student Center
BUrlington, VT 05405
802-656-0796
Alternative and demos.

Record Stores

Pure Pop Records
115 S Winooski Ave
Burlington VT 05401
802-658-2652
CD, CA

Sound Barrier
52-54 Center St
Rutland VT 05701
802-775-4754
CD, CA, LP, indie and alternative

Sound Effects
14 Church St
Burlington VT 05401
802-660-8080
CD, CA, T-shirts, Video

Music Stores

Advance Music Center
75 Maple St
Burlington VT 05401
802-863-8652
Full-line repairs and products;
PA rentals

Calliope Music
202 Main St
Burlington, VT 05401
802-863-4613
Sales, repairs, rentals

VIRGINIA
Richmond
Venues

Farmers Market Inn
1707 E Franklin St
Richmond VA 23223
804-344-8145
Capacity: 166
Blues and R&B.

Flood Zone
11 S 18th St.
Richmond VA 23223
804-782-0180
804-643-6006 Brett (bookings)
Capacity: 800
Alternative, rock

Irish Brigade
1005 Princess Anne St.
Fredericksburg VA 22401
703-371-9413
Capacity: 120
Alternative, rock

City Lights
6518 Horsepen Rd.
Richmond VA 23226
804-288-8963
Capacity: 400
Country, rock

Twisters
929 W Grace St.
Richmond VA 23220
804-353-4263
Capacity: 400
Alternative, college

Press

Richmond Times Dispatch
PO Box 85333
Richmond VA 23293
804-649-6731
Daily newspaper

Style Weekly
1118 W Main St.
Richmond VA 23220
804-358-0825
Weekly

Throttle
PO Box 250
Richmond VA 23202
804-644-0005
Bimonthly entertainment
magazine

Radio

WDCE 90.1 fm
University of Richmond
PO Box 85
Richmond VA 23173
804-289-8698
College

WCDX 92.7 fm
2809 Emery Wood Pkwy
Richmond VA 23294
804-672-9300
Urban contemporary

Record Stores

Peaches Music & Video
8018 W Broad St.
Richmond VA 23294
804-747-1755
CD, CA, Video

Plan 9 Records
3002 W Cary St.
Richmond VA 23221
804-353-9996
CD, LP, CA, Video
Recommended

Music Stores

Backstage
310 W Broad St.
Richmond VA 23220
804-644-1433
Sound sales, repairs, rentals

Don Warner Music
401 Libbie Ave.
Richmond VA 23226
804-282-9537
Guitar and electronic sales,
repairs, rentals

Guitar Works
3335 W Cary St.
Richmond VA 23221
804-358-0855
Sales, repairs, rentals

Virginia Beach Norfolk
Venues

Abbey Road
203 22nd St.
Virginia Beach VA 23451
804-425-6330
Capacity: 100, seated
Acoustic, rock

The Banque
1849 E Little Creek Rd.
Norfolk VA 23518
804-480-3600
804-460-0900 (bookings)
Capacity: 500
Country

Cogan's
1901 Colonial Ave.
Norfolk VA 23517
804-627-6428
Capacity: 100
Rock, R&B, and acoustic

Friar Tucks
4408 Hampton Blvd.
Norfolk VA 23508
804-423-2712
Capacity: 200
Reggae, alternative

The Jewish Mother
3108 Pacific Ave.
Virginia Beach VA 23451
804-422-5430
Capacity: 262
Acoustic

King's Head Inn
422 Hampton Blvd.
Norfolk VA 23508
804-489-3224
Capacity: 350
All styles

The Machine
118 Greenrun Square
Virginia Beach VA 23452
804-468-6324
Capacity: 300
Alternative

Press

Daily Press
7505 Warwick Blvd.
Newport News VA 23607
804-247-4744
Daily newspaper

Flash
1110 Atlantic Ave.
Virginia Beach VA 23451
804-461-6676
Monthly music magazine

Portfolio Magazine
5700 Thurston Ave., Ste 133
Virginia Beach VA 23455
804-363-2400
Weekly entertainment mag

Virginia Pilot/Ledger-Star
150 W Brambleton Ave.
Norfolk VA 23510
804-446-2000
Daily newspaper

Radio

WHRV 89.5 fm
5200 Hampton Blvd.
Norfolk VA 23508
804-489-9484
Alternative rock, jazz

WVAW
Virginia Wesleyan College
Wesleyan Drive
Norfolk VA 23502
804-455-3293

Record Stores

Birdland
957 Providence Square
Shopping Ctr.
Virginia Beach VA 23464
804-495-0961
CD, LP, CA

Factory Records
211 21st St.
Virginia Beach VA 23451
804-428-1615
CD, LP, CA

Fantasy
9823 Jefferson Ave.
Newport News VA 23605
804-595-1259
CD, CA, LP

Half Moon Music
1511 Pacific Ave.
Virginia Beach VA 23451
804-428-4072
CD, CA

Record Exchange
Coliseum Plaza
Hampton VA 23666
804-838-1200
CD, LP, CA

Skinnies Records
814 W 21st St.
Norfolk VA 23517
804-622-2241
CD, LP, CA

Unicorn Records
3214 Academy Ave.
Portsmouth VA 23703
804-483-0774
CD, LP, CA

Music Stores

A&E Music
3800 Holland Rd.
Virginia Beach VA 23452
804-498-8282
Most sales, repairs, rentals

Abbey Music
109 S Witchduck Rd.
Virginia Beach VA 23462
804-497-7777
Sales, repairs, rentals

Alpha Music
Southern Shopping Ctr, #9
Norfolk VA 23505
804-486-2001
Sales, repairs, rentals

Audio, Light & Musical
3301 N Military Hwy
Norfolk VA 23518
804-853-2424
Sales, repairs

Bay Music
7455 Tidewater Dr
Norfolk VA 23505
804-587-0057
Sales, repairs

WASHINGTON
Bellingham
Venues

3B Tavern
1226 N. State Street
Bellingham WA 98225
360-734-1881
Capacity: 260
Alternative

The Royal
208 E. Holly
Bellingham WA 98225
360-738-3701
Capacity: 275
All styles except country and
hard rock.

Radio

KUGS
Western Washington University
410 Viking Union Bldg
Bellingham WA 98225
360-650-2936
Alternative, Rap, Metal

Record Stores

Cellophane Square
115 E. Magnolia
Bellingham WA 98225
360-676-1404

Etc.

You're only 20 miles from
Canada. There's also plenty of
good hiking and rockclimbing
terrain here.

Olympia

Although there aren't alot of
venues to play (it's primarily the
Capitol Theatre) there is still
enough going on in Olympia to
make it worth a visit, even if
you don't have a show there.
Just hours away from Seattle,
Olympia is the stomping ground
for such alternative bands as
Unwound, Fitz of Depression
and Karp, and home to two
vibrant record labels, Yo Yo and
Kill Rock Stars.

Venues

Capitol Theatre
206 E. 5th St.
Olympia WA
206-754-5378
All styles.

Press

The Olympian
P.O. Box 407
Olympia WA 98507
206-754-5400

Radio

KAOS
Evergreen State College
TESC CAB 301
Olympia WA 98505
206-866-6000
All

Record Stores

Positively 4th Street
208 W. 4th Ave.
Olympia WA
206-786-8273
CD, CA, Vinyl

Rainy Day
2008 W. Harrison
Olympia WA 98502
206-357-4755
CD, CA, vinyl, clothes, videos,
skateboards.

Music Stores

Music 6000
2921 Pacific Ave. SE
Olympia WA 98501
206-786-6000
Sales

Moon Music
210 W. 4th Ave.
Olympia WA
206-705-4565
Guitars, amps and stuff.

Etc.

Olympia is a beautiful scenic
spot, and just the view of the
mountains could be enough. Try

a tour of the **Olympia Brewery** (you know..."it's the water") or just wander around by the Lake near downtown. **4th Avenue** offers restaurants, a movie theater, bars and places to play pinball. **The Spar** is an Olympia tradition for fine dining — which means a comfortable atmosphere and greasy french fries. Good for breakfasts and the milkshakes are even better. **Smithfield Cafe** on 4th serves breakfast all day and has both vegetarian and vegan menus.

Seattle
Venues

The Backstage
2208 NW Market St.
Seattle WA 98107
206-789-1184
Capacity: 450
All types

Ballard Firehouse Food
and Beverage Co.
5429 Russell NW
Seattle WA 98104
206-784-3516
Capacity: 350
Most styles

Colourbox
113 F Ave. S
Seattle WA 98104
206-340-4101
206-292-5181 Jennifer (bookings)
Capacity: 300
Alternative

Crocodile Cafe
2200 2nd Ave.
Seattle WA 98121
206-448-2114
206-441-5611 Terry (bookings)
Capacity: 200
Most styles

Jazz Alley
2033 6th Ave.
Seattle WA 98121
206-441-9729
Capacity: 275
Jazz

Moe's Mo'Roc'n Cafe
925 E Pike St
Seattle WA 98122
206-323-2373
Capacity: 540
Alternative, jazz, funk, indies

The New World
1471 N West 85th
Seattle WA 98113
206-789-6903/6830
206-522-8523 Kevin (bookings)
Rock

The Off Ramp
109 Eastlake Ave. E
Seattle WA 98109
206-628-0232
206-340-9322 Selena (bookings)
Capacity: 500
All styles

Re-Bar
1114 Howell St.
Seattle WA 98101
206-233-9873
Capacity: 262
Alternative, funk, rock

The Vogue
2018 First Ave.
Seattle WA 98121
206-443-0673
Capacity: 135
Alternative

Press

10 Things Jesus Wants You To Know
1407 NE 45th St. #17
Seattle WA 98105
Quarterly fanzine, punk and noise oriented

Pandemonium
917 Pacific Ave. #209
Tacoma WA 98402
206-272-3319
Monthly

The Rocket
The Rocket Towers
2028 5th Ave.
Seattle WA 98121
206-728-7625
Monthly entertainment mag with concert listings.

Seattle Post Intelligencer
PO Box 1909
Seattle WA 98111
206-448-8000
Daily newspaper

Seattle Times
PO Box 84647
Seattle WA 98124
206-464-2583
Daily newspaper

Seattle Weekly/Eastsideweek
1008 Western Ave. #300
Seattle WA 98101
206-623-0500
Weekly entertainment paper

The Stranger
4739 University Way NE
Ste 1516
Seattle WA 98105
206-547-7968
Weekly entertainment paper

Urban Spelunker
2319 North St., No 143
Seattle WA 98103
206-789-4112
Monthly music & arts mag

Radio

KASB 89.3 fm
Bellevue High School
10416 SE Kilmarnock St.
Bellevue WA 98004
206-455-6154
All styles

KBCS 91.3 fm
Bellevue Community College
3000 Landerholm Cir SE
Bellevue WA 98007
206-641-2424
Jazz, folk, blues, international

KCMU 90.3 fm
University of Washington
304 Communications Bldg
Seattle WA 98195
206-543-5541
Rock, rap, blues, R&B, jazz

KPLU 88.5 fm
Pacific Lutheran University
Tacoma WA 98447
206-340-1830
Jazz, news

Record Stores

Backstage Music and Video
2232 NW Market St.
Seattle WA 98107
206-784-9517
CD, LP, CA, Video

Bedazzled Discs
101 Cherry St.
Seattle WA 98104
206-382-6072
CD, LP

Bud's Jazz Records
102 S Trekson
Seattle WA 98104
206-628-0445
CD, CA

Cellophane Square Records
1315 Northeast 42nd St.
Seattle WA 98105
206-634-2280
CD, LP, CA, Video

Exotique Imports Inc.
2400 3rd Ave.
Seattle WA 98121
206-448-3452
CD, LP, CA, Video

Fallout Records/Skateboards
1506 East Olive Way
Seattle WA 98122
206-323-2662
CD, LP, CA

Park Ave. Records
532 Queen Anne Ave. N
Seattle WA 98109
206-284-2390
CD, LP, CA

Tower Records
500 Mercer St.
Seattle WA 98109
CD, LP, CA, Video

Music Stores

Al's Guitarville
19258 15th NE
Seattle WA 98155
206-363-8188
Sales, repairs, rentals

American Music
4450 Fremont Ave. N
Seattle WA 98103
206-633-1774
Sales, repairs, rentals

Embryo Stringed Instrument
76 W Washington #M106
Seattle WA 98104
206-232-2249
Repairs

Petosa Music
313 NE 45th St.
Seattle WA 98105
206-632-2700
Accordians, keyboards, and
electronic repairs; accordian
rentals; keyboard sales

Seattle Drumshop
843 NE Northgate Way
Seattle WA 98125
206-363-1853
Drum repairs, rentals, and sales

Steven's Stringed Instruments
1733 Westlake Ave. N
Seattle WA 98109
206-286-1443
All fretted instrument repairs; no
rentals

Etc.

Cyclops on Western Ave.;
vegetarian. **Flowers,** a hipster
hangout with vegetarian fare
and a buffet for $5.00. **Western
Cafe,** walking distance to OK
Hotel. **Fallout Records** has a
great selection of indie records
and comic books. For the best
thrift shopping try the **Fremont
District.** The **Pike Place Market** is
an open-air market full of street
musicians, fresh fruit and
vegetables, arts and crafts and
all kinds of cool stuff. Good bars
include **Mecca** on Queen Anne,
Five Points on Queen Anne,
Comet on Capitol Hill, **Night Line**
on 2nd Ave., **Frontier** on 1st
Ave. Look for cheap hotels on
Aurora Ave.

Spokane
Venues

The Big Dipper
S 171 Washington
Spokane, WA 99204
509-747-8036
John Lemon
21 and up

Press

Discourse Magazine
237 1/2 W Riverside #35
Spokane WA 99201
509-327-4041
Sky Kensok
Monthly fanzine, punk emphasis

Inlander
W. 539 Sharp #208
Spokane WA 99201
Bi-monthly, all styles

Radio

KAGU 88.7 fm
Gonzaga University
502 Boone
Spokane WA 99258
509-484-2820
Alternative

KWRS 90.3 fm
Whitworth College
Station 4302
Spokane WA 99251
509-466-1000
Alternative

Record Stores

4,000 Holes
1502 N Monroe
Spokane WA 99201
509-325-1914
CD CA LP

Food

Rasputin Cafe at S. 212 Wall in
Spokane, 509-624-2101, "Best
wierd place ever made!" **The
Shack** on 2nd, "Just ask!"

Shelter

"Don't stay at a hotel—too many fans with big old houses!"

Etc.

Mayfair Café; Bowl and Pitcher; Peaceful Valley; Value Village; Manitou Park; good pot is everywhere!

WASHINGTON D.C.
Venues

9:30 Club
930 F St., NW
Washington DC 20004
202-638-2008
Capacity: 199
Alternative
21 and up
Alternative. Very hip management.

15 Minutes
1030 15th St., NW
Washington DC 20005
202-408-1855
Capacity: 200
Alternative
Another very cool place to play, with friendlier management than some other places.

The Asylum
1210 U St., NW
Washington DC 20009
202-232-9354
Capacity: 200
Alternative, Rock

The Bayou
3135 K St., NW
Washington DC 20007
202-333-2898
Capacity: 500
Various styles

The Birchmere
3901 Mt Vernon Ave.
Alexandria VA 22305
703-549-5919
Capacity: 300
Blues, Rock, Acoustic, Jazz

The Black Cat
1831 14th St.
Washington DC 20036
202-667-4527
Capacity: 400
Alternative

Blues Alley
1073 Wisconsin Ave.
Washington DC 20007
202-337-4141
Capacity: 125
Blues, Jazz

Jack's
6355 Rolling Rd.
Springfield VA 22152
703-569-5940
Capacity: 500
Rock

Fat Tuesdays
10673 Braddock Rd.
Fairfax VA 22032
703-385-8660
Capacity: 350
Various styles

Food For Thought
1738 Connecticut Ave., NW
Washington DC 20009
202-797-1095
Capacity: 99
Folk, Blues, Rock, Country, Jazz

Grog and Tankard
2408 Wisconsin Ave., NW
Washington DC 20007
202-333-3114
Capacity: 200
Blues, Rock, Alternative

The Kilimanjaro
1724 California St., NW
Washington DC 20009
202-328-3839
Capacity: 600 in the restaurant;1,500 in the hall
Reggae, World Beat

Nick's
642 S Pickett St.
Alexandria VA 22304
703-751-8900
Capacity: 350
Rock, Dance

One Step Down
2517 Pennsylvania Ave., NW
Washington DC 20037
202-331-8863
Capacity: 75
Jazz

The Roxy
1214 18th St., NW
Washington DC 20036
202-296-9293
Capacity: 350
Reggae

Sylvia's Restauraunt and Palomino Club
11 Courthouse Rd.
Stafford VA 22554
703-659-8944
Capacity: 200
Country

Tiki Fala
160 Graham Park Rd.
Dumfries VA 22026
703-221-4146
Capacity: 250
Rock

Tres Amigos
10900 Lee Hwy
Fairfax VA 22030
703-352-9393
Capacity: 240
R&B, Blues, Rock

Zed
6151 Richmond Hwy
Alexandria VA 22303
703-768-5558
Capacity: 250
Country

Press

The City Paper
724 9th St., NW 5th Fl
Washington DC 20001
202-628-6528
Weekly newspaper

Country Plus Magazine
6933 Westhampton Dr
Alexandria VA 22037
703-765-7042
Monthly music magazine

Jazz Times
7961 Eastern Ave., Ste 303
Silver Spring MD 20910
301-588-4114
Monthly magazine

Mole
PO Box 5033
Herndon VA 22070
Quarterly fanzine

Northern Virginia Rhythm
Magazine
PO Box 2560
Merrifield VA 22116
703-912-7552
Fax: 703-912-7979
Biweekly entertainment mag

The Washington Post
1150 15th St. NW
Washington DC 20071
202-334-7540

Radio

WAMU 88.5 fm
American University
4400 Massachusetts Ave.
Washington DC 20016
202-885-1030
Alternative

WCUA 91.3 fm
Catholic University
Box 104 Cardinal Station
Washington DC 20064
202-319-5106
Alternative, Rap

WGMU 97.3 cafm 560 am
George Mason University
4400 University Dr
Fairfax VA 22030
703-993-2935
Alternative

WGTB 690 am cc
Georgetown University
316 Leavey Center
SAC Office
Washington DC 20057
202-687-3702

WHFS 99.1 fm
8201 Corporate Dr, #550
Landover MD 20785
301-306-0991
Commercial Alternative

WMUC 88.1
University of Maryland
Box 99
College Park MD 20742
301-314-7868
Various styles

WPFW 89.3 fm
702 H St. NW
Washington DC 20001
202-783-3100
Jazz, Blues, World Music

WRGW 540 am
George Washington University
800 21st St. #428, NW
Washington DC 20052
202-994-7314
Alternative

WVAU 101.7 fm
American University
Box 610 Eagle Station
Washington DC 20016
202-885-6162

WWDC 101.1 fm
8750 Brookeville Rd.
Silver Spring MD 20910-1801
301-587-7100
Commercial Rock

Record Stores

Go! Compact Discs
2507 N Franklin Rd.
Arlington VA 22201
703-528-8340
CD, LP, 7"

Joe's Record Paradise
2153 Bel Pre Rd.
Silver Spring MD 20906
301-460-8394
CD, CA, LP

Orpheus
3249 M St., NW
Washington DC 20007
202-337-7970
CD, CA, LP

Phantasmagoria
11308 Grandview Ave.
Wheaton MD 20902
301-949-8886
CD, CA, LP

PM Records
7221 Centreville Rd.
Manassas VA 22111
703-330-6270
CD, CA, LP

Record Mart
217 King St.
Alexandria VA 22314
703-683-4583
CD, CA, 7"

Smash
3279 M St., NW
Washington DC 20007
202-337-6274
CD, CA, LP

Vinyl Ink
955 Bonifant
Silver Spring MD 20910
301-588-4695
CD, CA, LP

Yesterday & Today
1327 J Rockville Pike
Rockville MD 20852
301-279-7007
CD, CA, LP

Music Stores

Ardis Music Center
1728 Conneticut Ave. NW
Washington DC 20009
202-234-6537
Most instrument sales, repairs
and rentals

Chuck Levin's Washington Music Center
11151 Veirsmill Rd.
Wheaton Md 20902
301-946-8808
Most instument sales, repairs
and rentals

Foxes Music
416 S Washington St.
Falls Church VA 22046
703-533-7393
Guitars, amps and some percussion sales

Music City
10969 Lute Court
Manassas VA 22110
703-368-0161
Sales, some repairs, rentals

Rolls Music Company
1065 W Broad St.
Falls Church VA 22046
703-533-9510
Fax: 703-533-9500
Most instrument sales, repairs,
and rentals

Southworth Guitars
7845 Old Georgetown Rd.
Bethesda MD 20814
301-718-1667
Vintage guitars sales, repairs

Food

Food For Thought is a vegetarian
place on Connecticut Ave.
Dante's also has vegetarian food
and they are open late. (They
are on 14th St. and P) **Zig Zag** is
a good coffee shop that is open
late.

Shelter

On 7th and E in Chinatown there
is either a **Quality Inn**, **Comfort
Inn** or **Days Inn**.

Etc.

I think the **Marlboro** factory is
somewhere in the state of
Virginia, not too far from D.C.,
but other than that, D.C. has
little to offer in the way of
tourism. Unless you like government buildings and monuments.
There may be a couple of free
museums or something somewhere in the area.

WEST VIRGINIA
Charleston Huntington
Venues

The Calamity Cafe
1555 Third Ave.
Huntington WV 25701
304-525-4171
Capacity: 200
Roy Clark - booking
Mainly an acoustic venue,
occasional electric shows.

Empty Glass
410 Elizabeth St
Charleston WV 25301
304-342-4412
Capacity: 100
Alternative, blues

The Graffiti
4615 Bomb Bl.
Pittsburgh WV 15213
412-682-4210
All styles

Players
2002 Third Ave
Huntington, WV
304-525-PLAY
Capacity: 200
Rock

Roper's
200 22nd St.
Huntington WV 25703
304-522-1298
Capacity: 1,000
Country

Sharky's
410 10th St.
Huntington WV 25701
304-697-5297
Capacity: 170
Blues, rock, and some acoustic

Press

Graffiti
1505 Lee St
Charleston, WV 25311
304-342-4412
Monthly alternative music paper.
Will review.

Radio

WMUL
Marshall University
400 Hal Greer Blvd.
Huntington WV 25755
304-696-2295
Various styles, Alternative.

Record Stores

Budget Tapes & Records
3708 MacCorkle Ave SE
Charleston WV 25304
304-925-8273
CD, CA

Davidson's Music
907 Fourth Ave.
Huntington WV 25701
304-522-0228
CD, LP, CA, Video
A highly recommended record
store

Music Stores

Gorby's Music
214 7th Ave
S Charleston WV 25303
304-744-9452
Sales, repairs, rentals

Herbert Music Co
920 Quarrier St
Charleston WV 25301
304-342-6121
Sales, repairs, rentals

Pied Piper
1200 Third Ave.
Huntington WV 25701
304-529-3355
Sales, repairs, rentals

Food

The Calamity Cafe has vegetarian and other similar dishes.
Chili Willie is a Mexican restuarant with $5 plates and a wide variety of food. Both of these places are good, cheap and not cheesey.

Shelter

The Coaches Inn, 12 blocks from clubs, is about $40 per night.

Etc.

The **Huntington Museum of Art** is a cool place to check out if you have a little spare time. **Eelie Art Gallery** is a privately owned gallery that frequently has shows worth seeing. **Dig's** is an alternative clothing store; they supposedly carry leather underwear. The **Rennaisance Bookshop** is combination art gallery, book store and coffee shop. It is also open 24 hours per day.

WISCONSIN
La Crosse
Venues

The Warehouse
PO Box 2044
La Crosse WI 54602
608-784-1422
Stephen Harm
The Warehouse is one of those rare finds in a venue — it seems to be geared to benefit any band. Not only is this all-ages space geographically helpful (2 hours from Minneapolis, 2 hours from Madison, and 4 hours from Chicago), but the space also provides a rehearsal space, recording studio, and soon to be installed record store. The Warehouse aims to please bands and make their time in La Crosse as effective as possible.

Press

Community Life
PO Box 367
Onalaska WI 54650
608-781-6700
Randy Erickson

Fall Down Go Boom
PO Box 2044
La Crosse WI 54602
A local/regional fanzine that does scene, live, and record reviews, etc, etc, etc.

La Crosse Tribune
401 N 3rd St.
La Crosse WI 54601
608-782-9710
Geri Parlin
Daily paper

Lumen
Viterbo College
608-791-0469
College paper

Racquet
University of Wisconsin
608-785-8378
College paper

Radio

KRPR 89.9 fm
Rochester Community College
851 30th Ave. SE
Rochester MN 55904
507-285-7231
This 100,000 watt commercial station has a Sunday Night Alternative show that is sponsored by the Warehouse Nightclub. This is a good place to be heard.

KQAL 89.5 fm
Winona State University
230 Performing Arts Center
Winona MN 55987
507-457-5226
Alternative

Record Stores

Def Ear
208 S. 4th
La Crosse WI 54601
608-782-7829

Face The Music
9348 Highway 16
Onalaska WI 54650
608-781-0070
CD, CA

Music Stores

Dave's Guitar Shop
1227 South 3rd
La Crosse WI 54601
608-785-7704
This place is truly world-reknowned. Everyone from Slash to Stevie Ray Vaughn has shopped here. The place is a museum for the most amazing collection of guitars you will see. Don't bring a credit card with any space on it, unless you intend to use it.

Food

Brew Note 327 Jay St., La Crosse; **Jules Coffeehouse**, 327 Pearl St.; **Zoo Twilite** in La Crescent, Minnesota.

Shelter

If the band plays at the Warehouse they can get corporate rates at hotels through the club. If you're not playing at the Warehouse, try the **Guest House**.

Etc.

If you go to La Crosse it's the law that you have to see the **A. Heileman Brewing Co**. and especially the **World's Largest Six Pack**. Call 608-782-2337.

Madison
Venues

The Chamber
114 King St.
Madison WI 53703
608-255-5402
Capacity: 150
Rock

Club de Wash
636 W Washington Ave.
Madison WI 53703
608-256-3302
Capacity: 250
Rock, blues, weird jazz

Crystal Corner
1302 Williamson St.
Madison WI 53703
608-256-2953
Capacity: 300
Mostly blues, some world beat, ska and reggae.

The Loft
112 N Fairchild
Madison WI 53703
608-251-0753
Capacity: 300
Hardcore, metal, rap, ska

O'Cayz Corral
504 E Wilson St.
Madison WI 53703
608-256-1348
Capacity: 250
Metal, blues, alternative.

Paramount Music Hall
103 N Park St
Madison WI 53715
608-256-1171
Capacity: 900
Alternative, experimental, jazz, blues

Rathskellar
Memorial Union
800 Langdon, Rm 514
Madison WI 53706
608-262-2215
Capacity: 800
Alternative, rock

The Terrace
Memorial Union
800 Langdon, Rm 514
Madison WI
608-262-2215
Capacity: 2,500+
Adjacent to the Rathskellar, this is set on the shores of Lake Mendota.

Union South
227 N Randall Ave., Rm 303
Madison WI 53715
608-263-5593
Capacity: 100
Jazz, reggae, techno/industrial at this University of Wisconsin student union.

Promoters

House of Toast
426 Algoma
Madison WI 53704
Tyler Jarman
608-249-7745
Loud stuff

Tom Layton
Lamebrain Productions
First Artists
1970 E Main St.
Madison WI 53704
608-242-8559
Rock

Memorial Union Music and Entertainment Committee
University of Wisconsin
800 Langdon St.
Madison WI 53706
608-262-2215
All styles

Really Productions
Ken Udell
608-276-7888
Industrial, Rock

Tag Team Productions
1110 Jennifer
Madison WI 53703
608-256-0622
All styles

Press

Badger Herald
550 State St.
Madison WI 53703
608-257-4712
Student daily paper

Capital Times
PO Box 8060
1901 Fish Hatchery Rd.
Madison WI 53708
608-252-6400
Daily newspaper

The Daily Cardinal
University of Wisconsin
2142 Vilas Hall
821 University Ave.
Madison WI 53706
608-262-5857
Daily newspaper

Isthmus
101 King St.
Madison WI 53703
608-251-5627
Weekly alternative paper

Night Sites & Sounds
2317 International Ln, Ste 212
Madison WI 53704
608-241-1144
Fax: 608-241-1167
Biweekly entertaiment paper

The Onion
33 University Square Ste 270
Madison WI 53715
608-256-1372
Weekly paper

Wisconsin State Journal
Box 8058
Madison WI 53708
608-252-6184
Daily newspaper

Radio

WORT 89.9 fm
118 S Bedford St.
Madison WI 53703
608-256-2695
Community radio - various styles
Call to set up an interview or
on-air performance

Record Stores

B-Side Records
436 State St.
Madison WI 53703
608-255-1977
CD, CA

Mad City Music Exchange
600 Williamson St.
Madison WI 53703
608-252-8558
Fax: 608-251-8668
CD, LP, CA, 7"

Music Stores

Good Music Company
5225 University Ave.
Madison WI 53705
608-231-5990
Sales, repairs, rentals

Sound Logic
2308 Atwood Ave.
Madison WI 53704
608-246-8742
Guitar, amp sales and repairs

Ward-Brodt Music
2200 Beltline Hwy
Madison WI 53713
608-271-1460
Sales, repairs, rentals

Food

There are good places all over
the city.

Etc.

Go to the **State Street** area for
sightseeing and thrift stores.

Milwaukee
Venues

Brett's
1501 N Jackson St.
Milwaukee WI 53202
414-277-0122
414-224-9123 Scott (bookings)
Capacity: 120
All styles. Decent venue if you
can get a guarantee

The Estate
2423 N Murray Ave.
Milwaukee WI 53211
414-964-9923
Capacity: 62
Jazz

The Globe
2028 E North Ave.
Milwaukee WI 53202
414-276-2233
Ian
Capacity: 175
All styles

Shank Hall
1434 N Farwell Ave.
Milwaukee WI 53202
414-276-7288
414-332-3061 Peter (bookings)
Capacity: 300
All styles. Recommended.

The Tamarack
322 W State St.
Milwaukee WI 53203
414-225-2552
Capacity: 200
Blues

T.A. Vern's
5401 N Lover's Lane
Milwaukee WI 53225
414-536-4222
Capacity: 700
Alternative, rock

The Unicorn
300 W Juneau Ave.
Milwaukee WI 53203
414-224-0123
Capacity: 300
Izzy does the booking
This is a great place to play.
Everyone affiliated with this club
seems to be cool and they really
cater to the bands. The owner of
this club also owns a Mexican
Restaurant upstairs and the food
is amazing, not to mention the
huge proportions. Even the
soundman is cool which, as you
will find, is a real hit and miss
issue.

Up & Under Pub
1216 E Brady St.
Milwaukee WI 53202
414-276-2677
Capacity: 200
Blues, reggae, rock

Press

Art Muscle
PO Box 93219
Milwaukee WI 53203
Bimonthly regional fine arts mag

City Edition
777 N Jefferson St.
Milwaukee WI 53202
414-273-8696
Weekly newspaper

Milwaukee Journal
PO Box 661
Milwaukee WI 53201
414-224-2000
Daily newspaper

Shepherd Express
1123 N Water St.
Milwaukee WI 53202
414-276-2222
Will cover any music, independent or major label. This is the best source for music in Milwaukee.

Radio

WMSE 91.7 fm
324 Juneau Ave.
Milwaukee WI 53202
414-277-7247
Mixed college format
Only alternative station playing independent music in the area.

WQFM 93.3 fm
633 W Wisconsin Ave., Ste 593
Milwaukee WI 53203
414-276-2040
Commercial rock

Record Stores

Atomic Records
1813 E Locust St.
Milwaukee WI 53211
414-332-3663
CD, LP
A highly recommended store

Earwaves East Limited
2218 N Farwell
Milwaukee WI 53202
414-271-8808
CD, LP, CA
This is also a very good store

The Exclusive Company
1669 N Farwell
Milwaukee WI 53202
414-271-8590
A record store chain that started in Osh Kosh Wisconsin, but is quickly expanding.

Rushmore Limited
2660 S Kinnickinnic
Milwaukee WI 53207
414-481-6040
CD, CA, LP

Music Stores

Cascio Music Co
13819 W National Ave.
New Berlin WI 53151
414-786-6249
Sales, repairs, rentals

Crown Music
2637 S Kinnickinnic Ave.
Milwaukee WI 53207
414-481-3430
Sales, repairs, rentals

Faust Music
414-744-1112
The ultimate drum shop, if you can handle old Mr. Faust. The guy is totally insane, but he knows drums better than anyone. I think Max Roach even bought his instruments of percussion there.

Uncle Bob's Music
10220 W Greenfield Ave.
West Allis WI 53214
414-453-2700
Repairs and sales. The main store.

Food

Ma Fischer's is good, but rather expensive, especialy if you are on the old $5 per diem. **Beans and Barley** on Arlington is a good, cheap vegetarian place. **Gyro Express**, around the corner from Beans and Barley on North Ave. has good Greek food and a decent vegetarian menu. **Jalisco's** has "Burritos as big as your head for a buck!" **The Fuel Cafe** is the "hepcat" hangout for poets and punkers alike. Good

cheap coffee and plenty of cool atmosphere. **Brewed Awakenings** has good coffee and is open late.

Shelter

The **Hotel Wisconsin** is in Downtown Milwaukee; it is a cool, cheap, old hotel with the **Cafe Roulange** downstairs. This is the type of place Tom Waits would probably hangout at. **The Belmont**, across the street, is a $15-$20 per night flophouse.

Etc.

Milwaukee is the city for beer. There are three huge breweries to check out: **Pabst, Blatz,** and the **Miller Brewery**. There are also a million bars. The **Zurkrone**, a German bar located in Walker's Point, has more beers on tap than you could possibly stuff into your tiny little beer gut in one evening. Also home to Walker's Point are about 5 other bars in a 2 block radius. **The Landmark** is combination amusement park, bowling alley, bar and bum fest. It is located in the basement of **The Oriental**, a movie theater. There are also a couple of interesting museums to check out. One is the **Milwaukee Public Museum**, which has a spectacular Rainforest exhibit. The other is the **Milwaukee Arts Center** on Lake Front, for you, well, artist types.

WYOMING
Laramie
Venues

Club-U-Dub
University of Wyoming
Campus Activities Center
Wyoming Union
PO Box 3625
Laramie WY 82071
307-766-6342/6340
Capacity: 200
Jazz, folk, new age, acoustic

Blind Dog City
201 Custer St.
Laramie WY 82070
307-721-5097
Capacity: 263
Country, blues, rock

The Ranger
453 N 3rd
Laramie WY 82070
307-745-9751
Capacity: 120
Blues, occasional reggae.

Press

The Branding-Iron
University of Wyoming
PO Box 4238
Student Publication
University Station
Laramie WY 82071
307-766-6190
Newspaper

Radio

KUWR 91.9 fm
University of Wyoming
PO Box 3984
Laramie WY 82071
307-766-4240
Classical, folk, rock, R&B

Record Stores

Music Box
300 S 2nd St.
Laramie WY 82070
307-742-3774
CD, CA, Video

Top Notch Records
212 Ivinson St.
Laramie WY 82070
307-742-7270
CD, LP, CA

Music Stores

Scorpio Music
300 S. 2nd St.
Laramie WY 82070
307-745-7013
Sales, guitar & horn repairs,
rentals

Food
Jefferies Bistro, Overland Deli,
and **Elmer Lovejoy's**, a bar and
grill that does quite a variety, no
smoking.

Shelter
The Travel Inn, The Sunset Inn
(Comfort Inn chain), a number of
other cheap places to stay.

CANADA
Montreal
Venues

Cafe Campus
57 Prince Arthur E
Montreal QUE H2X 2B4
514-844-1010
Capacity: 500
Alternative

Cat House
1459 St Alexander St
Montreal QUE H3A 2G3
514-848-9306
Capacity: 1200
Alternative, metal

Purple Haze
3699 A St Laurent
Montreal QUE H2X 2V7
514-982-1859
Capacity: 500
Alternative

Rage
5116 Park Ave
Montreal QUE
514-951-6149
Capacity: 130
Alternative, funk

Press

Hour
4130 St Dennis St
Montreal QUE H2W 2M5
514-848-0777
Weekly alternative paper

Montreal Mirror
400 McGill St
Montreal QUE H2Y 2G1
514-393-1010
Weekly

The Voice
275 St Jacques #20
Montreal QUE H2Y 1M9
514-842-7127
Monthly music, entertainment

Radio

CKUT
3647 University St
Montreal QUE
514-398-6787
Community alternative

Record Stores

L'Oblique
4333 Rivard St
Montreal, QUE H2J 2M7
514-499-1323
CD, CA, LP, imports

Music Stores

Steve's Music Store
51 St Antoine
Montreal QUE H2Z 1G9
514-878-2216
Sales, repairs, rentals

Etc.

The **Plateau Mt. Royale** area is a good place to hang out, lots of stores and restaurants. **San Tropol** on Duluth has "big sandwiches, many kinds." **Frite Alors** on Rochelle and Rivard has Belgian french fries and great meat and veggie burgers.

Toronto
Venues

Cabana Room
460 King St W
Toronto ONT M5V 107
416-368-2864
416-368-0729
Capacity: 150
All styles

Cameron House
408 Queen St W
Toronto ONT M5V 2A7
416-703-0811
Capacity: 200
All styles

Classic Studio
12A Ossington St
Toronto ONT M6J 2Y7
416-533-5595
Capacity: 120
Punk, rock, reggae

Clinton's
693 Bloor St W
Toronto ONT M6G 1L5
416-535-9541
Capacity: 175
All styes

El Mocambo
464 Spadina Ave
Toronto ONT M5T 2G8
416 928 3566
Capacity: 750
Rock

Horseshoe Tavern
370 Queen St W
Toronto ONT M5V 2A2
416-598-4753
Capacity: 300
All styles

Lee's Palace
529 Bloor St W
Toronto ONT M5S 1Y5
416-532-7383
Capacity: 500
Rock

The Phoenix Concert Theatre
410 Shelbourne St
Toronto ONT M4X 1K2
416-323-1251
Capacity: 1000
All styles

Rivoli
332 Queen St W
Toronto ONT M5V 2A2
416-596-1908
Capacity: 150
All styles

Ultra Sound Show Bar
269 Queen St W
Toronto ONT M5V 1Z9
416-593-0540
Capacity: 100
All styles

The World Famous Gasworks Rock Bar
585 Yonge St
Toronto ONT M4Y 1Z2
416-922-9367
Capacity: 400 upstairs, 300 downstairs
Rock

The Zoo Bar East
2714 Danforth Ave
Toronto ONT M4C 1L7
416-699-9888
Capacity: 850
Alternative

Press

Eye Weekly
57 Spadina Ave #207
Toronto ONT M5V 2J2
416-971-8421
416-971-7786 fax
Weekly news

ID
69 Wyndham St N #211
Guelph ONT N1H 4E7
519-766-9891
Biweekly news, entertainment

NOW
150 Danforth Ave
Toronto ONT M4K 1N1
416-461-0871
Weekly news, entertainment

Radio

CFNY 102 fm
83 Kennedy Rd S
Brampton ONT L6W 3P3
905-453-7452
Commercial alternative

CHRY 105.5
York University
258A Vanaer College
4700 Keele St
North York ONT M3J 1P3
Community, all styles

CIUT 89.5 fm
U of Toronto
91 St George St
Toronto ONT M5S QE8
416-595-0909
College, all styles

CKLN 88.1
380 Victoria St #A71
Ryerson Polytechnic
Toronto ONT M5B 1W7
416-595-1477
Community, all styles

Record Stores

Play De Record
357A Yonge St
Toronto ONT M5B 1S4
416-586-0380
CD, CA, LP

Rotate This
620 Queen St W
Toronto ONT M6J 1E4
416-504-8447
CD, CA, LP, 8 track

Music Stores

Long and McQuade
925 Bloor St W
Toronto ONT M6H 1L5
416-588-7886
5 other locations. Sales, rentals, repairs

Song Bird Music
801 Queen St W
Toronto ONT M6J 1G1
416-362-7664
Sales, rentals, repairs

Etc.

The **Queen Street Strip** is loaded with thrift, vintage and record stores. **Buddha's** downtown has veggie and health food, try the fake duck. **Sneaky D's** is a cool bar. If you can afford it, stay at the **Royal York Hotel** on Carlton in the city center.

Vancouver
Venues

The Falls Pub
435 W Pender St
Vancouver, BC V6B 1V2
604-688-7574
Capacity: 300
Punk, alternative

Gastown Music Hall
6 Powell St
Vancouver BC V6A 1E7
604-685-1333
Capacity: 125
Alternative, pop

Hungry Eye
23 W Cordova
Vancouver BC V65 1C8
604-688-5351
Capacity: 225
Alternative, punk

Malcolm Lowry Room
4125 E Hastings St
Burnaby BC
604-685-0143
Capacity: 100
Alternative

The New York Theatre
639 Commercial Dr
Vancouver BC V5L 3W3
604-254-3545
Capacity: 750
Alternative. This place puts on most of the big punk and alternative shows.

Railway Club
579 Dunsmuir St
Vancouver BC V6B 1Y4
604-681-1625
Capacity: 176
All styles

The Starfish Room
1055 Homer St
Vancouver BC V6B 2X5
604-682-4171
Capacity: 400
Alternative

Press

Discorder
U of British Columbia
c/o CITR Student Union Bldg #233
6138 S Bl.
Vancouver BC V6T 1Z1
604-822-3017
Monthly alternative music mag

Terminal City
825 Granville St #203
Vancouver BC V6Z 1K9
604-669-6910
Weekly news, entertainment. Recommended. Definitely send your stuff for concert listings.

Radio

CFRO 102.7 fm
337 Carroll St
Vancouver BC V6B 2J4
604-684-8494
Community, all styles

CITR 101.9 fm
U of BC
6138 Sub Bl
Vancouver BC V6T 1Z1
604-822-3017
College, all styles

Record Stores

Track Records
552 Seymour St
Vancouver BC V6B 2N4
604-682-7976
CD, CA, LP.
Lots of new vinyl. Recommended.

Scratch Records
317 A Cambie St
Vancouver BC V6B 2N4
604-687-6355
CD, CA, vinyl

Zulu Records
1869 W 4th Ave
Vancouver BC V6J 1M4
604-738-3232
CD, CA, LP, alternative

Music Stores

Drums Only
2060 Pine St
Vancouver BC V6J 4P8
604-736-5411
Sales

Not Just Another Music Shop
1228 Granville St
Vancouver BC V6Z 1M4
604-669-6768
Sales, rentals, repairs

Etc.

The **Commercial Drive** area of East Vancouver is full of funky shops and tons of great cafés. **Albion Books** and **Carson Books and Records** have lots of beat lit and secondhand jazz vinyl.

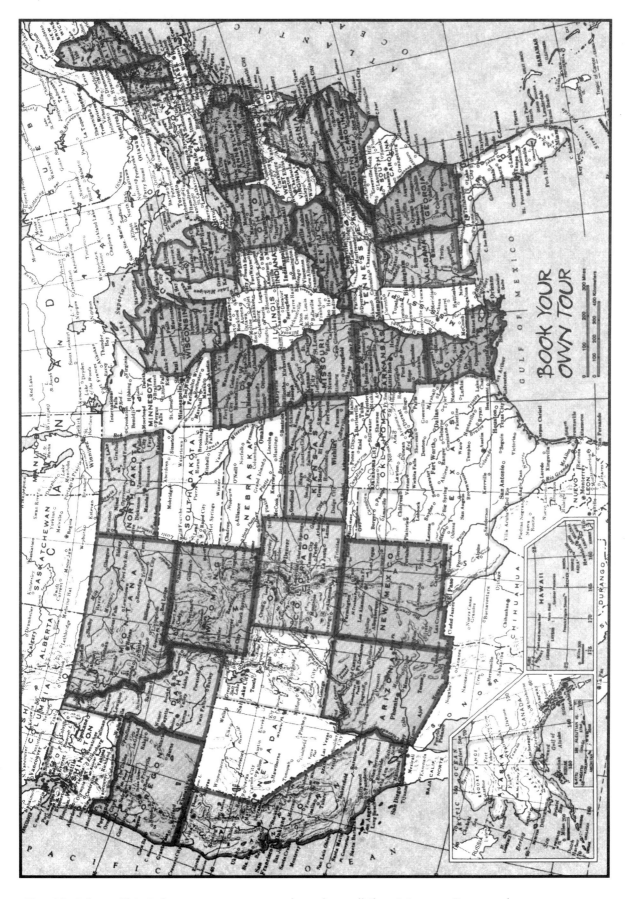

Map Disclaimer: This is just so you can remember where all the states are. Buy a real map.

CONCLUSION

So, do you *still* want to take your band on the road? It's a challenge but by all means it is possible. I hope this touring "how-to" guide helps you get started and get out there. Always keep in mind the essentials of booking a successful tour: Preparation and set-up time, persistentence, follow-through and communication. Oh yeah, being able to play your music helps, too!

Becoming a successful touring band or artist takes time. Don't expect to go out on your first tour and make a ton of money playing to packed clubs. The more you tour, the bigger your base of fans and contacts in other cities will be. This will lead to more records sold and more friends made.

Let us know what you find. Maybe the hip club in Portland has turned into a sports bar by this time next year, or that great record store we bragged about in New York now only sells CD-ROMs. This book will be updated often, so if there are any additional contacts or places or sights or stories you want to share, let us know!

So get in that van and go, and remember to send us a postcard.

Thanks.

Liz Garo
c/o Restless Records
1616 Vista Del Mar
Hollywood CA 90028-6420

Rockpress
P.O. Box 99090
San Diego CA 92169

Thank You

A huge thanks goes out to all of the following people who submitted information to this book. In no particular order: Jennifer (Ragin' Records, Fresno), Charles Cox, Zack Matheson, Lori McKee, Krista Kansas, Laurie Bilden, Kagin Lee, Terry Conrad, Dave Sullivan, Martin Haw, Lucia Corace, Wade Tolleson, Lucy Kerley, Bill Jennings, Carol Schutzbank, Bob Gulla, Bliss Blood, Denton Anderson, Keith Lyle, *The Splatter Effect*, Jade Nielsen, John Book, Mark Abernathy, *Fizz* Magazine, Karen Weil, Claudia at *Homotiller*, Greg Vegas, Debbie Caponera, Var, Jon Hardman, Hillary Meister, Doug Roberson, Chris Porter, Al Quint, Paul Hutzuer, Marlon Butela, John Livingstone, Jim Testa, Eric Weilander, Jeremy Steckler, Samir (Charlotte, NC), Davit Souders, Stephen Anderson, Margit Detweiler, Bryan (Philly), Ty Jesso, Luann Williams, Malcolm Mayhew and Teresa Gubbins, Sky Kensok, Michael (Rotate This), Randy Ballwahn, Eric Gladstone, David Reinders, Byron (*Terminal City*), Luc (L'Oblique), Bob Baker.

And to everyone else who contributed information: **THANKS!**

NEW BOOKS FROM ROCKPRESS

BOOK YOUR OWN TOUR, BY LIZ GARO

The new bible for bands who want to plan and execute a cost-effective, successful national or regional tour. Features listings for over 100 U.S. cities, with information such as venues, local press, radio stations, record and music stores, vegetarian food, cheap lodging and much more. Plus sample press releases, tour schedules, tour routes, booking contracts, interviews, and advice from the road. ©1995. 181 pg., $19.95.

GETTING RADIO AIRPLAY, BY GARY HUSTWIT

NEW SECOND EDITION! The definitive guide to getting your music played on college, public and commercial radio. Features interviews with radio station Music Directors, record label promo staff and independent artists who've done it, plus mailing lists for 900 stations, including address, phone, and style of music. An important book for anyone who wants to make a nationwide impact with their music. ©1994. 130 pg., $19.95.

RELEASING AN INDEPENDENT RECORD
BY GARY HUSTWIT

NEW FOURTH EDITION! The only book published with the current contacts and information you need to release and market your own music on a national level. Gary Hustwit, formerly with SST Records, backs his advice with experience, concrete examples and invaluable directories (radio stations, booking agents, stores, distributors, manufacturers, press, record labels, 3000 contacts in all) to help musicians from all styles release their own records, tapes and CDs. New for 4th Edition: music publisher directory, sample contracts and updated directories. ©1994, 182 pg., $22.95. Coming in August, 1995: RELEASING AN INDEPENDENT RECORD, 5TH EDITION.

NETWORKING IN THE MUSIC INDUSTRY,
BY JIM CLEVO AND ERIC OLSEN

Examines the inner workings of the music industry and "networking" within it, through text and interviews with over 80 music professionals; from Mike Watt, Brett Gurewitz and Greg Ginn to Paul Sacksman, Howie Klein and Bob Guccione Jr. Learn how to use music conferences, video, computer BBSs, music associations and press to make valuable new contacts. Includes discussions about artist/label relationships, music publishing and the indie scene. ©1993. 238 pg., $19.95.

101 WAYS TO MAKE MONEY RIGHT NOW IN
THE MUSIC BUSINESS, BY BOB BAKER

Whether you're an aspiring musician, a music professional or just fascinated by the music industry, this book offers over 101 honest, down-to-earth ways to make a living independently in the music industry. These often overlooked areas can be pursued part-time for extra cash, or full-time for an even bigger payoff. There are bound to be at least a few topics here that inspire you, or perhaps trigger still more money making ideas. ©1993. 140 pg., $14.95.

To order any of these books, or for a free catalog featuring hundreds of music-related books, call Mix Bookshelf at 1-800-233-9604, M-F, 9-6 PST.